Jessica Adams began her career at *Elle* and is the astrologer for international editions of *Vogue* and *Cosmopolitan*, as well as *The Australian Women's Weekly*. She is the author of six novels and a team editor on the *Girls' Night In* and *Kids' Night In* series, which have raised $2.5 million for the global children's charity War Child.

ESSENTIAL
ASTROLOGY
FOR WOMEN

HarperCollins*Publishers*

HarperCollins_Publishers_

First published in Australia in 1997 as _Astrology for Women_
This revised edition published in 2006
by HarperCollins_Publishers_ Australia Pty Limited
ABN 36 009 913 517
www.harpercollins.com.au

HarperCollins_Publishers_
25 Ryde Road, Pymble, Sydney NSW 2073, Australia
31 View Road, Glenfield, Auckland 10, New Zealand
77–85 Fulham Palace Road, London W6 8JB, United Kingdom
2 Bloor Street East, 20th floor, Toronto, Ontario M4W 1A8, Canada
10 East 53rd Street, New York NY 10022, USA

National Library of Australia Cataloguing-in-Publication data:

Adams, Jessica.
  The essential astrology for women : to 2025.
  Rev ed.
  Bibliography
  ISBN 13: 978 0 7322 8365 0.
  ISBN 10: 0 7322 8365 5.
  1. Astrology. 2. Women – Miscellanea. I. Adams, Jessica.
  Astrology for women. II. Title.
133.5082

Cover design by Natalie Winter
Image courtesy of Shutterstock
Author photo: Peter Clarke
Internal design by Natalie Winter
Typeset in Charter 9/13 by Helen Beard, ECJ Australia Pty Limited
Printed and bound in Australia by Griffin Press
on 79gsm Bulky Paperback White

5 4 3 2 1   06 07 08 09

*This book is dedicated to
Miss Peggy Popovic of Hastings
and Miss Allegra Allen
of London.*

CoNTENTS

PREDICTING THE FUTURE

BIRTHDAY TABLES

RESOURCES

INTRODUCTION

Astrology is different for women. Our Moon signs and Venus signs say more about us than our Sun signs, because they are female planets — consequently, they receive a lot of space in the new edition of this book, which was first published ten years ago.

This updated version of *Astrology For Women* will enable you to predict your future to 2025 — and it also contains information on your Chinese Zodiac Sign and Indian Moon Sign, as Asia is destined to play a powerful role in our lives over the next two decades.

You will also find a new section on chemistry and compatibility in this edition — not only with partners and dates, but also with friends, family, employers, colleagues, flatmates and clients.

Revising this book after ten years has also given me a chance to streamline some sections, remove others which are dated — and add some brand new sections. If you're an astrologer, please note: both solar charts and natal charts are used in this version of the book.

I would like to thank my editorial consultant, the BBC radio astrologer and teacher Julian Venables — and Clare Barker, Keven Barrett, Diana Beaumont, Andreina Cordani, Helen Daly, Fiona Inglis, Jonathan Lloyd, Pippa Masson, Amruta Slee, Karen Spressor, Deborah Thomas, James Williams, Helen Beard, Kate O'Donnell and Natalie Winter.

I would also like to remember some astrological pioneers in this edition — America's legendary researcher Lois Rodden; my predecessor at *The Australian Women's Weekly*, Athena Starwoman; and Ananda Bagley from Electric Ephemeris in London, who provided the planetary tables in the first book.

Jessica Adams
Brighton, England, 2006

YOUR FIVE
STAR SIGNS

You have five star signs, not one.
They are your Sun sign (which you probably know), your Moon sign, your Mercury sign, your Venus sign and your Mars sign. Each of these has something to say about your personality, destiny and relationships.

Your Sun sign describes what will make you well-known or admired. It shows where you're likely to shine in life, and what could make you famous. Your Moon sign describes what kind of mother you are, to your own, or other people's, children. It also shows the sort of home life you need, and your lifestyle in general. Your Mercury sign points to your working life. How do you conduct meetings, talk to clients or customers, give speeches, send e-mails, write documents, or manage negotiations? Your Mercury sign shows how. Your Venus sign describes who you are when you're in love. It shows your charm, your style and your femininity. It's the essence of your womanhood, and for the female of the species it is absolutely essential knowledge! Your Mars sign shows how you defend who or what is important to you. It describes what you're like in a fight, no matter if it's with work rivals or your partner.

Ready to go? Turn to the tables, which begin on page 379, and write your five star signs down here:

Sun Sign

Moon Sign

Mercury Sign

Venus Sign

Mars Sign

Sun Signs

SUN SIGN ARIES

* You identify with women who are brave, tough, strong and absolutely fearless.

* Your proudest moments include career triumphs or sporting victories.

* You shine when you're fighting the good fight — or just throwing tomatoes.

* You seem like a redhead to a lot of people, no matter what colour your hair is.

* By forty you will become well-known for your dynamic, feisty, energetic style.

SUN SIGN TAURUS

* You identify with women who are wealthy — at the other extreme — female alternative lifestylers.

* Your proudest moments include getting rich — or refusing to sell out.

* You shine when you're bargaining, buying, selling or investing.
* You have a fetish for certain objects — anything from jewellery to art.
* If you become famous, it will be for your business sense — or strong values.

SUN SIGN GEMINI

* You identify with women who are witty and clever — real-life Lois Lanes.
* Your proudest moments involve speeches, interviews or being published.
* You shine when you're writing or talking — or just getting a message across.
* You are hooked on e-mail, phone texting or keeping a blog or diary.
* By forty, you will become well-known for your way with words.

SUN SIGN CANCER

* You identify with mothers, the caring professions or property moguls.
* Your proudest moments involve real estate triumphs or children.
* You shine when you're looking after people and may be a great cook.
* You have a passion for redeveloping and improving gardens and homes.
* Even if you never have kids yourself, you'll make a star godmother/aunt.

SUN SIGN LEO

★   You identify with the great and the good — you're motivated by famous people.

★   Your proudest moments involve your creative talents and self-expression.

★   You shine when you're playing queen or diva in any professional situation.

★   You spend a lot of money on hairdressers or hats . . . you love a tiara too.

★   Of all the twelve signs you are best equipped to handle being well-known.

SUN SIGN VIRGO

★   You identify with hard-working women who get the job done perfectly.

★   Your proudest moments involve successful diets or big health victories.

★   You shine when you're slogging away on detailed plans or intricate projects.

★   Times of low self-confidence usually accompany poor health or work issues.

★   Born in the '60s? Your obsessions are typical of your generation.

SUN SIGN LIBRA

★   You identify with famous couples, romantic heroines or glorious brides.

★   Your proudest moments involve milestones in your love life — like a proposal.

* You shine when you're immersed in beauty; from gardens to fashion shows.
* You will have a well-known romantic or business partnership one day.
* You're famous for your diplomacy skills and could easily work in an embassy.

SUN SIGN SCORPIO

* You identify with powerful women like Condoleezza Rice or Hillary Rodham Clinton.
* Your proudest moments are those where you were in complete control!
* You shine in any crisis, as you are unafraid of raw, human issues.
* You could get quite a reputation for your secrecy or need for privacy.
* You come into your own when you finally get the sex life you deserve.

SUN SIGN SAGITTARIUS

* You identify with travellers, explorers, teachers, students and writers.
* Your proudest moments involve education, or self-education, milestones.
* You shine when you're being funny — you're a natural comic or cartoonist.
* Of all the signs, you are most likely to emigrate, travel or work overseas.
* You will become well-known for your attachment to another culture/place.

SUN SIGN CAPRICORN

* You identify with women who have made it to the top through sheer hard work.

* Your proudest moments involve awards, promotions or record sales figures.

* You shine when you are asked to give the benefit of wisdom/experience.

* Nobody can ever pin your age down, no matter how old/young you are.

* You are famously cautious and make a savvy grandmother . . . or wise aunt.

SUN SIGN AQUARIUS

* You identify with feminists, eccentrics, female rebels and alternative types.

* Your proudest moments involve group projects or shared achievements.

* You shine when you can show off your originality, and your unique abilities.

* Even when you're not trying, you stand out from the crowd; you're different.

* You may become well-known for being years ahead of your time!

SUN SIGN PISCES

* You identify with poets, painters, photographers, psychics and saints.

* Your proudest moments are those where you show off your imagination.

* You shine when you are making unconditional sacrifices for people/animals.
* You are famously sensitive, which makes you sympathetic — or very fragile.
* Over time, you will become well-known for your predictions or hunches.

MoON SIgNS

MOON SIGN ARIES

- ★ Your mother was a fighter, not a lover, and she wasn't scared of a battle.

- ★ You need fast food — not junk food, just anything which takes five minutes.

- ★ You're competitive when it comes to real estate, and *pulverise* the Joneses!

- ★ You look after other people by staging World War Three on their behalf.

- ★ Emotionally, you are short on patience, and big on impulse and speed.

MOON SIGN TAURUS

- ★ Your mother was rich, a collector, hung up on cash — or a hippy drop-out.

- ★ You need food which either comes in under budget or costs a bomb (like caviar).

* Your home is your biggest investment; you believe in bricks and mortar.
* You look after people by spending on them, or advising them on finance.
* Emotionally, you need your precious things around you to feel safe.

MOON SIGN GEMINI

* Your mother had a way with words, and was a great reader, writer or talker.
* You need food which won't get in the way of your book or TV program.
* Your home is a communications HQ — from the computer to the cell phone.
* You look after people by making them laugh, or by talking them to death.
* Emotionally, you must have excellent communication — or it all falls apart.

MOON SIGN CANCER

* Your mother was a real mother — a feeder, a breeder, or a comforter.
* You need food which reminds you of childhood; it makes you feel secure.
* Your home is your nest, your haven, your castle and your sanctuary.
* You look after people by cooking for them, nursing them or holding them.
* Emotionally, you fall into parent–child scenarios. You play both roles too.

MOON SIGN LEO

* Your mother was special, and had a creative job —
  or creative hobbies.

* You prefer food and drink which is gourmet,
  expensive or five-star.

* Your home will never be ordinary or commonplace.
  You need luxury too.

* You find security through recognition — you need
  the spotlight to feel okay.

* Emotionally, you are motivated by pride. You're
  dignified, even in a crisis.

MOON SIGN VIRGO

* Your mother was hard-working, and her
  health/wellbeing was a real issue.

* You need food and drink which suits your body; it's
  got to be just right.

* Your home will be clean, well-organised, and often a
  second office after five.

* To feel secure, you must have your routines and
  rituals in place.

* You need to keep striving for perfection — in
  everything from your figure to your work.

MOON SIGN LIBRA

* Your mother was feminine, diplomatic, tactful and
  really needed a partner.

* You prefer food which other people like! You're a
  people-pleaser by nature.

* Your home will be beautiful, and you won't skip the flowers or the artwork.
* To feel secure, you need a partner: a soulmate.
* You need to live in a fair and just world, so causes will often attract you.

MOON SIGN SCORPIO

* Your mother was powerful, secretive, intense and just a little bit obsessive.
* At various stages in your life you will have wild food/cookbook fixations.
* Your bedroom is the nerve centre of your home — it's where the sex is!
* Emotionally, you are the deepest and darkest of the twelve Moon signs.
* No wonder you picked up this book; astrology's secrets compel you.

MOON SIGN SAGITTARIUS

* Your mother had foreign roots, or was a traveller. She was funny too.
* You globetrot, and bring home foreign food preferences/recipes.
* You will only feel at home when you emigrate, or have constant travel in your life.
* You look after people by telling them about your philosophy or life/beliefs.
* You need to study, or educate yourself, over the course of your lifetime.

MOON SIGN CAPRICORN

* Your mother was serious, wise, cautious, and big on status or achievement.

* When entertaining influential people, you work incredibly hard to impress.

* Your home is a status marker. You'd rather rent in Bel Air than buy a hovel.

* You will never feel at home in the world unless you're right at the top.

* You need to have ambitions to strive for or you feel empty and incomplete.

MOON SIGN AQUARIUS

* Your mother was independent, eccentric and always ahead of her time.

* You're a mad cook and nobody can ever predict the results of your recipes.

* Your home life will be unique, and your house, flat or lifestyle will be unusual.

* To feel secure, you need to be free. You need tons of space and me-time.

* You need to make the world a better place or you'll feel weirdly unfulfilled.

MOON SIGN PISCES

* Your mother was wafty, sensitive, intuitive, imaginative and kind-hearted.

* You're only interested in fantasy food — the rest of it is rather boring.

* You'll aim to live by water, or make a focus of the bath/pond/pool/fishtank.

* Escaping from reality makes you feel safe, but try to skip drugs or alcohol.

* You need television, film, books, music and/or meditation to help you cope.

Mercury Signs

MERCURY SIGN ARIES

* You think quickly in attack–defence situations — like a military commander.

* You're a fast talker, or become noticeably snappy when you're stressed.

* Your e-mails don't waste any time getting the message across.

* At school you argued the point with the teacher and got bored easily.

* A brother or sister was an action man/woman, or a competitive type.

MERCURY SIGN TAURUS

* You think in terms of how much things will cost you — on every level.

* You are a down-to-earth communicator who takes a practical angle.

- ★ Your e-mails revolve around dollars and cents, euros, or pounds and pence.
- ★ At school you aimed for subjects which you knew would help your career.
- ★ A brother or sister was hung up on money, or rejected capitalism altogether.

MERCURY SIGN GEMINI

- ★ You think like a born writer or scriptwriter, as words are your domain.
- ★ You use wordplay when you talk, and are a witty conversationalist.
- ★ Your e-mails often reveal words or terms you have made up yourself.
- ★ At school you did well in English, or related areas like debating/drama.
- ★ A brother or sister was virtually born with a cell phone in his/her hand.

MERCURY SIGN CANCER

- ★ You think like a mother/grandmother — always in terms of looking after others.
- ★ You tend to talk in terms of feelings and emotions, rather than cold logic.
- ★ Your e-mails often centre on your clan — be it family or flatmates.
- ★ At school you may have done well in cooking, history or carpentry!
- ★ A brother or sister wanted kids young, or has adopted a pet as a baby substitute!

MERCURY SIGN LEO

*   You think like a born leader or commander and dramatise every issue.

*   You tend to talk with your head held high, your chin up, or in a posh accent.

*   Your e-mails dramatise events and situations — almost to TV show level.

*   At school you were brilliant in amateur plays — even when playing a sheep.

*   A brother or sister was a natural leader type, or extremely creative.

MERCURY SIGN VIRGO

*   You think about details more than other people and file things in your mind.

*   You tend to talk precisely — no sloppy language, vagueness or generalisation.

*   Your e-mails are run through spellcheck and you dot i's and cross t's.

*   At school you were astonishingly hard-working on subjects that mattered.

*   A brother or sister was concerned with his/her health, fitness, diet or wellbeing.

MERCURY SIGN LIBRA

*   You think in terms of win–win situations as you prefer balanced scales.

*   You tend to talk diplomatically and tactfully, winning people over.

* Your e-mails are a fantastic tool in your social life; you're a networker.
* At school you preferred subjects/projects which involved how things look!
* A brother or sister was a charmer, whose appearance really mattered.

MERCURY SIGN SCORPIO

* You are secretive and never reveal what you are really thinking or planning.
* You tend to talk less and listen more — it gives you more power with others.
* Your e-mails never give away too much information, as it could be used against you.
* At school you became quite obsessed with certain subjects/projects.
* A brother or sister was intense, passionate and kept secrets extremely well.

MERCURY SIGN SAGITTARIUS

* You think with your sense of humour first and foremost — it's your filter.
* You always insert a bit of homespun philosophy into your conversations.
* Your e-mails often come with a joke or a funny spin — or a cartoon.
* At school you loved teachers/subjects which opened up the world to you.
* A brother or sister was a natural traveller and drawn to far-off places.

MERCURY SIGN CAPRICORN

* You think carefully and cautiously and always for the long-term picture.

* You ask questions which get you places professionally or socially.

* Your e-mails are strictly business most of the time.

* At school you persevered with any subject which could lead to success.

* A brother or sister was ambitious and wanted big things from his/her life.

MERCURY SIGN AQUARIUS

* You think in your own unique way which others seldom truly understand.

* You can surprise, or even shock, people around you with what you say.

* Your e-mails are your lifeline. Or, at the other extreme, you're anti-internet.

* At school you rebelled against any teacher or subject you disliked.

* A brother or sister was a one-off, with quite a few eccentricities.

MERCURY SIGN PISCES

* You think in images and pictures — your mind's eye dictates how you process facts.

* You have inspired quite a few people with your conversations and ideas.

* Your e-mails can be rather vague, flaky or forgetful — or full of white lies!
* At school you were the class dreamer in subjects which bored you.
* A brother or sister was highly imaginative and rather sensitive.

VENUS SIGNS

VENUS SIGN ARIES

* You love action men, and action women — wimps or wibblers can go away.

* Your version of femininity is feisty, fearless, fast and sometimes furious.

* If you are passionate about someone, you will fight for them/against them!

* You're popular with people who appreciate high energy and drive.

* Your wardrobe contains at least one outfit which is pure 'dress to kill'.

VENUS SIGN TAURUS

* You love people who are wealthy, or rich for spiritual or ethical reasons.

* Your version of femininity is grounded, down-to-earth and unpretentious.

* If you are passionate about someone, you'll spend on them/give them stuff.
* You're popular with people who appreciate your natural money sense or your firm values.
* Your wardrobe contains at least one ridiculous bargain — worth much more.

VENUS SIGN GEMINI

* You love people who are the talkers, thinkers or writers of the world.
* Your version of femininity is brainy, entertaining and witty.
* If you are passionate about someone, you'll e-mail and text them endlessly.
* You're popular with people who appreciate your way with words.
* You prefer clothes, shoes or bags which send clear statements.

VENUS SIGN CANCER

* You love anyone who cares — doctors, nurses, cooks, charity-givers, mothers.
* Your version of femininity is old-fashioned girl, or yummy mummy.
* If you are passionate about someone, you'll feed them or breed with them.
* You're popular with people who appreciate your caring, protective style.
* Your wardrobe contains at least one vintage or family heirloom piece.

VENUS SIGN LEO

* You love anyone with star quality, from local guitarists to Hollywood names.

* Your version of femininity is dignified, classy and absolutely five-star.

* If you are passionate about someone, you'll be proud to be seen with them.

* You're popular with people who appreciate your sense of drama/display.

* Your wardrobe contains at least one link to a celebrity — by label or look.

VENUS SIGN VIRGO

* You love anyone who works hard to be fit and healthy — wellbeing is crucial!

* Your version of femininity begins and ends with the body beautiful.

* If you are passionate about someone, you'll give them diet/vitamin advice.

* You're popular with people who appreciate how incredibly hard you work.

* Your wardrobe contains at least one piece of yoga/fitness-related gear.

VENUS SIGN LIBRA

* You love anyone who is good-looking or beautifully dressed or groomed.

* Your version of femininity is all-girl. You don't do asexual or tough.

* If you are passionate about someone, you'll do anything to make it work.

* You're popular with people who appreciate your charm, tact or diplomacy.

* Your wardrobe contains pastels, pink, frills, bows and/or flowery patterns.

VENUS SIGN SCORPIO

* You love anyone who is obsessive about what or who they value most.

* Your version of femininity is sexy beyond belief — from the lingerie up.

* If you are passionate about someone, you'll be jealous of exes or rivals.

* You're popular with people who appreciate how powerful you really are.

* Your wardrobe contains at least one item with a good sex story behind it.

VENUS SIGN SAGITTARIUS

* You love anyone who has travelled, emigrated or has a foreign connection.

* Your version of femininity is global — your style comes from all over the place.

* If you are passionate about someone, you'll book airline tickets with them.

* You're popular with people who appreciate your sense of humour.

* Your wardrobe contains plenty of items you've picked up overseas.

VENUS SIGN CAPRICORN

* You love anyone who's made it to the top by climbing slowly up the ladder.

* Your version of femininity is practical, successful, ambitious and grounded.

* If you are passionate about someone, you'll think long-term about them.

* You're popular with people who appreciate your wisdom and serious side.

* Your wardrobe contains work outfits which double as investment pieces.

VENUS SIGN AQUARIUS

* You love anyone who's alternative, eccentric, radical or ahead of their time.

* Your version of femininity is your own. You make it up as you go along.

* If you are passionate about someone, you'll treat them as your friend — always.

* You're popular with people who appreciate your humanitarian principles.

* Your wardrobe contains some wild charity shop/market/vintage discoveries.

VENUS SIGN PISCES

* You love anyone who's imaginative, sensitive, compassionate and emotional.

* Your version of femininity is inspired by photographs and films you love.

*   If you are passionate about someone, you will make big sacrifices for them.

*   You're popular with people who appreciate your intuition and sixth sense.

*   Your wardrobe contains at least one pure fantasy outfit to dress up in.

MaRS Signs

MARS SIGN ARIES

* You survive by being first off the blocks, and often see life as a short sprint.

* You're a tough fighter and can be a real Amazon when you're in the mood.

* You're an energetic, fearless competitor — in love, at work, or in sport.

* You get what you want by pushing and shoving, if necessary.

* You get angry by rolling up your sleeves and taking immediate action.

MARS SIGN TAURUS

* You survive by using your money, property or possessions as your weapons.

* You're a stubborn fighter and know how to hang on — and on — if necessary.

* You're a financially aware, business-minded competitor, even in love.

* You get what you want by paying for it, or doing clever money-saving deals.

* You get angry by waving a chequebook, suing, or flaunting your wealth.

MARS SIGN GEMINI

* You survive by using your intelligence and your clever way with words.

* You're a witty fighter and will use your sense of humour to score points.

* You're an articulate competitor and always know what to say, or write.

* You get what you want by using letters, e-mails, faxes or text messages.

* You get angry by choosing words that hurt, or by hurling obscenities.

MARS SIGN CANCER

* You survive by falling back on family members, or clinging to your home.

* You're an emotional fighter and can be furiously protective of your clan.

* You compete by using your parents, kids, close relatives or flatmates!

* You get what you want by using your role as mother — or property owner.

* You get angry by playing super-mother, especially if men are involved.

MARS SIGN LEO

* You survive by being more creative than those who are your nearest rivals.

* You're a dramatic fighter and can lapse into acting or attention-seeking.

* You compete by using your confidence and dignity to outclass others.

* You get what you want by being superior to everybody around you.

* You get angry by being condescending or patronising.

MARS SIGN VIRGO

* You survive by working harder than anyone else to win a particular battle.

* You're a critical fighter or opponent and always find flaws or imperfections.

* You compete by being fitter and healthier than others — or by having more extreme illnesses!

* You get what you want by going over every detail, almost exhaustively.

* You get angry with a list in your head, and file every point you make.

MARS SIGN LIBRA

* You survive by finding a partner or ally who can support you when necessary.

* You're a diplomatic fighter, as you know a fair result is achieved by tact.

* You compete by using your husband, lover or business partner to help.

* You get what you want by pure charm, and seduce people into saying yes.

* You get angry with difficulty, as you prefer balance and harmony.

MARS SIGN SCORPIO

* You survive better than any other Mars sign — you're a phoenix figure.

* You're a passionate fighter and can become obsessed by your enemies.

* You compete by using your power — and then manipulating situations.

* You get what you want by using sex, or other people's money or property.

* You get angry on the deepest level and can be emotionally intense.

MARS SIGN SAGITTARIUS

* You survive by moving, finding new places to visit, or just running away.

* You're a fighter with a sense of humour and can always see the joke.

* You compete by using two weapons — humour and your vast general knowledge.

* You get what you want by drawing on what you've read or studied.

* You get angry over philosophical, religious, moral or ethical points.

MARS SIGN CAPRICORN

* You survive by using your advanced position on the career or status ladder.

* You're a practical fighter and attack or defend cautiously at all times.

* You compete by using your job, or your social position, as a weapon.

* You get what you want by waiting, working and being extremely patient.

* You get angry, but never lose your temper if it will damage your ambitions.

MARS SIGN AQUARIUS

* You survive by doing it your way, and inventing new rules as you go along.

* You're a rebellious, unpredictable fighter who often shocks or surprises.

* You compete by using your brilliant originality and advanced ideas.

* You get what you want by rebelling, or just by following a unique path.

* You get angry, but not in a way that people have experienced before!

MARS SIGN PISCES

* You survive by using your intuition, sixth sense and hunches — or tarot cards.

* You're a deceptive fighter who will lie, fake it or fudge the truth at times.

*   You compete by being more imaginative than your rivals or enemies.

*   You get what you want by making sacrifices — for others, or in general.

*   You get angry with difficulty, as you know how it feels to be your enemy!

LIVING WITH YOUR FIVE SIGNS

You can solve problems by using your five signs as you need them. It's rather like having a wardrobe of useful clothes. Drag out what works and put it on. By 'inhabiting' your planet signs to the fullest, you'll be in sync and life will be easier.

If you're feeling invisible, read all about your Sun sign. These are the qualities which will gain you recognition. If you are feeling insignificant or overlooked in your life — maybe you've become a mother rather than a person, or perhaps you're stuck with a horrible job — do some research on what your Sun sign is all about. These are the traits you need to work on, and show off, to really make people look twice.

Famous women live out the qualities of their Sun signs in an obvious way, because they are permanently in the spotlight. Princess Diana had the Sun in caring Cancer — she is most remembered as the mother of William and Harry, and the patron of children's and AIDS charities. Madonna has the Sun in Leo — she's famous for her star quality and her boundless creativity. The Queen has the Sun in Taurus — she is famous for being the wealthiest woman in England. Anne Frank had the Sun in Gemini — she is famous for her diary. Germaine Greer has the Sun in Aquarius — she is famous for her radical views.

If you are going through an insecure patch, then you need to express your Moon sign and 'feed' it properly. Feeling emotionally wobbly is a sure sign that you are forgetting what your Moon sign needs. Do you have the Moon in Virgo? Look at your daily routine, your diet, your health and your wellbeing. Do you have the Moon in Libra? You need a partner. If it's not possible in your sex life, find a work or business partner instead — or maybe a dance class partner.

Occasionally, you will be thrown into work or academic projects which lean heavily on your communication skills. This applies even if you normally do a lot of writing or talking. When the pressure is on, return to your Mercury sign and try to get in touch with its qualities. Using your Mercury sign consciously will make it easier for you to get your message across.

Single women looking for love need to use their Venus sign to get what they want. It's their seduction tool. If you are in a relationship which isn't working, you can also use your Venus sign to create more harmony in the partnership.

Is someone determined to fight with you or attack you on any level? Then you need your Mars sign. Never forget that it's there. Getting in touch with your Mars qualities will empower you and give you the energy and strength you need to defend yourself, or even work towards a win–win outcome.

THE REaL YOU

Astrology is different for women. You know your Sun sign, of course — but did you know it's a male planet? For women, it's the Moon sign and Venus sign, combined, which really hold the key. These are the two female planets, and when read together will give an instant snapshot of who you really are. This might take some getting used to if you're used to your magazine or newspaper 'sign' being the whole story. Nevertheless, the female planets will sum you up in the most amazing and accurate way.

If your Sun sign is the same as your Moon sign or Venus sign (it happens sometimes), then you'll just feel an extra sense of recognition. Now read on!

YOUR ARIES MOON/VENUS

Aries is a goal-oriented, fearless sign and having it as your Moon/Venus sign is like having a tiger in your handbag. It also helps you in those situations where you must defend and protect yourself. And along with the tiger in the handbag, there is a set of red designer armour in there!

> **Are you typical?**
> You're sporty or athletic, or do strenuous dance or yoga
> You take adventure holidays
> You never give in without a fight
> You're competitive in your career

An Aries Moon or Venus sign for women is rather like having an outboard motor attached to some part of you — providing the muscle and adrenaline you need. Forget women who run with the wolves. Your Aries planets guarantee you'll run with virtually anything. If this side of you is strongly developed, you'll probably be one of the very few women who can develop a passion for male sport as well.

One of the basic things I notice about people with planets in Aries is that they always feel better after they've walked things off or sweated them out. You don't have to be an athlete or action woman to live out this sign in your life, but you will find that everything seems to come together better when your body is being stretched. Apart from anything else, it gets rid of the frustration, tension or anger that you naturally accumulate — thanks to the family, your girlfriends or your love life!

The Versus Factor

Aries Moon/Venus signs in your chart create you-versus-them situations more frequently than any other sign. Some Aries-influenced women consciously enter into fights; others don't ask for them, but seem to get them anyway. You will often be in two-way contests or three-way triangles, and the following scenarios are especially common:

Husband versus wife
Mother versus daughter
Father versus daughter

Husband versus wife versus mistress
Husband versus first and second wives
Lover versus ex-lover
Business partner versus business partner
Friends versus friends of friends
Nation versus nation
Neighbour versus neighbour
Team versus team
Employee versus boss
Brand versus brand
Business versus business
You versus the world!

Mars — Ruler of your Moon/Venus

Aries is one of the least acceptable signs in our society, because its ruling planet, Mars, is so brutal. Mars was the God of War and represents pure aggression. In mythology and astrological tradition, he is dripping with blood and hungry for battle. The socially acceptable face of Aries is sport and organised war machinery — the Army, the Navy, the Air Force. Also, sanctioned places where aggression, attack and defence can be played out — like the police force, politics and the legal arena. Corporate aggression is okay too. And how about other action-woman pursuits, like rescue/emergency services?

If you are strongly Aries-influenced, these general areas and themes may have already played a part in your life. Still, it is unusual for little girls to be told that scrapping in the playground is a fabulous idea, that becoming a general is the way to go, and that tough girls are good girls.

Society as a whole has always had a problem with women who have Aries planets. Its preference is generally for nice women, and I really don't think the word 'nice' is what your Aries side is all about. Strong, tough, assertive, feisty and fearless are adjectives which are much closer to the mark.

If you try to pretend that your Aries Moon or Venus isn't there, it will squeeze in through the back door. Then, in what appear to be circumstances beyond your control, you have to face all manner of stresses, irritations, bitchfests and snarling relationships — all of which seem to take ages to resolve.

These long-running snarlfests are a total negation of what your Aries side is all about. Aries Moon/Venus fury should be honest, plain, obvious, and both aired and finished with as quickly as possible. It also needs to go back to its *true* source. Complications seem to arise for Aries-influenced women when they either: a) ignore the original source of their anger and end up venting their spleen on inappropriate targets around them; or b) stretch out the purity of quick fury into something niggling and time-consuming — like nagging, sniping, passive aggression or secret bitching sessions.

Handling the Anger

I don't think any astrologer would recommend that an Aries Moon/Venus type should just march over and bop someone on the nose — or throw a frying pan at them. But to pretend that you were not born with an Arian side, and have no connection with Mars, God of War, could end up making life very complicated. Perhaps unhealthy too, as misdirected anger becomes stress, and anger turned back in on the body has been known to reveal itself as illness.

There are many ways to deal with the inevitable battles or miniwars that affect your Aries side. One way is to write it all down. There will be times when you must *genuinely* attack or defend, though, in which case your Aries side will be very useful, maybe even life-preserving. Finally, forget the personal: your Aries 'Tank Girl' side is a fantastic plus for whichever good cause or group goal you lend it to. It's your

Aries planets which make the difference between sitting on the couch worrying about things, and actually being motivated enough to do something about them.

Self-Starters

A tremendous number of women with Aries Moon/Venus signs succeed in their own businesses, or in fields where they are pretty much left to their own devices. You have enough energy, courage and confidence to make it on your own. The Aries number is one. It also rules the First House of the horoscope wheel. Being number one, and doing it by yourself, is a constructive way of channelling your aggressive Aries planets.

Some of you run one-woman shows inside larger organisations. It's also very common for Aries-influenced women to set up under their own names or to be strongly identified on a first-name basis with their clients or customers. If you have an Arian side, people tend to relate to *you* first, and what you have to offer becomes entwined with your personality. Your name leads the product or service.

Spiritual Redheads

If you have the Moon/Venus in Aries, and strongly identify with the sign, then you are a spiritual redhead. Mars, the ruler of Aries, has long been associated with the colour red. It's interesting to see how this colour turns up in the lives of the Aries-influenced too.

Some of you are almost auburn — or almost auburn again. The fates may become your personal hairdresser if you are born with an Aries planet, or a strong Mars signature in your horoscope. You may develop a thing about red cars, red lipstick or red flowers as well. It doesn't matter what colour your hair is, though — you may still seem like a redhead if you are strongly Arian. This vibrant colour (which can also lean towards hot pink) may also turn up in your home.

Aries Moon/Venus Inspiration: Scarlett O'Hara

The sassy, independent and occasionally aggressive heroine of *Gone with the Wind* is one of many fictional Aries women (Lucy van Pelt in the *Peanuts* cartoons is another). Scarlett's most famous feud was with Rhett Butler, but her cinematic spats are many and varied. Her name also contains the famous Arian allusion to red. Her style is very Arian — impatient, brave, tough and full of pioneering spirit. If you need to revive the Aries side of your personality, hire the video, see the film on the big screen, or read Margaret Mitchell's book.

Pioneering Spirit

If you were born with the Moon/Venus in Aries, it allows you to be right *on the edge* of the first wave. This sign gives you a charge signal that can lead you into some pioneering areas: never too far ahead of the trend, but always on top of it. Your Arian side enjoys being first, or being involved with the first wave of anything. This side of you likes to race off in new directions as quickly as possible.

It's partly your competitive side that dislikes being left behind, but it's also a genuine desire to champion new ideas or new trends, explore new territory and lead the field. This side of you is unafraid and enjoys risks. Other signs in your astro-package may be slower or more cautious, but your Aries planets will always push you forward.

You were probably *living* affirmative action even as governments were inventing a word for it. You don't do sexism. This Moon or Venus sign is often identified with equality, breaking the glass ceiling or advancing women's progress. It may — or may not be — the ethical questions surrounding feminism and equality that concern you, but you are unlikely to tolerate being last in any race, or the last to follow any new idea. The fact that you are a woman is irrelevant.

Tougher than Tough

Your Aries Moon/Venus lend you a toughness that does your image no harm at all. It's a kind of jodhpurs-and-leather-boots swagger, and it exists no matter what you're wearing. I suspect Aries-influenced women could wander around in pink frilly kaftans and still look tough. Mars, the ruler of Aries, was also known as Gradivus, or the Strider. The ancients associated your sign with striding out into battle. Many women project their striding Arian side straight into their wardrobes and live their lives in pants or jeans. More importantly, they tend to stride and swagger through life itself.

A Sense of Self

The words 'me' and 'I' are strongly associated with Aries, because this sign rules House One of the horoscope, where women develop a sense of self. Aries gone mad can be notoriously self-centred for this reason. Handled properly, though, an Aries planet can be wonderfully assertive. Most of you who have developed your Arian side will have no problem using the 'me' word or the 'I' word. Women who sing or write songs for a living tend to lean hard on this Arian sense of self to push their personalities across.

YOUR TAURUS MOON/VENUS

You instinctively know the value of things. You may express this in the traditional way, by becoming a collector or an investor, or you may develop your value system to include the things that money cannot buy. For this reason, some of you become conservationists — as you believe nature cannot be bought and sold. Others become world-class bargain-hunters or sharp-eyed collectors. Your Taurean side increases your enjoyment of art, music, food, fashion, jewellery, furniture and beauty. It helps you appreciate quality.

> **Are you typical?**
> You love beautiful things
> You are good at giving and receiving massage
> You have your finances — and your value system — sorted out
> You are continually finding new pleasure in art or music

A Head for Business

Successful businesswomen figure heavily in the Taurus story, and so do thoughtful investors. Taurean-influenced women become expert in areas like commerce and economics — and there are also a few 'women at the top' who have a canny appreciation of their own worth, and value, in the market. Having a planet in this sign does not guarantee a gold-plated existence, but it will help you to recover better from financial lows, and give you a finely tuned understanding of supply and demand. Taurus is associated with the stock market through bullion, and also through bull markets. It is common in the charts of high earners, wealthy investors and small business success stories.

Here's a little of what you need . . . or love:
Security and certainty — unless you give up your money
for an ideal, you'll opt for home ownership every time *
A beautiful garden * Collectible furniture * Original art *
Home insurance * Beautiful bargains * A financial
safety net * A personal code of values * Above all, perhaps,

a good accountant. You are very *thingy* about your things,
and you need to be able to afford them!

Finding a Value System

Non-material values are arguably the most sophisticated
expression of a Taurus planet. This does not negate your
understanding of market forces, or your eye for all that is
beautiful and 'priceless'. Taureans often transcend money
and materialism to settle on something bigger, though.

For some of you, this is your professional integrity.
Taurean types often struggle with the idea of selling out. In
other cases, Taurean types put a higher price on human
values — commonly, human lives. If you have a planet
here, you may typically find that you follow both roads.
One part of you is the instinctive collector and owner —
money-minded, swayed by beauty and longing for security.
The other part of you has a highly sophisticated
understanding of a different kind of marketplace. Here,
you are trading in other values: the price of a rainforest,
the cost of saving a life, or the value of your own
credibility and integrity.

What price reputation? Your Taurus planets probably
understand this issue quite well. Many Taurus-influenced
women are well known for dealing in an alternative value
structure that has absolutely nothing to do with money or
materialism. *Priceless integrity* is the domain of Taurus, above
all other signs. Getting there seems to involve a lot of trial
and error, but when your Taurean side has fixed a price on
the things that cash cannot purchase, it's exceedingly hard to
go back.

If life is an auction, then it's this Taurean side of you that
refuses to sell out to the highest bidder: you leap over money
into a value system that is personal and precious to you. It
doesn't mean that you lose your Taurean awareness of money

— far from it. But if you choose this 'elevated' Taurean pathway, then you'll also have an awareness of quite a different value system. Destiny says you'll be obliged to choose, however. 'For love, not money' is often the mantra of the Taurus Moon/Venus woman!

The Taurean Bull

The ancient astrologers could have chosen any symbols for their constellations. In all honesty, the stars that make up the Taurean Bull could just as easily make up the Taurean Aardvark or the Taurean Ferret. The symbolism of the bull suits your Taurean side rather better, though. The ancient astrologers noticed that people born when the Sun appeared to be passing through this part of the sky were slower to move and more stubborn than most. Today, astrologers notice the staying power and persistence of women who have a planet in this sign. You drive a hard bargain. You never take the first offer!

Your Taurean side slows you down, and the image of the bull describes this steady, powering side of you quite potently. To really tap into Taurus, walk up to the fence and gaze at the next bull you see in a paddock. That ambling style, those dug-in heels, that slow watchfulness . . . It all changes, of course, when the bull charges. Your Taurean side can be awfully slow to react — and to act — but it is quite forceful when a decision has been reached.

Staying Power

Your Taurean side has a steady, relentless quality that is very hard to beat. The steadiness and slowness of Taurus results in a stubborn refusal to give in or give up. Women with planets in Taurus have proven, over the years, that they are in it *for the distance.* The bounce-back qualities of the sign are justifiably famous, and only a Capricorn planet makes you a better long-term stayer. This reveals itself in business — or property.

YOUR GEMINI MOON/VENUS

Use the famous Gemini wit and you will charm or distract absolutely anybody into absolutely anything. Your Geminian side also brings a passion for reading which you can enjoy from childhood to old age.

Are you typical?
You love the telephone and your e-mail
You travel whenever you can, even for brief getaways
You write for sheer pleasure or even for profit
You've worked out precisely why sibling issues are so important to you

---

I have never met a woman with planets in Gemini who was not known by another name at some stage in her life. If you have Gemini planets, you may find that you are quite happy about the name your parents gave you, but everybody else feels moved to re-christen you as quickly as possible. It's almost as if you really have been split into one or two sets of twin personalities, and each time someone different sees one of these multiple versions of you, they give you a different name.

Some Geminian women change their names for professional reasons. Some of you may not feel entirely comfortable with your given name, so you make an adjustment. With the right name, you can end up with quite a variety of alternative labels. If you have friends who also have Gemini planets, a whole chain of nicknames and alter egos can develop between you. If you have quite a few

Gemini-influenced people in your social circle, then when you all get together outsiders won't have a clue what or whom you are talking about!

Siblings and Twins

Your Geminian side can also be expressed through a sister or brother figure, or real-life sibling issues. Brothers or sisters may have a huge impact on your life if you were born with Gemini planets, or you may find the fates throw you someone who acts as your symbolic twin, or other half. Many women with Gemini planets have platonic, sisterly relationships with men for this reason. For better or worse, this is the sign of the sibling.

If your Geminian side is strongly developed, it may be hard for you to think of yourself, or your life and times, without immediate reference to a brother or sister. Astrologers who are also qualified psychologists invariably ask about brothers and sisters if a Gemini-influenced client turns up for counselling. Sometimes, the issue is that there was no sibling at all, and psychologists find it has influenced the whole family dynamic. The myth of Castor and Pollux also describes cousins, and your Gemini planets may bring strong issues around the children of your mother's and father's siblings.

On Castor's 'off' days, Pollux would take his place. If you have Gemini planets, your relationship with a sister or brother may reflect the myth. You may live parallel lives, you may be rivals, there may be a difficulty if both of you occupy the same position or place in life, or there may well be another strange twist of fate going on.

Language is a Virus

Singer and performance artist Laurie Anderson (Gemini Sun) had two hits. One, 'O Superman', was largely based around an answering machine (typically Gemini) and the other, 'Language is a Virus', sums up the wordy, verbal obsessions of the sign. Your Geminian side is the one that inspires you to make up names or nicknames for other people (or objects). Mercury, your ruler, is associated with *naming things* and many women who have Gemini planets seem to delight in fixing humans, animals or even cars with a title.

Your Geminian side may be the one that lets you create catchphrases, or pick them up. Most Gemini-influenced women have a pet phrase or expression that family or friends associate with them. Words just seem to stick with Gemini, and if you have planets here you will continually supply those around you with your aural 'signatures' and quotable quotes. Crosswords, dictionary games, Scrabble, diaries, journals, poems, letters, postcards, books, memos, Post-it notes, texts, sign language, switchboards, telephones, pagers and puns are Gemini's domain too.

Gemini famously gives you a *way with words* above all other things, and a love of language. Your place in the astrological tribe is to articulate, refine, polish and play around with your language of choice. For this reason, your Geminian side may be equally entertained by scripts, song lyrics, poetry, fiction, prose, non-fiction or journalism. If new words or slang start to float around you, the chances are you either started it, or some other Gemini-influenced female is spreading the verbal virus. Gemini planets help you to pick up foreign languages more easily too. Just as you can transmit information, you also seem to absorb it effortlessly. No wonder the Geminian self-education process is lifelong.

Doubles and Multiples

I have known many people with Gemini planets who have a kind of 'multiple choice' lifestyle which results in these doubles and multiples: it's because there are two of you, and sometimes more!

Two identical teapots
Five nicknames
Two passports
Three television sets
Six pseudonyms
Two fax machines
Four jobs
Eight identical black poodles
Two sexual preferences
Four telephones
Two houses

Gemini Moon/Venus types split themselves into different people, pursuing different lifestyles, countries, social circles and professions simultaneously. Dual passports, or dual citizenship, is another example of Gemini's tendency to double up. Your Geminian side is a natural juggler.

Travelling Light

Gemini is strongly associated with short journeys — the kind where you can boomerang back to your original starting point very quickly. Gemini's ruler, Mercury (also identified with Hermes), spent a lot of time zipping around with winged sandals, but never really went very far. If you are strongly Gemini, your life may be full of short hops, either for professional or personal reasons. Your Geminian side inclines itself to city–country hops, interstate journeys, neighbourhood circuits and short treks to other countries. Flight attendants with Gemini planets always seem to stick to short hauls. And I know a vast number of women in the media with Gemini planets who spend their lives in the back of taxis! (Gemini rules taxi drivers and couriers too.) The more your Geminian side dominates your life, the more likely you are to get around town, or the planet, more than other women.

Gemini planets incline their owners towards the neighbourhood above all other things, perhaps because that is originally where Mercury felt at home. There is often a lively, local feel in the lives of strongly Geminian women, and the sign has traditionally been associated with neighbours. If your Geminian side is active, you may be quite involved with your neighbours, or have a definite network locally. You will tend to identify with, and feel at home in, the few kilometres around your home.

Gemini and Comedy

Behind the best comedy lies a Gemini Moon/Venus. Part of your Geminian inheritance is an extremely sharp sense of humour. Many Gemini-influenced women are brilliant mimics. You'll either 'do' a voice to make your point, or use silly accents for selected parts of your sentence. If you develop your Geminian side, you may end up being a professional funnywoman.

YOUR CANCER MOON/VENUS

Are you typical?

You're totally in touch with the part that childhood and home plays for you

Turning a house into a home is a mission of love for you

You've found at least one human or animal in your life to protect and nurture

The Mother Role

The word *mother* resonates with Cancer-influenced women for all kinds of different reasons. Some are positive reasons, some are more complicated, and some are downright difficult.

Moon/Venus in Cancer describes how you feel about being a mother, how you feel about your own mother, and the role of women as mothers in general. If you decide to go ahead and have a child, it will be a bigger deal for you than for most other women. If you skip parenthood, then, similarly, it's going to be a very big deal.

Your Cancerian side will be clan conscious. This means your own parents and siblings and close relatives — or the family you create by yourself. It can also mean your ancestors — the roots in your family tree. There will be very little that you do which can take place without reference to your family, to your place in the clan and to your relationship with those people.

Some astrology books have described Cancer Moon/Venus women as stove-bound, baby-sprouting, soup-making matriarchs. Having a planet here does make you family-conscious, yes, and certainly extremely sensitive to the notion of mother–child relationships. Your own maternal instincts, though, will be strongly influenced by your particular experience of the family set-up, and this is one of the most complicated areas of life as an astrologer knows it.

All we know when you walk in the door with your birthday on a piece of paper is this: if we barge in with insensitive comments about your family, your mother, or your feelings about children, we are likely to lose a client.

For every woman with a Cancer planet with three children at school and another on the way, there is one who has a problem with the notion of motherhood.

Of course, some of them are powerful matriarchs; but most are just intricately involved with their families and clans because destiny has intervened. Family trees, and the family name, is big with you if you have the Moon/Venus in Cancer.

Dynasties and Family Trees
Princess Anne — Venus in Cancer
Princess Margaret — Moon in Cancer
The Queen Mother — Venus in Cancer
Judy Garland — Venus in Cancer
Nancy Reagan — Moon in Cancer
Nancy Sinatra — Moon in Cancer

Interpreting Cancer
Women with planets in Cancer who have a problem with the traditional image of child-bearing hips and pots and pans prefer it when the notion of motherhood is analysed a little more thoroughly. Cancer has described different maternal roles at different stages in history. Once it may have been about endless baby-popping and apron-tying, but today Cancer's maternal feelings encompass a variety of different roles. You will probably recognise an aspect of yourself here, yet all of these roles are also aspects of modern motherhood. They may be applied to your own family, if you have one, or to the world outside your front door:

Nurse ★ Doctor ★ Psychologist ★ Counsellor ★ Chef ★ Sports coach ★ Courier ★ Taxi driver ★ Entertainer ★ Mediator ★ Switchboard operator ★ Waitress ★ Cleaner ★ Interior decorator ★ Accountant ★ Security guard ★ Vet ★ Children's storyteller ★ Home renovator ★ Teacher ★ Nanny ★ Electrician ★ Plumber ★ Nutritionist ★ Caterer ★ Tailor ★ Masseuse ★ Party organiser ★ Defence minister ★ Food entrepreneur ★ Restaurateur ★ Psychic healer ★ Hotelier ★ NGO or charity worker ★ Babysitter ★ Adoption agency/fertility expert.

All of these roles, in Cancerian terms, are done for love. And they are accomplished *protectively*. As with all things associated with this sign, the accent is on caring and caretaking — or feeding and homemaking.

You may be a traditional mother taking on a variety of these modern roles, or you may take on responsibility for others, in which case you may gravitate towards a career where you are caring for others in a wider sense, or towards interests which extend to others' welfare. This will be particularly obvious if you have more than one planet in Cancer, too. The Cancerian thing is *looking after other people*.

What you need with the Moon in Cancer is this:
Security ★ Your own home ★ A family, or substitute family ★ A sense of place ★ The food you love ★ Old photo albums ★ Peace of mind about your mother/stepmother ★ Something to nurture or care for.

Home is where life begins and ends, as your house or flat is the centre of everything you need. You need a signed document to say that the place is yours, above all other things, as the insecurity of renting is not really your ideal. Peaceful surroundings, or a door that slams on the outside world, are very important. The bathroom is full of potions, lotions, luxuries and gadgets, and only the kitchen comes up for the same kind of attention.

With the Moon in Cancer, you either inherit family recipes, or create classics which are then passed on through the clan. Your mother or grandmother always seems to be floating over your shoulder when you cook too — literally or symbolically! You're good at doling out food for the five hundred, and shine at those 'gathering of the clan' functions. You're especially fond of food you grew up with, or associate with your homeland. You're a nostalgic cook.

Food and Diet

The Moon rules Cancer, and this planet is associated with food and eating issues by astrologers. You may express this in different ways. Some of you are expert cooks, some of you just love food. Others have difficult issues around eating, and dieting, and food consumption: if this sounds like you, an astrologer will look at the position of the Moon in your personal horoscope for initial clues.

Most of you are enthusiastic cooks or natural entertainers, have a fine appreciation of good food, and some of you even make a career out of it: a strong Moon or Cancer emphasis in a horoscope usually describes a natural cook or gourmet. The comfort food of childhood and adolescence is usually a big trigger for you.

The Home Environment

This sign increases your interest in, and enjoyment of, your own place. It may give you a concern for the housing or accommodation given to other people too — charities for the homeless might touch you, for example. Women who earn their livings in real estate, the hospitality industries, architecture, interior design and building often have a Cancer Moon/Venus.

You don't have to work in the area of property to like it, though. Most of you with a Cancer planet are perfectly happy to stand in front of real estate agents' windows, or cart home DIY equipment from the hardware shop on the weekend. All of you seem to adore turning empty houses or flats into havens. This is an intensely home-oriented, shelter-seeking, cave-retreating sign . . . and you just love pulling up the drawbridge.

Your Homeland

My country, right or wrong, is a phrase that seems particularly appropriate to Cancer planets. Your ancestry may be Aboriginal, Irish or fifth-generation Australian; Quaker American, Scots, Japanese or Welsh, but a strong sense of homeland seems to come with the territory.

A deep sense of roots, history and belonging is necessary for your Cancerian side, which may beam out strong messages about your culture, origins or nationality to people who meet you. This is never more obvious than when you are far from home, or a long way away from your roots.

It's an intensely tribal thing, even if your 'tribe' happens to be living in the middle of deepest, darkest Manchester in a high-rise flat! Not surprisingly, Cancer planets lend an incredible patriotism, and a strong identification with familiar slang, customs, food and cultural preferences. Identifying with your roots in this way could influence everything from your favourite recipes to the kind of accent you speak with. It may influence you on election day, or when you switch on the television to watch the news — or the sport.

I have noticed that there are a few women with Cancer planets who cannot bear the idea of living in their own country (sometimes for painful reasons) yet create a sense of belonging elsewhere. They become flag-wavers or enthusiasts for other people's homelands, cultures and beliefs. Strange but true — but then your Cancerian side will always need roots, even if they are borrowed from elsewhere.

Some of you with a Cancerian side are so interested in your origins that you turn your attentions to history, even becoming historians.

Children and Teenagers

Those of you who do feel comfortable expressing your family-conscious, child-conscious side often gravitate towards areas where you can do something to reach children and teenagers in a practical way. It's virtually a rule with this Moon or Venus sign!

Mary Poppins is a good Cancerian Moon/Venus icon. She adopted a clan — or perhaps they adopted her — when she landed, via umbrella, in the home of a London family. Her 'spoonful of sugar helps the medicine go down' technique is typically Cancerian, and so is her extreme Englishness — Cancerian types 'speak' their nationality very strongly.

YOUR LEO MOON/VENUS

Your Leonine side makes it easier for you to approach life in a confident way, and it helps your self-esteem. Leo planets are also invaluable when you need to out-class the opposition. Something about your Leonine side intimidates others very easily, and in the right time and place this 'class act' can be helpful. Leo's other bonuses? Rampant creativity and self-expression. This is the sign which gives birth to schemes, performances, dreams and projects.

Are you typical?

You're proud of who you are and what you're
    doing with your life

You have an outlet for expressing yourself
    (Some may call it showing off!)

You have a position of leadership somewhere

You walk tall

Glittering Connections

If you have planets in this sign, there may literally be some royal or aristocratic link in your life. What does your family tree say? A touch of Hollywood, showbiz, television, music, entertainment, royalty or the White House/10 Downing Street/the Lodge often turns up in the strangest ways in the lives of Leo Moon/Venus women.

I have known women with Leo Moon planets who can claim OBEs, royal chefs, Scottish aristocrats and medieval courtiers in their family trees. In the United States and in Argentina, the Leonine connection also works towards the president, and in Australia and the UK towards the prime minister.

The symbolism is the same — it stands for rank and privilege, divine leadership, and all that those things entail. Your planets in Leo incline you towards the world of the special, the exclusive and the elite. In Hollywood, this means superstars. In London, this means Buckingham Palace. In swimming pools and stadiums across the land, Leo leads to gold medals and the company of winners. It's about knowing or being related to *special* people — or being special yourself!

Very commonly, women with Leo planets have a connection to people in the world of film, television, music, internet stardom, sporting success, politics, radio or media — which is where the new kings and queens come from. They shift you towards the gods, in theatrical terms. The upper echelons of the Establishment, and the top ranks of corporate life, are also Leo's domain.

Pride and Dignity

This really is the sign of invisible height, and wherever Leo planets fall in your chart, you are likely to live your life from a slightly elevated perspective. Your Leonine side expresses itself proudly and with dignity because of the link with female royalty. It has always been necessary for queens to appear proud and dignified to inspire the confidence of the people — and to intimidate pretenders to the throne and rival powers.

There's always a mild head-toss about Leo Moon/Venus women, no matter how cool they are!

Your Leo planets will express themselves with dignity very convincingly, but there is usually some perspiration under the crown. Many women with Leo planets have told me that it feels automatic and natural to approach life in a dignified way — but they are also aware of the performance that goes with the territory, and sometimes it's a strain.

This may be another reason why Leo is associated with creativity and entertainment. Every modern queen is an actress at heart (Otherwise, how does one face the TV cameras on Christmas Day, my dear?) and if you have planets in this sign, you will come to know this 'stagey' feeling in your working life, and perhaps in your private life as well. Every time you have to be on display, even if it's just at a meeting, your Leo Moon/Venus will show itself.

Dignity is everything with you. The writer Nancy Mitford, who had the Moon in Leo, wrote *The Sun King* and *Noblesse Oblige*. More tellingly, she always preserved what other people saw as a 'perfect shopfront', even when facing marital breakdown and illness. Elevated posture, elevated views, elevated speech and an elevated nose (!) are all deeply Leonine. It's the brave-face sign.

Do you have the Moon in Leo? Then you need all this:
The spotlight ⋆ A child — or a brainchild ⋆ Special treatment ⋆ Luxury ⋆ Authority ⋆ Loyalty ⋆ A leading role ⋆ Five-star accommodation ⋆ First-class tickets ⋆ A home to show off.

Your house or flat is designed for parties, children or creativity (or perhaps all three). There is usually a playroom in a Moon in Leo home, and it may be a 'nursery' for various hobbies, interests and talents, or — if you have children —

the real thing. Leo Moon homes always contain something grand, impressive, rare or expensive. You are house-proud and really need a palace or a castle. Chairs matter too — the throne symbol! No cheap plastic for you.

You are a creative cook if you have the Moon in Leo, and really come into your own when you are trying to impress people. In a perfect world, cooks and maids would do it all for you, but Moon in Leo women don't mind washing up afterwards if they receive well-chosen compliments when it's all over. You prefer impressive menus and are quite a confident cook. You'll end up with Alessi or Wedgwood eventually! And you rate TV chefs.

The Chanel Connection

The Leonine links in the life of Coco Chanel are full of mysterious synchronicities. And it's fitting that the Chanel label still symbolises VIP status today — very Moon or Venus in Leo!

Mademoiselle Gabrielle 'Coco' Chanel (Leo Sun) designed the pink suit Jackie Kennedy (Leo Sun) was wearing on the day President Kennedy was assassinated. Two decades later, Madonna (Leo Sun) was also wearing Chanel designed by Karl Lagerfeld (Leo Mercury). Claudia Schiffer (Leo Mars) was a favourite Chanel model too. Marilyn Monroe (Leo Rising) also became the face of Chanel No. 5 (the Leo number) in perfume advertisements. Coco Chanel is buried in Lausanne, beneath a tomb carved with *lions*.

There are many other Leonine words and images in Chanel's life: the Chanel men's fragrance L'Egoiste (ego is certainly Leo's domain); the name of Coco's orphanage — Sacred Heart of Mary (Leo rules the heart, Mary is a royal name); one of her first clients, Elizabeth, the Queen Mother, and a later one, Metro Goldwyn Mayer, whose logo — of course — is the lion. Many of her clothes are held (where

else?) at the regal Victoria and Albert Museum in London —
including a very famous evening dress and cape worn by Mrs
Leo D'Arlanger.

If you have Leo planets, your life and times may not be
quite as laden with symbols as Chanel's, but you may
appreciate her perfume, or her little black dress, nevertheless.
It's certainly remarkable how often Moon/Venus Leo women
find a little (or a lot) of Chanel dropping into their lives.

Leonine Luxury

Embellishment, decoration and self-expression accompany
your Leonine side. This is partly because ancient monarchs
had to be myth-builders. To build an aura around a monarch,
symbols, images and designs must be constructed — rather
like those surrounding religious icons. To protect the
sacredness and power of the monarch's position, personal
seals, stamps and coats of arms must be made. Precious
jewels must be worn, robes must be sewn and gold must be
hammered.

The act of personalising something to suit oneself — or
of choosing the rare and exclusive — is inherently Leonine.
The art of being widely imitated is also woven into the sign.
Invariably, clients I have seen who are strongly expressing
their Leo planets seem to have tremendous flair. There is a
preference for putting a stamp or a seal on things — and this
may be done by adopting a memorable trademark style, or
by doing things more dramatically, creatively or distinctively
than usual.

You don't do cheap, ordinary or boring . . . that's for other
people!

The Creative Impulse

Leo rules the Fifth House in astrology, which is where
babies are conceived and born, children are raised, and

great ideas are also delivered and nurtured. If you have planets in Leo, then you need to grow some kind of seed, and what that seed becomes will be entirely reflective of your genetic make-up, your bloodline and the environment you inherit.

On the most obvious level, this seed will be a child — or you may adopt a child. But the creative impulse is so strong with Leo planets that it is never enough for a Leo-influenced mother merely to conceive and give birth to a baby: the creative process may still be going on during the child's adolescence. Leo types enjoy the bending, shaping and guiding process that parenting involves. They also take particular enjoyment in the drawings, stories and scribbles of their offspring.

There are many women with Leo planets who are childless by choice or circumstance, and their creative impulse goes into a very different kind of conception, birth and nurturing. These are the women who begin with a blank sheet of paper, an empty desk, a bare garden or house, a vacant stage, a bare table or a blank canvas.

Essentially, your Leo planets represent that side of you which has the urge to enjoy yourself and reproduce. That may be why women with a strongly developed Leonine side either make a vocation out of love and motherhood, or, alternatively, out of all that their brains or bodies can express.

Leonine Authority

The Sun, Leo's ruler, is associated in astrology with authority and leadership qualities. Wherever you have a planet in this sign, you will find a side of you that is convinced it can captain the team, steer the meeting, deliver the interview or head up the business. If you are strongly Leo-influenced you may become head of your own company, or take a position of influence and importance in someone else's — or just become a minor, or major, celebrity.

Little girls with a Leo planet seem to remember the times they do well and are praised, and ignore the occasions where they fail. When you grow up, you tend to do what you're good at and avoid the rest. The subjects you struggle with — or are embarrassed by — at school are left behind for good when you graduate.

Your Leonine side is interested in shining and in being complimented and acknowledged by other people. You'll even consider taking a salary drop in order to do something fabulously well, with maximum applause. Just as long as you can still afford your luxuries, of course.

Be careful — queens lose their heads (or their tax havens) when they lose touch with real people, real issues and, above all, their own failings and faults. If you have the Moon/Venus in Leo then part of you is definitely a queen, but too much ego or 'me, me, me' and the masses might just accuse you of behaving like an impossible princess.

Lady Penelope, the puppet heroine of *Thunderbirds*, is a classic Venus/Moon Leo by the way. She has a family crest, aristocratic heritage, a family mansion, a chauffeur and a pink Rolls Royce. She is also a British secret agent, working for queen and country. Sylvia Anderson, who created Lady Penelope and her costumes (and provided the character's voice in the original series), was kind enough to confirm to me that Penelope was indeed 'born' between July and August, making the character a Leo type.

Myth Building
Do myths occur naturally around Leo planet women, or do they create the myths deliberately? Your Leonine side attracts

stories, gossip and 'legendary' anecdotes about you, but only you can say if you consciously encouraged the story or found it had just woven itself around you. Your Leonine side is a brilliant editor. It cuts out the drab bits, censors the clumsy scenes, and omits the ordinary, the awful or the less-than-glorious.

A toothpaste advertisement shown on Australian television in the seventies reminds me of this trait in Leo types. An air hostess was being interviewed. 'How's your love life?' the voice asked. 'Wonderful,' the air hostess enthused, 'London, Paris, New York . . .' The voice persisted. Finally, the air hostess admitted her love life was terrible (no doubt because of her appalling halitosis).

The Moon/Venus Leo woman *likes* myths. Misery, failures, embarrassments, humiliations, poverty and disappointments do not go on display because they spoil the act. Perhaps the myths around you come from this. It certainly creates mystery and curiosity, and when this happens, myths follow.

With planets in this sign, you can literally make yourself up. (You don't believe this? Find your resumé or CV. Your Leo planet will have left its signature somewhere on page three . . .) You may not even realise you are doing it. Either way, when you exit the room, people will say, 'Did you know that she . . .?'

YOUR VIRGO MOON/VENUS

Virgo is associated with precision and perfection.

Typically, you're in touch with health, fitness and body issues. You enjoy detailed work or interests that challenge your brain. You're a reader, or a writer. You can't leave any project unfinished or less than perfect. Many Virgo-influenced women enjoy stretching the English language like a piece of elastic and make a beeline for education, media, publishing or similar industries, or they thrive in computer-based businesses and companies where communication is everything, even if it's exporting raspberry jelly.

Do you have the Moon in Virgo? You need:
Routine, routine, routine ⋆ Productivity bonuses ⋆ A water cooler ⋆ Your own space in the fridge ⋆ Ergonomic chairs ⋆ A designer filing cabinet ⋆ Colleagues with high standards ⋆ Space for your writing skills ⋆ An organised workspace ⋆ The best cleaner in town.

Delivering the Message

Virgo thrives on information, communication and the world of words. Only planets in Gemini and Sagittarius are as deeply concerned with knowledge (if you have these in your astropackage too, you may as well decamp to a library or radio station and live there).

Getting the message across correctly is a chief concern of Virgo. Your Virgoan side is there to question, record, nod, contradict, agree, check — and then transmit. There is a strong sense of dedication and responsibility surrounding your messenger role. It's not enough to write it, or say it, casually. Information is never just flicked with a towel when Virgo is behind it — you assess information critically.

Whatever is passed on to others by your Virgoan side has to be researched, checked, double-checked and *word perfect*.

Many of the world's greatest writers, educators and media figures have Virgo planets for this reason. So do many women who act as messengers and information agents for those in the communication, education and information industries — and women who are the informal news services for their families and friends.

Some of your interests and abilities will be defined by the other signs that are in your birth package. The talent for getting it all across, though, is definitely Virgo's domain. Whatever field you find yourself in, you will often find fate asks you to be the courier or reporter who kicks the information across.

Moon in Virgo women also need this:
Pure food, without additives or toxins ⋆ White sheets ⋆ An eco-friendly lifestyle ⋆ A job that is a calling ⋆ Order and organisation ⋆ Books ⋆ A laptop ⋆ A trusted doctor or naturopath.

If you have the Moon in Virgo, then you create order out of clutter. You know exactly where everything goes and enjoy sorting it all out. People move your bathroom things into new places and you just move it all back again. You like having bits of nature around you, even if you live in an urban setting. The Virgoan essentials? Vitamins, white things, herbs. The Moon in Virgo cook likes piling everything up on the chopping board, like an illustration from a five food groups pyramid chart. Here are the onions, here are the mushrooms, here are the organic lettuces . . . egad! Your kitchen is a shrine to neatness and order and you feel physically ill when the rubbish collectors go on strike. You're a good breadmaker, even if you don't know it. Your herbs are *fresh*.

Body Maintenance
Virgo planets often conspire to create the classically health-conscious or body-conscious woman. You may develop an interest in health and healing, or a strong connection to your own body. Along with the typical Virgo-influenced clients I see (mineral water, yoga and vitamin B

girls), I also know a few who are interested in recreational drugs. Body-consciousness with Virgo does not always take the form of a mineral water habit or a penchant for massage.

Your Virgo side knows about poisons and toxins, botany and biology, the sea and the air, the soil and the plants, the blood and the bones. Your experiences with illness, or more serious crises within your body, will be turning points in your life, because they bring your Virgoan side into sharp focus. Often, the woman with a Virgo Moon/Venus is superbly body-conscious because illness has made her that way.

If you have Virgo planets, you will eventually develop the ability to 'read' your body and understand the equation that leads you to peace of mind and mental equilibrium — or to low energy and personal downtime. You may also be able to do this, quite shrewdly, with those around you — even animals — especially when they are suffering.

It is the *intelligent handling of the physical* that defines Virgo. Your own body is the initial practice ground for this, but eventually it may extend to others as well. Even a Virgo type with a junk food habit will be able to tell you the fat content of the junk, the effect she expects it to have and the kilojoule conversion rate!

The Natural World

Part of your Virgoan inheritance is a profound understanding of the natural world. Many women who have Virgo planets are concerned with environmental and ecological issues as they specifically affect the atmosphere, the sea, the food chain or the ozone layer. Your garden is important to you if you have planets in Virgo, but the world is the biggest garden of all. Virgo the virgin is about purity.

If you have the Moon and/or Venus in this sign, you show you care by making sure that the mineral water is sparkling, the rubbish is recycled, the eggs are free-range — and the subscription to Greenpeace, PETA or The Wilderness Society is in the mail.

The Work Ethic

Inheriting the sign of Virgo in your astrological package is something that needs careful consideration. Part of it is certainly about finding value and pleasure in what can be achieved by letting the clock and the calendar dictate your efficiency and productivity. However, there are many women with a strong Virgoan side who find that routine takes them over, or that the work ethic becomes their whole life.

You will see your Virgoan side most strongly when you begin your first full-time job, choose to embark upon motherhood for the first time, or even tackle unemployment for the first time. You relate to people by working hard for them — or by encouraging them to work as hard as you do. But is this eating your life?

Order and Organisation

Virgo rewards thoughtful organisation. In your own life, it is the filing, sorting, weighing, cleaning, judging, filtering, classifying, marshalling, cataloguing and tidying that counts. I have heard an awful lot of women with a Virgo planet groan when they hear this. It does — on the surface — sound fairly dull. Some spectacular things can occur when Virgoan types create order out of chaos, though. Your influence in a marriage, a parent–child relationship or a professional double-act is always obvious, as there's a bedrock of method and order underlying everything you do.

YOUR LIBRA MOON/VENUS

Libra is the public relations sign, and if you have a planet here, you have a natural ability to make peace or win people over. Libra planets also intensify your enjoyment of music, art, design and beauty. Having a planet in this sensual sign increases the pleasure frequency!

Are you typical?

You make room for romance in your life

You have a strong feeling for colour, texture, design, shape or form

You're happy to play the role of peacemaker

You feel good about your attractiveness and appearance

Partnerships are your Oxygen

In France, the sign of Libra is known as 'Balance' and if you have the Moon/Venus here, then your romantic relationships will be the first big balancing acts of your life. You really need, or desire, a partner with this sign in your chart — other women *say* they do, but you really, really, really do!

The ultimate expression of Libra is a successful partnership, and having one or more planets in this sign encourages you to pursue it, either through business ventures or professional double-acts, or through marital or de facto relationships.

Crossing Boundaries

Libra planets make it difficult to fly solo, because they describe an alliance between two sides. It is common for strongly Libran women to marry across their social class, across their nationality, across their background or across their status. Why? Because Libra wants the perfect formula that will make two radically different species appear to be equal. Also, perhaps, because the Libra inside you needs the challenge of differences in order to understand what equality and balance are really all about.

Using patience, trickery, subtlety and native intelligence, your internal Libra will ultimately balance the scales, particularly in romantic relationships. The Libra inside you is interested in getting the red needle in the partnership to wobble in the middle — not to swing violently from left to right. The process of partnership is often as meaningful as the end result for Libra Moon/Venus. Perhaps for that reason, strongly Libran women seem to gravitate towards relationships or marriages where their partner comes from a different world.

The same principle exists in the professional partnerships formed by women with Libra planets. It is easy for you to fall into a double-act. Libra really translates as the ampersand, (or the 'and') in your life. It describes two parts of a whole. Commonly, what makes the alliance so interesting in its own right is the fact that it is clearly bridging some kind of gap. This is the source of the 'different but equal' message spelled out by the sign.

Women with planets in Libra are also responsible for some of the world's most successful professional partnerships. Two is your magic number.

Do you have the Moon in Libra? Here's what you need:
Peace, harmony and co-operation ⋆ A place for
everything that is aesthetic or easy on the eye ⋆
Above all else? Loving relationships.

Your house or flat tends to be a setting for your social life above all other factors. Appearances will be unusually important and you may spend a long time selecting the colours, shapes and textures you prefer. Typically, you are less interested in the structure or foundations than the colours or design of the guest towels. A mansion designed for good manners is really your dream home.

The Moon in Libra cook specialises in beautifully presented food, gracefully handed over. Flowers are *de rigueur*. You prefer restaurants where chefs are artists, and find it hard to resist the romanticism of low lighting and foreign menus. You're a tactful cook, always finding ways to let your guests off the culinary hook. Who caters for vegetarians, carnivores, dieters and chocaholics without flinching? A Moon in Libra woman.

The Ampersand Sign

Many women with Libra planets seem to slide into partnerships where two names merge into one, and are connected only by an ampersand. This does not take away your independence or identity. However, there will be times in your life when you must also weigh up the differences between you, the other person involved and the partnership itself, which often seems to become as complicated and as real as a third person in its own right.

Jane Austen, who had the Moon in Libra, never married but spent her entire career writing about engagements. In her most famous novel, *Pride and Prejudice* (there's that ampersand again!), she described the chemistry between the proud Mr Darcy and the prejudiced Miss Bennet in a way that sums up the capacity of Libra to create partnerships and marriages which are so complex, so colourful and so intricate, that they become entities in their own right. If you have planets in Libra, it is very likely that you have created your own Jane Austen novels from the various alliances, romances, double-acts and duets in your own life.

Give Me Beauty!

Libra is associated with the visual arts, fashion, beauty, design, packaging, presentation and, above all, taste. This theme seems to run through the lives of most women with planets in Libra. In the Libran universe, appearances really do count. Planets in Libra lend themselves to expression through colour, form, shape, design and texture. If this sign really is strong in your chart, then you may personally become a kind of modern Venus in your own right — adored by men and admired by other women. There are plenty of Libran women who are well-dressed, beautifully packaged, and quite literally born beautiful. There are also quite a number who have a passion for texture, colour, design and shape. Libra is certainly over-represented in the beauty, art, fashion and design-based industries!

Finding a Balance

Your planets in Libra are there to help you develop your taste, to increase your appreciation of beauty, and to encourage you to build partnerships. Most importantly, Libra planets are also there to help you build bridges. This sign abhors imbalance and injustice. Why should rabbits be used in laboratory experiments because they were born in the animal kingdom and not the human one? Why should working-class children receive a different education from upper-class children? Why should one country reserve the right to invade another one? Why should the First World exist at the expense of the Third World? Why do whites receive more opportunities than blacks? Why should women be treated differently from men? Why aren't fat women and thin women equal? These are all essentially Libran questions, although you will find your own way of framing them. It's really a matter of finding the particular injustice that rankles most.

I suspect women with planets in Libra only come into their own during times of war, because that is precisely the moment that diplomats and peacemakers are required. Today, women with planets in Libra turn their attention to other battles. Racism, class warfare, animal exploitation and sexism are just some of them. Wherever there is prejudice, bias, unfair treatment or discrimination, your Libra planets will jump in. Your Libran side has a sharp eye for a flaw in the system, and it will seem natural for you to try and restore balance, order and harmony. Some women with Libra planets have told me they cannot bear to look at prejudice, bias or discrimination in the world, as they find it physically ugly and offensive. Whatever offends the eye with you is likely to be the same thing that offends your sense of fairness and justice.

War and Peace

Not every woman with planets in Libra becomes involved in political or ideological battles, although many do. However, if you are expressing yourself at least partly through this sign, you are unlikely to ignore the unfair, the ugly and the brutal in this life.

The difficulty for you, with planets in Libra, is to find a way to protect your principles without ending up in a fight. Occasionally, it will be possible to do this. The real test for Libra-influenced women is to weigh up the cost of battle against the price of peace. In a perfect world, it would be sufficient to sweetly point out the injustices, give a nice smile and hope that human intelligence will prevail. Inevitably, there comes a point when even a peaceful protest will not do, and it is then that the famous Libran ability to weigh and measure will appear.

If you are expressing your Libra planets quite strongly, you may already be aware that you have diplomatic skills and a talent for negotiation. Libra is interested in finding the common ground, not the differences. If you are really living this sign, then a lot of your energy will go into peace treaties, bargains, deals and double-acts. The Libra inside you is a charmer, a peacemaker and a diplomat. However, it is also true to say that your Libran side is prepared to put on armour when all else fails — *especially* if your sense of justice is offended. Your first preference is to find a useful ally. Forming alliances is natural if you have planets in Libra. If all else fails, you will resort to conflict as a last option. Classically, you will be more prepared to fight if someone else is on your side or wedded to your cause, and a great deal of energy goes into these kinds of mergers.

If war is the price of peace, then your planets in Libra will ultimately decide if you must pay it. This applies in your private life, in your career, or, in a wider context, in causes and principles you believe in. If it really does seem to be right, then your Libran side may well have to decide to fight for it. Campaigns of one kind or another are a common theme with strongly Libran women — but peace and balance are always driving the decisions. As Moon in Libra politician Golda Meir said, 'A leader who doesn't hesitate before he sends his nation into battle is not fit to be a leader.'

Libran Venus/Moon Myths

In Shakespeare's play *Henry V*, the French Princess Katherine is fated to marry England's King Henry as part of the peace settlement between the two countries. She is the perfect Libran bridge between two worlds. Were she not beautifully packaged and diplomatic, she would not be considered a good peace offering by Henry, but she is quickly accepted. The fashionable, feminine, charming Katherine agrees to the marriage not only in the interests of forming a romantic partnership, but also in the interests of a diplomatic accord between the two sides, France and England. If you have planets in Libra, the symbolism of Katherine's story may also reflect aspects of your own life and times.

Hanging on to your Womanhood

Destiny says that many Libra-influenced women end up in all-male environments, or break ground — as a female — in a male-dominated area. For some, this sense of womanhood means perfume, lipstick and heels. For others, being defiantly female means choosing to incorporate the traditional strategies of the wife or girlfriend — charm, negotiation, conflict resolution — into professional life.

Some Libra-influenced women use love, care and feminine intuition in their working lives as an acknowledgement of female principles. For you, with planets in Libra, a lot depends on how you define femininity and womanhood. It may be wearing white lace lingerie under your suit, putting flowers in your office, or simply refusing to play it like a man even if you're moving in a male environment. Women with planets in Libra who spend time together invariably send one of two strong messages to the world: either very girly or strongly feminist.

YOUR SCORPIO MOON/VENUS

This definitely gives you depth, soul, a little darkness, a lot of passion and a huge dose of intensity. You can channel this into the goals which are most important to you, with powerful results. Single-minded passion is Scorpio's domain, and having a planet in this sign makes it simple for you to express yourself powerfully and with enormous focus. Controlled obsession for the goals which matter most will not only bring them closer, but also with results that deepen your understanding of life.

> **Are you typical?**
> You get wholly involved with people and projects, or not at all
> You respect intense emotion, from passion to pain
> You're in touch with your sexuality at the deepest level — including all the taboos
> You understand that being human is all about acknowledging our darkness

Mistress of the Dark

If you have planets in Scorpio, then for professional reasons, or intensely personal reasons, you will come into contact with all our dark sides. The Seven Deadly Sins are your domain! Sometimes the dark side just happens to Scorpio-influenced women of its own accord. Consciously, you may be pursuing the most uncomplicated life: living in the light. Then, one day, you wake up with the sinners — or the sinned-against — on your doorstep. You do not have to have a planet in Scorpio to be in opera — but it helps.

This sign is about power, femme fatales, crisis, rebirth, survival, secrets, passion, sex, death, race and money . . . and indecent obsession, as well as decent obsession.

Do you have a Scorpio moon? Here's what you need:
Intensity ★ Passion ★ Dramatic and powerful music ★
Emotional purges ★ Mystery ★ Secrets ★ Sexuality with
depth ★ A walk on the wild side ★ Mutual obsession ★
Above all — privacy.

Your house or flat is one of those places where everything leads back to the bedroom. You have little boxes and locks and special drawers, and what isn't hidden there is pushed under the bed. Depending on the state of play with family members, flatmates or neighbours, your home will either crackle with atmosphere or be drenched in the strangest vibrations!

You like the sensuality of food, and get a great deal of enjoyment from the oral component of cooking and eating! Scorpionic cooks can become quite manic about their recipes and usually have to be dragged away from their culinary masterpieces. You are passionate about your favourite flavours and scents. You also tend to cook for love, or prepare food or drinks with a view to sex. In your dreams, you have a *9½ Weeks* kind of kitchen to play in.

Let's Talk About Sex

Some of you will meet your Scorpionic 'sex' side through your careers. Some of you may meet Scorpio directly, in the most difficult way, through your own experience of the unacceptable face of human sexuality. However you experience sex, it is part of the Scorpionic inheritance to drag taboos into the light.

Scorpionic sexuality reflects the deeper issues — nothing that can be dismissed as shagging or bonking, but the intensity of our entire sexual underworld. From the taboo — masturbation — to the non-mainstream — homosexuality, tantric sex, S&M — to the dark side — sexually transmitted disease, sexual abuse, incest, sex addicton and rape — everything is fair game in Scorpio's domain. If you have planets in Scorpio, then in astrological terms you are one of the very few women who are qualified to address this 'underworld'.

The theme of *sexual appetites* and *forbidden fruit* also seems to resonate with Scorpio-influenced women. If you have a planet in this sign, you may experience both sides of the Pluto myth which rules Scorpio, either hungering for forbidden fruit or feeding it to others. Some women with a Scorpio planet do this 'feeding of the forbidden' in a professional way — as sexual advice columnists. The rest of you just advise your friends over a bottle of wine.

Cosmopolitan founder and sexual revolutionary Helen Gurley Brown has the Moon in Scorpio.

Race and Colour

For as long as racism and bigotry continue to be taboo issues in society, Scorpio planets will seek out the awkward, uncomfortable issues around them. Many of the women on the Scorpio Moon/Venus list are involved with Aboriginal or African–American issues. Others are concerned with racism on other levels. If you have Scorpio planets you won't be afraid of any difficult or taboo questions.

It is no accident that the planet Pluto was discovered and named in the 1930s, just as race hatred was on the rise. If you have a Scorpio planet, your experiences with race or colour will trigger many of the questions in you that polite society would prefer to forget about. If race or colour are the 'dark horses' of modern life, then it is unlikely that your Scorpionic side can simply allow them to run away without closer inspection.

Secrets and Mysteries

Why is your Scorpionic side so famously secretive? Some astrologers argue that it lends you the power, or control, that you seek in life: rather like the playground chant of 'I know something you don't know', it gives you considerable influence! There may be something in this. Knowledge is power, and your Scorpionic side does give you an ability to draw out sensitive information from other people without ever revealing too much of yourself in return. This in itself makes you a rather powerful figure, although not every woman with a Scorpio planet is conscious of her behaviour patterns.

There is another explanation for your secretiveness, and that is the intervention of fate. Destiny singles you out for intense experiences which really cannot be tossed around like so much gossip. Consequently, you get into the habit of censoring large parts of yourself and, by a chain reaction, become discreet or silent on other matters too. No wonder you have such a weakness for murder mystery — on television or at the cinema. You understand the deep, dark, deadly secret thing better than any other Moon or Venus sign.

Planets here give you an appetite for ghosts and disappearances, murder and magic. Scorpio is strongly associated with everything that takes place from midnight to dawn — including the late-night horror shift and the slow tread of the vampire. Women who are strongly Scorpio-influenced are often familiar with the occult, and have a slightly 'witchy' feel or appearance about them.

Serious Money

Scorpionic money is the kind one dies for, the kind that is hushed up or kept confidential, the kind that carries power, splits families, breaks marriages or runs deep. It is *power* money at its most basic level, and really not the same money at all as Taurean cash — which goes on perfume, wine and pearls. Scorpionic money has nothing to do with the shopping centre; it is about sex, power or death, or all three.

Invariably, when clients used to see me with a big Scorpio (Eighth House) cycle going on, they inherited money from a dead relative, entered into binding financial agreements with their husbands or partners, were involved with hush-hush stock market deals, or found themselves surrounded by bankers and taxmen and lawyers!

The more complex side of money is your domain. (If you have planets in Taurus too, then business or money management will be a major part of your life.) With Scorpio planets, you will find that serious money leads you on a trail to your other Scorpionic qualities. There are women with Scorpio planets (and money) who marry men with nothing or men with everything! They become sharply aware of issues like power and control in connection with finance. There are a few female bankers and stockbrokers around with a complete understanding of the legend that Scorpionic money is hush money.

Death and Dying

Civilised society is most comfortable handling death inside the walls of life insurance offices and quiet, enclosed hospitals. Any discussion of Scorpio has to include death, though — and not only because Pluto ruled the realms of the dead in mythology. Women with Scorpio planets or Pluto chart signatures have a deep understanding of death and dying issues. This sign is deeply concerned with questions about heaven and hell, spirits and resurrection, death and rebirth. No wonder so many writers and actors with Scorpio planets gravitate to tales of ghosts, murder and the church. No wonder so many women in the caring professions end up working with *life and death* situations, courtesy of their Scorpio planets. Something about this sign is pulled towards — or pulled into — these issues. More than any other sign, Scorpio seems to know and understand them.

Scorpio Transforms

Your Scorpionic side is rather like the phoenix. You die, symbolically, and are then reborn from your own ashes after being transformed. Many of you will have experienced this process between the years 1984–1995, as Pluto passed over your Moon or Venus. Do you remember? Or, more likely, can you ever forget Pluto's effect on you in those years?

Scorpio Moon

You appear to have gone through an emotional purging session. Family, house or flat crises have coincided with the most intense period of soul-searching and change. You are not who you were.

Scorpio Venus

A relationship that killed off the old you, and gave birth to the new you — via a crisis. Alternatively, you got involved with a partner whom you totally transformed — once again because of a crisis.

One of the reasons you seem to carry such a depth charge around with you is this: you've been through crisis, survived and *changed*. Perhaps it is these qualities that attract you to others going through intense experiences and transformations, or maybe they gravitate towards you because of the signals they read that you cannot see!

Scorpio-influenced women seem to find themselves around people who are in crisis, on the edge, or bravely facing tremendous healing in their lives. Some of you do this because you seek it out. Whenever people go through great changes and a rebuilding of the inner or outer self, you're usually around.

Female Power

Scorpionic power generally seems to channel in two distinct ways with women. Some of you find it by forming friendships, close relationships or marriages with extremely powerful people. You receive your influence by proxy. Another group of you trade on your sexual charge and female identity — and combine it with career skills or financial acumen.

Women with Scorpio planets are sometimes a magnet for people with money, power or influence of their own. Sometimes you seek this out quite deliberately. At other times, these people just seem to 'happen'. There are many Scorpio-influenced women who are powers behind their partners' thrones.

Scorpio Moon/Venus Myths

Shakespeare's Lady Macbeth has female power in abundance. Her story also sums up all our dark sides — sex, mystery, obsession and death. *Macbeth* is a tale of taboos on all fronts, and Lady Macbeth is the supreme femme fatale, holding invisible controls. Lady Macbeth is a tragic Scorpio type, whose crisis leads to a dark transformation — from queen to madwoman. Despite the tragedy, there is still something awe-inspiring about Shakespeare's version of the Scorpionic female. Finally, did you know that Anne Rice, author of *Interview with the Vampire*, has Venus in Scorpio?

YOUR SAGITTARIUS MOON/VENUS

Drag out your Sagittarian side when a difficult or trying situation needs to be broken up with a joke. Next to Gemini, this sign is strongly associated with a talent to amuse. Your Moon or Venus in Sagittarius is also about the printed word, knowledge and learning. If you make space for Sagittarius in your life, you may become one of the best-read and most knowledgeable women in the zodiac. Finally, Sagittarius is associated with all that is global and international. Having a planet in this sign will well and truly give you the big picture and a wide perspective, which can only make your journey easier.

Are you typical?

You travel or explore whenever you can possibly get away

You are committed to a strong sense of meaning or purpose in your life — your personal philosophy or 'ism'

You exercise your sense of humour wherever possible

You are continually learning and educating yourself

Sagittarius and Size

Women with Sagittarius planets have a preoccupation with size. Not just being too fat or too thin — which you might expect in our fat-phobic society — there is also height (too tall, too short) to consider, and then the individual size of each body part. This sign has size issues to deal with because your symbol, the centaur, looks so uncomfortable with a human upper body and a horse's hindquarters below. Everything is out of proportion.

Sagittarius-influenced women often have issues about their own, or other people's, bodies to deal with. If this sign is especially strong in your chart, you may always have felt as if bits of you were too tall, too short, too fat or too thin. You may also be sensitive to other people around you being giants or midgets, skeletons or beachballs.

Comedy and Humour

With you, dramatic situations become tiny. Trivia becomes over the top. In plain English, this is comedy. In situation comedy, the funniest characters are usually the ones who are larger than life. Extreme and excessive, over-the-top characters. If you have a Sagittarian side, you also possess a talent for amusing people. By over-stressing the trivial and underplaying what is serious, you create comedy. You can stretch a joke, keep a straight face, or wave your hands around to make a point.

Do you have the Moon in Sagittarius? Here's what you need:

Wide open spaces ∗ Freedom to come and go ∗ Weekend getaways ∗ Overseas hauls ∗ A philosophy, belief system or sense of meaning ∗ People who share your sense of humour ∗ Family, flatmates or even a pet who makes you laugh out loud.

You definitely need a room with a view, and can become edgy if you feel too locked in. Bits and pieces from your travels or periods of wanderlust end up in drawers and on shelves. You need something cross-cultural, imported, exotic or different around you to remind you of the world beyond your window. Bags, rucksacks or suitcases are never very far out of reach, and your bookshelves are crammed with the most mind-expanding non-fiction you can find. You really *need* an answering machine.

As a cook, you're optimistic and like taking gambles. Exotic and imported ingredients are irresistible, but if you're running around too much to cater in-house, you'll send out for Asian, Indian or possibly Outer Mongolian. You have a thing about serving size — too much? too little? — but you're a genius at campfire cooking and barbecues. You like exchanging the kitchen ceiling for the stars and the results are delicious. Smorgasbords suit you — if everyone helps themselves, that frees you up completely.

Travellers and Explorers

Sagittarius rules the Ninth House in astrology. In the Middle Ages, the Ninth House described foreigners and exotic, unseen places. After NASA played golf on the Moon in the 1960s, the Ninth House also started to describe extra-terrestrial places. Until you actually get offered a ticket up there, though, your interests may remain with Europe and Asia if you are based in Australia, and just about anywhere if you are one of the roaming Sagittarian types.

If you have planets here, you may end being a lifelong traveller, a fulfilled migrant (who never goes back) . . . or work in a field where distance dialling codes become part of your life. Of course, you may stay put (for financial reasons) or work in a less than adventurous career — but you will get your global 'fix' by subscribing to the internet, watching foreign films or reading foreign writers.

Sagittarius planets really do not like the neighbourhood, the corner store and the local scene. They incline you towards the world of the unexplored and exotic, the ethnic and cosmopolitan. There are many Sagittarius planet women around with passports which look like abstract artworks, they are so overlaid with stamps. And if Sagittarius is strong in your chart, you may always have your bag packed ready to go, or a suitcase flung under the bed. In a small, small town it is always the Sagittarius-influenced woman who is first to jump on the first available bus out of there.

The Great Outdoors is also part of Sagittarian territory. This sign needs to *literally* look beyond the horizon. If you have planets in this sign, you may be a four-wheel driver, a long-distance walker, a keen sailor or an unstoppable climber. You may enjoy the endless horizon that appears over the ocean at sunset, or the suggestion of pure space that is found in the desert.

If your Sagittarian side is particularly strong, you may emigrate, work in a field which involves a lot of interstate or international juggling, or 'adopt' somewhere suitably far-flung or exotic.

It is in the nature of the sign to be interested in other cultures, other customs and other perspectives. World citizens and international bright young things really can't afford to be xenophobic. It's common to find women with a Sagittarius planet shaping careers where the adjective 'international' becomes part of their job description. Sagittarius's association with size also lends itself to this all-encompassing view of the world. But even if you're not that ambitious, the big picture will be an important part of your mindset.

The Meaning of Life

When I was studying philosophy one of our courses was actually called 'The Meaning of Life'. When the rather brilliant prof asked the members of the class what they thought it was, someone stuck their hand up and said, 'A Monty Python film'. Sagittarius *is*, however, strongly associated with the search for a belief system, a sense of meaning and some kind of faith. As an astrologer, I have yet to meet a woman with a Sagittarius planet who is content to wander around in a meaningless universe. Demented though it may sound, having a planet in this sign *will* send you looking for The Meaning of Life, sooner or later.

Along with Pisces, this is the sign most associated with conventional religion. For every one of you who finds your meaning or moral order in set religions, though, there is one who looks for something less structured. I have had Sagittarius-influenced clients who have taken up meditation as part of their inner search, touching on Eastern philosophy. Some have found meaning in life after experimentation with LSD, which they believe has helped them see the universe differently.

Your Sagittarian side will not let you accept a void. Jupiter, your ruler, lorded it over the heavens and anything 'up there' is part of Sagittarian territory too. The idea that we are all here for no purpose, that life is a chaotic, random mess and that suffering is without purpose seems to horrify Sagittarian types. It may take you years to find your own sense of meaning. Alternatively, you may grow up having a strong personal philosophy, and I have known women with Sagittarius planets to borrow 'bits' of philosophy and religion to make sense of it all.

For some women with Sagittarius planets, the only code or philosophy which fits is the one contained in the constitution or inside the law of the land. What's yours?

The Printed Word

Sagittarius is associated with the mass media, education, academia, mass communications, the net and all aspects of the printed word. Having a Sagittarius planet is a little like having a library of the best fiction and non-fiction locked inside your head, and when you are not planning your next trip, you will probably be curled up with a book. Fate may send you in directions where the printed word is the biggest part of your life, and your other planets — and your Rising sign — will give more information about this. Alternatively, you may just be one of those well-read women the rest of us are happy to sit next to on planes. Sagittarius planets seem to pick up information as a professional librarian does — in a kind of broad, interdisciplinary way. Jupiter, the ruler of Sagittarius, governs anything with the word *mass* in front of it. It connects your sign to the big, global picture.

A Matter of Principle

Sagittarius rules moral principles and ethical principles, but above all, it rules the *law* — as it applies to your own life. Some women with a strongly Sagittarian side do go on to become solicitors, barristers, judges, politicians and trade union officials. But a peculiar thing happens for any Sagittarius-influenced woman: every so often, between the joking, the travelling and the reading, it all comes to a screeching halt *on a matter of principle.* You will bite on this simple fact several times in your life: someone *else's* word is law. Some women with Sagittarius planets meet this in the course of their working lives; some meet it through their love lives or family experiences. Some of you end up believing that the law really is an ass; others find something very pure in it.

Your Sagittarian side may become triggered quite sharply if you find yourself having to run things through a legal department, or being on jury duty, or tackling other points of law. Similarly, any experiences you have with religion will drag out your inner Sagittarius. She, above all other sides of yourself, has to define what justice really is. Also, perhaps, what is moral and ethical, fair and correct. If you want to destroy your own dinner party in five minutes flat, invite a group of women with Sagittarius planets in their charts to talk about politics, religion or the constitution!

Eternal Optimists

Jupiter, the ruler of Sagittarius, is also known as Jove in ancient mythology. From this comes the word *jovial*, which my trusty, coffee-stained thesaurus defines this way: 'merry, joyous, joyful, sparkling, mirth-loving, waggish, jocular, witty, gay and frivolous'. It also suggests kittenish and rackety, but I'm not sure how you feel about that. Having a planet in this sign is like having a recorded message in your head saying 'never surrender'. Even when you're feeling black, your Sagittarian side will come through and find that famous *sense of meaning* which turns negatives into positives.

YOUR CAPRICORN MOON/VENUS

This sign helps you take the job seriously, and no matter what else may be going on in your life, things will always come back to your job! Your Capricorn Moon and/or Venus lends you ambition, organising ability and patience. It makes you resourceful and in control. It gives you, above all other things, a reality check. It's an aid to accomplishment, no matter how high you aim. What does it take to become a director — of anything? Capricornian qualities seem to lend themselves to leading positions.

Are you typical?

You have amazing ambition and are prepared to work to see it fulfilled

You have older people, or respected role models, around you

You understand that nothing happens in this life without self-discipline

You respect hierarchies and structures

My Brilliant Career

Sometimes, looking at the career paths of Capricornian types, it's difficult to imagine how they got here from *there*. If you have a planet in this sign, you stand a better than average chance of pole-vaulting way, way above the place you started from.

There are many Capricorn-influenced women who have rags-to-riches life stories. And there are those who have seemingly achieved the impossible — gone from actor to director, or from small-town girl to Big City Empress.

The rare combination of frank ambition, combined with the persistence and shrewdness of this sign, often produces women of remarkable achievement. It's the beginnings in the lives of Capricornian types which matter as much as the endings: be you suburban or working-class at the start, you will end up several classes above that at the end!

Do you have the Moon in Capricorn? Here's a little of what you need:

People who are as organised as you are ∗ Family, flatmates, lovers or friends who know the form ∗ A job where you can truly achieve ∗ Friends or contacts in high places ∗ Professional mentors.

At heart, you're a home owner, not a renter. You need those firm foundations, and the prospect of throwing everything into a removal truck every few years makes you depressed. You like good, solid construction and like it if you can see the plans. You're modest about your house or flat, but anybody can see the place is the result of amazing hard work on your part. You like a workspace at home too, and because you so often bring things home with you, will develop one part of your living space as a kind of floating desk or office.

You try harder if someone amazing is coming to dinner, but you're always organised. You're a cautious cook — you stick to recipes you know, or give everything a run-through before a big dinner party. You're loyal to certain brands and products, and won't switch easily. You have one or two tried and true things which you *always* make, and have a wonderful knack of getting other people to help you when they're not entirely sure that's what they've been doing!

Guides and Mentors

With a Capricorn planet, you like attaching yourself to people who can teach you something. The figure of the guide or mentor is crucial to women with a Capricorn Moon/Venus.

During the course of your life, you may find that it is one remarkable, much older 'destiny figure' who turns things around for you — or you may collect all sorts of guides, mentors, teachers and helpers along the way.

Part of the reason for this is your Moon/Venus ruler, Saturn. This planet — and archetype — is the wise elder. Your guide may be male or female, but this person will inevitably be more experienced than you. You may feel that you have a lot to live up to with them, or that you must test yourself as you struggle to meet their standards or expectations. It is seldom an easy process, but then Saturn, your ruler, has never been known for producing easy learning experiences.

Frequently, Capricornian types have a series of mentors or guides throughout their lives. Cher, a Capricorn Moon, has had several — including Oscar-winning actress Meryl Streep, with whom she worked on *Silkwood*. A few years later, Cher won an Oscar of her own, for *Moonstruck*. Writer Dorothy Parker, a Capricorn Moon, also had many mentors, including

Frank Crowninshield, who chose her as his protégée on both *Vogue* and *Vanity Fair* magazines.

The Getting of Wisdom

Henry Handel Richardson, a Capricorn Sun, wrote *The Getting of Wisdom* (later made into a film), which perfectly describes part of this sign's legacy to you. Destiny says you often have to do it the hard way. Your Saturn Return, in particular around of the ages of thirty and sixty, is going to have a major impact on you.

Some of you seem to gain strength from hardship. Having suffered, you learn — and fast. Single parenthood, divorce, bankruptcy, redundancy, serious illness — nothing rocks you. You always learn from it, and it makes you wiser than other women. The grounded, savvy quality of Capricorn Moon/Venus women is one of their trademarks.

Having a planet in Capricorn does not automatically qualify you for one of those 'We were so poor, we lived in a cardboard box on the middle of the road' types of stories. Nor does it mean that life has to be one long and difficult haul. On the contrary, what it does do is give you a kind of freedom. When you hit a bad patch, your Capricornian side will feel more comfortable with it, more prepared to handle it — and more interested in the challenge — than any other part of you.

I have often noticed that clients with a Capricorn planet seem to turn struggle into success. It is when they hit a low of insecurity, or real-life practical problems, that the process begins, as their Capricornian side wakes up and rallies round. With a planet here, you are in the unique position of being able to use your hard-won experience to fuel something bigger and altogether better for yourself. Things which leave other women feeling helpless actually become a source of strength for you, and this in itself is a kind of protection, as well as a kind of freedom.

Utterly Professional

On the job, a Capricorn planet helps you to be utterly professional. The same traits, though — reliability, commitment, common sense — are also likely to filter through into your private life. There is something wonderfully sensible, earthed and true about Capricornian types, and it is these women who help the rest of the zodiac maintain a sense of standards!

Some women loathe having a planet in Capricorn. They feel it's too boring, too staid or too hungry for success. In the greater astrological tribe, though, Capricorn's values and strengths are desperately needed. Without your mature approach, your love of hard work and your cautious good sense, a great many things would begin to fall apart. Lean harder on your other signs if you have decided you really want something a little more adventurous, dramatic or colourful. Then channel your Capricornian side back in to provide the staying power and common sense you are going to need to get there from here.

Women Growing Older

Because Capricorn is ruled by Saturn, the Lord of Time, the issue of being the right *age* for anything is a particularly big one for you. Clients with Capricorn planets have often told me they feel too old when they are young (sixteen going on forty) and then too young when they are growing older. But — and here's something to look forward to — Capricornian types grow into their forty-plus years far more comfortably than the rest of us seem to. The writer George Eliot, a Capricorn Moon, published her most famous novels — *The Mill on the Floss* and *Middlemarch* — in her forties and fifties.

Your appreciation of the time that solid achievements take also explains the way you glide up the ladder. It's all about gradual success, built block by block, or climbed rung by rung.

Having a planet in this sign helps you to understand hierarchies. Not only professional hierarchies, but also the social strata around you. Without trying too hard, you will probably understand where everyone fits in just by looking at them. Women I have known with a strongly developed Capricornian side who move through the Establishment, or the glitterati, have an instinct for the social pecking order and social propriety. You not only know what's what, you know who's who. Most of you are determined to respect that structure, and some of you may become a part of it. Others stay on the outside, but still keep a shrewd eye on the form.

Serious Young Insects

You may have planets in other signs which are lighter or wackier, like Sagittarius or Aquarius. Having a Capricornian side, though, means having a distinctly serious side. This sign slows you down and steadies you. You can bring this out whenever you need to — to prove to others that you mean business, to make the right impression on more conservative people, or to persuade those around you that order must be restored.

The flipside of occasionally being a serious young insect is that it can tip you over into serious pessimism — negative thinking. Being cautious, careful, controlled and seeing the hard realities, not the champagne corks, is okay in proportion. However, I have seen enough Capricorn-influenced women dropping in for chart readings over the years to realise that this famous propensity for seriousness can also lead to depression and worry.

If you have planets in other signs, you can use them to help lift yourself out of the Capricornian glooms when you need to. It's quite common for women with a Capricorn planet to also have something in Sagittarius or Aquarius, for example: these signs will push the humour back in and help you to adjust things.

'I'm prone to periods of unhappiness,' Cher (a Capricorn Moon) told an interviewer once. 'I'm not an extrovert, I'm quite introverted and I can be really morose. Not for long periods but sporadically.' She leans hard on her more flippant, forever-young Gemini Venus to get herself out of those kinds of doldrums.

YOUR AQUARIUS MOON/VENUS

This side of you will help you to break new ground, explore some highly experimental territory and convince all those around you that you are part genius, part visionary. Your Aquarian side is utterly original and prefers to do its own thing. Make the most of this side of you whenever you need to excel professionally — it is in the nature of Aquarius to have sudden insights and to make innovations and discoveries which will help you to stand out from the pack. It is the things which are most unique about you — even if they are a little eccentric — which you need to feel confident enough to express.

Are you typical?
You have a wide circle of friends and contacts
You refuse to conform or compromise just for
    the sake of fitting in
You enjoy your own eccentricities
Aspects of your life are downright alternative
    or radically different
Freedom is your oxygen!

Utterly Individual

Without Aquarius, women would not have had feminism. But this sign is linked to highly individual viewpoints of all kinds. If you have planets in Aquarius, you are, above all, an extreme individualist. It is your Aquarius planets which strive for something which is brilliantly clear, honest and true — but principally *for you*. There are women with Aquarius planets who are radical conservatives, and there are women with Aquarius planets who are radical radicals.

For many women with Aquarius planets, the decision to be their own woman, or follow their own unique course, is easy. Inside, they know they are right. Life only becomes difficult when eyebrows are raised, objections are made and people become threatened.

Aquarius is a sign that often makes people feel uncertain or unsafe. One of the biggest challenges for you is finding a way to accommodate your own unique ideas, opinions, life and values in a way that other people can accept. Most of the time, this live and let live approach will work successfully. However, it is in the nature of this sign to be stubborn. The freedom that you crave to be yourself, and the changes and new ideas that you long for, may never happen unless you can find some kind of bridge that will lead you to the rest of the population. Your Aquarian side absolutely detests compromising and faking it, smiling politely and falling into line. But a small amount of social lubricant will be necessary if your ideas, principles and plans are going to be accepted.

Ahead of Your Time

Your Aquarian side is always living in the future. Sometimes it cannot resist looking into it, either. (If you bought this book, your Aquarius planets may have to take full responsibility: this sign, along with Scorpio, is linked to astrology.) Mostly, though, Aquarius planets are always a few decades ahead, and quite unknowingly.

Aquarius planets are very useful if you are in a career where you must be sensitive to the *Zeitgeist*, the spirit of the time, or the invisible movements, trends and preferences that drive us all on. Your Aquarian side will 'get' things before the rest of the population even knows they are desirable. Bear in mind that sometimes you will be *too* far ahead of your time. You might be establishing a tradition for the year 2050 without knowing it — which is why the rest of the world backs off nervously.

In a Majority of One

You exist as a majority of one. What you need and love — or who you need and love — makes you different from everybody else. You stand out from the crowd either quietly or in the most public way, and your idea of hell is probably filling in a form — Aquarian Moon/Venus women never fit all the boxes.

The strongly Aquarian woman often literally takes a solo journey — living by herself, travelling by herself, working by herself or taking a lone stand. Sometimes your Aquarian side will make this choice quite consciously. You follow the single life, or the solo path, because your strong need for freedom and independence allows you to see that happiness is not necessarily about clinging to the clan (or a partner) indefinitely. Sometimes your Aquarius planets will put you on this solo voyage when you would honestly prefer not to take it. Repeatedly, I have heard this from women with Aquarius planets: whether they choose time alone or apart, or whether they have it forced upon them, solitude is always a route to discovery. If you have the Moon/Venus in Aquarius, you are unlikely to be dependent on any lover for long — you're accountable to yourself, and you are a free spirit who doesn't necessarily always like the game-playing of relationships or the restrictions of being someone's partner or wife. Typically, you don't fake or compromise — that often means you end up by yourself!

Women Who Don't

Your Aquarian side expresses itself most strongly through what you don't do. Here are some Moon/Venus in Aquarius traits I've noted over the years, from clients and from the charts of the rich and famous:

Not driving ★ Not having a TV set ★ Not eating meat ★ Not carrying change ★ Not collecting the mail ★ Not cooking ★ Not using washing-up liquid ★ Not wearing a watch ★ Not wearing underwear ★ Not having sex ★ Not wearing lace-up shoes ★ Not paying parking fines ★ Not wearing anything red ★ Not admitting to being female.

The things that your Aquarian side actually *does* do are probably just as personalised. Eccentricity is never forced with you, if you're typical. It just happens. It takes an outsider to notice it and point it out to you.

All Change!

Your Aquarian side can be quite perverse. It can desire change when hardly anybody else sees the need for it, and absolutely *refuse* to change if there is a sense that you are being pressured or forced. You are a reformer at the same time that you are quite a stubborn defender of your own position. Once you have made up your mind to be an Aboriginal supporter, a Republican, an Anti-Republican, a Radical Celibate or a member of the Flat Earth Society . . . well, that's it. Having placed your vote on Our Common

Future, you are unlikely to allow yourself to be forced into an alternative position.

You may also find this happening to you: you turn sharp right (or left, or sideways) and then other people start following you, whereupon you swing around dramatically in another direction. I really believe this is not conscious perversity. Your Aquarius planets often seem to be responding to some mysterious signal the rest of us cannot see or hear. You go your own way and do your own thing.

Feminism is the best example of that mysterious Aquarian perversity. Some of you with planets here are absolutely feminists of the Old School. Some of you think many of the feminists got it wrong. Mostly, women with Aquarius planets do pick up on the basic aspects of feminism — freedom and independence are really what it's about, and Aquarius craves these. Remember the perversity, though? You'll find just as many fellow Aquarian types who will happily argue about the finer points until one of you falls over.

Gloria Steinem has Venus in Aquarius, so did Simone de Beauvoir, and so does Erica Jong. Anne Summers has the Moon there. It's the free-form feminist sign.

Do you have the Moon/Venus in Aquarius? Here's a little of what you need:
A room of your own ⋆ Freedom ⋆ Machines that go *ping* ⋆ Strange hobbies ⋆ Your funny little ways ⋆ Independence ⋆ Mad clothes ⋆ Men who treat you as an equal — or superior.

You have the most peculiar domestic set-up in the zodiac. Even Aquarius Moon homes which appear to be quite normal are based around something very . . . slightly . . .

odd. It's hard to generalise about your house or flat set-up, because this sign is so intensely individual. However, whatever your friends or family have, you don't want. Whatever the home and lifestyle shows tell you to do, you won't. The rule with the Aquarian home is that you need lots of space to yourself, and freedom to do things your own mad way.

You tend to shock people on a regular basis, either because your kitchen set-up is not what they expected, or because you put food on the table which they frankly hadn't dreamed of seeing *even* under the effect of hallucinatory drugs. You can be a shockingly good, or shockingly awful, cook. But you do like new gadgets and whizzy equipment that looks like it should be in the galley of the Starship *Enterprise*.

Experimental Thinkers

What draws you most?
The internet and its possibilities — or the Luddite revolution * Alternative lifestyles * New ideas * Progressive political reform * Radical theories and proposals * Real-life experiments, either involving the New Age or new technology.

Your Aquarius planets reach into the atmosphere and pick out whatever is strange, new — even shocking — and definitely 'out there'. It's natural for you to be different, and to innovate wherever you can. Frequently, you'll dive into new technology to be able to do your own thing. It's not so much the wires and the bytes that are sexy to your Aquarian side, it's the fabulous things they can do.

If you have planets in this sign, you may become a regular Lieutenant Uhura — or ignore the technical bits and leap straight into playtime. Incidentally, your Aquarian-influenced brothers tend to be into the classical 'male' sciences (and science-fiction) side of things. You may do this, but on the whole I have found Aquarius-influenced women prefer the 'female', people-oriented sciences — psychology and sociology. Still, anything with a hypothesis, an experiment and a conclusion will probably do!

Total Freedom

The principle of freedom is part of what you are all about. Some of you will push for this freedom for other people — sometimes for other living things. Princess Diana had an Aquarius Moon, and there are some who think she paid the price for her freedom-fighting (particularly on landmines) with her death. Janis Joplin had Venus in Aquarius, and sang that freedom was just another word for nothing left to lose. Absolutely!

Women with Aquarius planets tend to worry when things look unfair — when one group is treated in a second-rate way because of their appearance, race, class, sex or even their species. Your Aquarian side becomes horrified at the idea of anything being trapped or confined or hampered. Your Aquarian side will often ask: 'Why can't I?' and 'Why shouldn't they?' and 'What's stopping us?'. You don't understand racism or sexism.

If you're typical of your Aquarian Moon and/or Venus sign, you'll be genuinely horrified by what you see as all those old-school dinosaurs out there.

Born to Shock

You often end up leaving all around you reaching for the brandy and groping for a chair. It is almost a rule with Aquarius-influenced women. It's in your nature to shock, jolt, disrupt, dislodge and challenge — even when you don't mean to.

Your Aquarian side encourages the most surprising decisions, the most unlikely possibilities and, sometimes, the most shockingly sudden events. Uranus, your ruler, is associated with lightning. If you have ever watched a storm in its entirety, you will have seen something of your Aquarian side played out in the sky. Lightning may literally strike not just once, but several times, in your own life and times. In a word, you get zapped.

There will also be occasions when things do not happen to *you,* but you seem to happen to *them.* After a few decades of being around you, I believe those who know you well will hardly be surprised at what you do or say any more. 'You've decided to give yourself up to an inter-galactic alien breeding scheme? How wonderful for you.'

On the Outside

Your Aquarius planets may well show you this classic scenario: everyone seems to be speaking one language or sharing one reality and you don't understand, or fit into, any of it. Your Aquarius planets will tend to guide you into situations where you are separated from the majority in a very clear way. Here are some examples:

Country mouse in the city
Beautiful in a family of plain sisters and brothers
Dyslexic at school
Black in a white legal firm
Lesbian in a straight family
Punk in a religious family
Stranger in a strange land

From time to time, your Aquarian side will place you firmly, but gently, in a world where you are immediately and obviously quite different. The irony of all this? You love having friends and belonging to a loose tribe or network. With your fair, friendly style, a cool and easy popularity among a large and casual series of connections is ensured. It's just that, from time to time, you really will be stuck on the outside looking in, either because you have chosen that role, or because it has been chosen for you by what the Ancients called Fate. Women with Aquarian planets — like you — will always be different from everyone else (and ahead of everyone else too).

YOUR PISCES MOON/VENUS

Pisces rules the feet in astrology, and you find it easy to put yourself in other people's shoes. As a result, you're hopelessly sentimental and easily moved and are frequently involved in helping others. The traditional church is important to many Piscean-influenced women, and so are alternative religions and philosophies. You also identify with a sense of oneness with us all. Then there are those of you who are neither Christian nor Buddhist, but unable to be anything but selfless.

This side of Pisces comes from your ruler, Neptune, which dissolves boundaries and increases your sensitivity. You 'just know' what is going on in other people's heads or behind an animal's eyes, and you really *feel* for them. The leap of the imagination that is required to identify with all creatures great and small is part of the Piscean package. Women with Pisces planets do seem to have a special regard for other creatures — even dinosaurs! Joy Adamson, who shared her life with lions, and found fame in *Born Free*, was born with Venus in Pisces. Your connection might be to jungle animals or goldfish at the school fair — or to the people in your personal or professional world — but when you feel for something, or someone, you really do *feel* it.

Fantasy and Reality

Your Piscean side does not see the real world as other people see it. This may be literal — your eyesight may be out — but the distortion can also take place behind your eyes, and there are many Pisces-influenced women who have perfect eyesight but enjoy a kind of coloured slide show going on behind each iris, thanks to their habit of daydreaming, drinking or drugging themselves up to the eyeballs.

The pictures or films running in your head can be remarkably useful if you are in a field where imagination is necessary. If you are working in a strictly practical job, and surrounded by strictly practical people in your private life, you may need consciously to find a place and a space to dream and escape. If not, your Pisces side may help you to excuse yourself from practical reality by inviting vagueness, lateness or daydreaming. At its most extreme, this 'slipping away' syndrome can result in drug or alcohol dependency for some — and even prescribed drugs can fall into this category.

Drugs and alcohol typically produce one of two polarised reactions from strongly Piscean women. Some of you avoid them because of the alarming effect they have; the rest of you enjoy them in moderation, and love the effect, as the Piscean inner cinema or slide show becomes more colourful.

Betty Ford was born with both the Moon and Venus in Pisces. A double whammy! The world's most famous addiction clinic is named after her.

If you have a Pisces planet, you may already have found ways to incorporate fantasy into your reality. You may discover this by losing yourself in photography, films, music, art or fantasy. Perhaps you enjoy diving into a swimming pool or gazing at fish through a glass mask. Or you may have found a professional or after-hours pursuit which allows you to see pictures in your head or chase — quite literally — a 'fantasy' career.

Pisces planets have a reputation for being elastic with the truth. When others demand the 'bare facts' or 'raw truth', something in you just wants to soften the story or even slip away altogether. The classic vagueness — and sometimes quite conscious evasiveness — that surrounds Pisces is a pretty mild 'wobble' on reality. When your unconscious is saying, 'Enough reality already, someone get me out of here!'

Something most women with a Pisces Moon/Venus must face is this: at some point your reality will clash with other people's. For Billie Holiday and Drew Barrymore, both Pisces Venus women, this played itself out in addiction problems.

Above all, perhaps, a Pisces planet gives you enormous sensitivity — to everyday atmospheres, but also to the pain or problems in the world around you. In much the same way that sensitive skin is layered with cream and protected by cotton wool, a Pisces-influenced woman needs to find some kind of layer and protection against the pain in the outside world. Finding a sense of meaning, or a sense of spirituality, will become increasingly important as you go through life. In common with those who have Sagittarius planets, you cannot bear to live in a void.

Some of you are so sensitive that you are psychic. You pick up tarot cards and make stunning predictions on your first try — or you have dreams where people in spirit are giving you messages about the future. You may already know you're a medium or psychic, of course, or be using the kind of astrology which depends on the sixth sense as much as it does on computers.

Do you have the Moon in Pisces? Here's a little of what you need:
Music ★ Poems ★ The ocean ★ Art ★ Escapes ★ Dreams ★ Psychic friends ★ Creative interests ★ People or animals to care for ★ Plenty of time ★ Fantasy ★ No pressure.

Your creative efforts, or those of artists or photographers you admire, will be important features of your house or flat. Some of you may have books on spiritual matters on the shelves. Other books will reflect your favourite escapist interests. You like whimsical bits and pieces around you too. You definitely need fantasy in your reality! The Pisces Moon home is usually decorated in an inspired and imaginative way. If you can, you'll live near water, or have a pool or pond. All creatures great and small — in the garden or indoors — will make a difference to you. Candles, incense and spiritual objects matter too.

If you're okay about wine and spirits, you'll either throw them into the recipe or have a glass while you cook. Those of you who are teetotallers (and there are a few) will still pour in essences, oils and vinegars — this sign rules liquids. At best, you are the classic 'hunch' cook; at worst, you are chaotic and prone to losing vital ingredients — like the cutlery. You enjoy having music playing in the background while you clean or cook too. You're inspired by glossy food illustrations and especially by soft-focus TV chefs.

Your Childhood

Your Piscean side probably found a place to breathe in your childhood, above all other times in your life. At an age when fairy tales are read aloud, picture books seem true, pets are cared for and imaginary friends made up, Pisces-influenced little girls seem quite well catered for. There is also the familiar world of Doctors and Nurses (rescuing people, dolls and animals) and the fantasy world of the Tooth Fairy, Santa Claus and the Easter Bunny.

If you feel your childhood wasn't that colourful or happy, your Piscean side may have helped you escape by encouraging daydreams or long wishing sessions. The inner life of a Piscean-influenced child is often very rich, and can sometimes make an effective substitute for reality. Women with Pisces planets have told me that these childhood experiences were particularly important and special to them:

Imaginary friends

Reading books to escape sadness

Believing in fictional or imaginary characters

Vivid dreams — still remembered today

Raising money for charities

Animal friends who are almost human

Dressing up dogs and cats

Curiosity about God and heaven

Creating outfits from the dressing-up box

Finger painting

Nonsense rhymes

Saviours and Victims

If you have a planet in Pisces, then at various times in your life you will feel moved to save, help or rescue people whom you see as victims. Identifying with all that is vulnerable, suffering, in trouble or defenceless in the world is a common

Piscean experience. You cry a lot, but you still have to give up your time, energy or money!

You may spend time in the helping, healing, counselling or caring professions for this reason, or find yourself in situations in your domestic or personal life where you must perform the role of what we commonly know to be a saint! You may, or may not, be a religious or spiritual person. But you'll know what karma is intuitively — and understand what the Buddha and Christ were all about.

At what point does a Piscean type cease being a saviour and turn into a victim? And is it a happy and healthy state of affairs to be a martyr to anything? This is one of the most baffling areas of Piscean experience, and astrologers often find themselves grappling with the contradictions. The two fish in the Piscean glyph do not swim in opposite directions for nothing. The contradictions in the victim–saviour patterns that you will experience in your lifetime are rather like those fish.

Confusion — a very Piscean word — is the common result of these discussions, which are basically ethical in nature, and will make far more sense to you on a personal level than words on a page ever will! Perhaps it is true to say that you may find it useful to analyse your own ideas about what a victim is, what a martyr is and what a saviour should be doing.

The Non-Material World

You may also be a meditator, a lifelong wisher, a mantra chanter or even a spell-caster. Pisces describes the unseen and the non-material world. There is something deeply mysterious — and basically 'sensed' — about this area of Piscean experience. Joan of Arc had the Moon in Pisces, and Shirley MacLaine has Venus in Pisces. The blind and deaf

Helen Keller, a Pisces Moon, spent most of her time in a world which was literally unseen by others. In this letter to a friend in 1899 (published in her autobiography, *The Story of my Life*), she describes 'seeing' statues of mythological figures. 'Venus entranced me,' she wrote. 'She looked as if she had just risen from the foam of the sea, and her loveliness was like a strain of heavenly music.' To Helen Keller, imagination was sight. Running her fingers over a sculpture, she saw her own reality.

What you *perceive* as part of your Piscean experiences may be a result of your sixth sense, or a sense beyond that. You may be one of the Pisces-influenced women who also sees ghosts, registers the spirit within yourself, knows God, or experiences lucid dreaming. You may *feel* atmospheres, or simply sense the *Zeitgeist*, the spirit of the time, which manifests itself in the invisible trends and changes in the wind which affect us all. Piscean hunches can be highly accurate and quite profitable.

Above all, your Piscean side has an extreme sensitivity to all that cannot be measured, charted or tested in a laboratory. Sometimes it is impossible for strongly Piscean experiences to be articulated, just because they lack this measurable, material quality.

Many Pisces-influenced women feel drawn to the esoteric, mysterious side of astrology, and have little interest in sceptics demanding proof and data. Some of the best astrologers I have known have Pisces planets, because they bring intuitive gifts to the field. They also have a rare ability to sympathise and empathise with their clients, and to feel their way around a chart.

If you are strongly Piscean, and there are no Earth signs — Taurus, Virgo, Capricorn — around your birthdate, then you may find you need to earth yourself, because the influence of the non-material world may very well take over.

Going out of your way to sink your hands into the soil or put your feet on the ground is one way of doing it. The symptoms of Pisces gone mad? Unpaid bills, professional or domestic chaos, and a general feeling that the practical details of life are eluding you.

Neptune's Sacrifices

The myth surrounding Neptune, the ruler of your Moon/Venus sign, involves several images of sacrifice. Black bulls and horses were thrown into rivers for the god, and Neptune was occasionally given human sacrifices as well.

Both the idea and the reality of sacrifice will be an important part of your story. What has been given up by you, or lost by you, may be totally involuntary, or it could be a conscious decision. A Pisces planet, however, lends the sacrifice a kind of depth and richness as well.

If you have the Moon in Pisces, you will care for your children or partner by giving up time, energy or money for them. Of course, every woman does this, but you go the extra mile. If you don't have a partner, the sacrifices for the people, or creatures, you care about will be just as big — but you may channel your feelings through a charity, or by giving up your weekends or evenings for someone who needs you.

If you have Venus in Pisces, you love your partner by giving things up for them. You seduce potential dates by giving way, or giving in. This Venus sign is notorious for producing human doormats, but you don't have to give in that way. On a more spiritual note, you can sometimes get involved in relationships or marriages which involve the most beautiful and compassionate acts. There is a sense that if you love someone, you are prepared to lay down your life for them.

To discover where you are destined to make sacrifices in your life, find your chart at www.astro.com and look for this symbol Ψ which is Neptune, the planet of sacrifice. The house it is in shows you the area of life where you will be prepared to martyr yourself if necessary — and, most of all, where you act from unconditional love of another human being or creature. It will have a phenomenal influence on your life, so take a look.

The houses are horoscope slices — sections of the circle. The First House is at the 9pm slot, and they follow in anti-clockwise order, with the Tenth House typically coming at the midnight position on the wheel.

Here's the lowdown:

First House Neptune — Your sacrifices will be linked to your image, appearance and reputation.

Second House Neptune — You'll sacrifice money, possessions or property for a purpose; or, alternatively, make enormous sacrifices in the name of wealth.

Third House Neptune — You'll make sacrifices for a brother, sister or cousin. In order to get your message across to others, you'll also have to give up/give in.

Fourth House Neptune — You'll make sacrifices for a parent or other close relative. Your house or flat may involve quite a few sacrifices from you too.

Fifth House Neptune — Your sex life will involve several sacrifices. The world of children and babies (yours or others) will also call on you to give up or give in.

Sixth House Neptune — Your job and working life will involve quite a few unconditional sacrifices. You'll also have to give up, or in, for your health.

Seventh House Neptune — You'll make sacrifices for your lover or partner here. Sometimes a professional or business partner also finds you giving in/up.

Eighth House Neptune — The world of other people's money, houses, flats and possessions is where you'll be making sacrifices.

Ninth House Neptune — Destiny says that travelling, or your involvement with other cultures and countries, will bring about some sort of sacrifice from you.

Tenth House Neptune — You could give it all up for your career, or even sacrifice your job or status at various points. You'll give up a lot for success.

Eleventh House Neptune — Your friends or the group you are involved with will find you making unconditional sacrifices and putting others before yourself.

Twelfth House Neptune — Your most important sacrifices will be those you keep secret, as it is impossible for you to ever share what you've really given up!

YOUR CHINESE
ZODIAC SIGN

As East is destined to meet West in a major way in the years ahead, knowing how China and India see you is both fun and necessary.

Here's a Western take on your Chinese Zodiac Sign to start with. Because Chinese signs revolve in approximate twelve-year cycles, they also tally with the cycles of Jupiter, which throws new light on the meaning of each sign.

Note: if you were born before or after the dates listed here, please visit www.jessicaadams.com for more. You can also visit my site to read your Chinascope — your Chinese Zodiac Sign prediction.

THE MOUSE

January 28 1960–February 14 1961
February 15 1972–February 2 1973
February 2 1984–February 19 1985
February 19 1996–February 6 1997

THE SIXTIES MOUSE

* In your professional life — or at home — you have total control and rulership.

* You are a powerful woman who knows how to discipline herself at all times.

* You are a natural leader and you're big enough to accept responsibility.

* You could easily become a prime minister or president if you enter politics.

THE SEVENTIES MOUSE

* You are extremely approachable and friendly, but you're a tough cookie too.

* Your willpower is amazing and you can do anything once you commit to it.

* You're a natural networker and are always open to new faces in new places.

* You love meeting people halfway, but you are also a formidable character.

THE EIGHTIES MOUSE

* You're a spiritual mouse and you have a strong feeling you're being guided.

* You're genuinely lucky, with Jupiter on your side, and are always protected.

* You can also work as a guardian angel for others — your job may reflect this.

* You're a helper and a healer figure for people in trouble — a safety net!

THE NINETIES MOUSE

* There are two sides to you. One is the explorer, the other is the Amazon.

* One half of you wants to see the world; the other wants to win at any cost.

* You make a dramatic impact on people and intimidate quite a few of them.

* You're an action woman, and your career, or your interests, reflect this.

THE OX

February 15 1961–February 4 1962
February 3 1973–January 22 1974
February 20 1985–February 8 1986
February 7 1997–January 27 1998

THE SIXTIES OX

* You are a creative person who needs peace and quiet to find inspiration.

* You've always got time to stop and smell the roses — in fact, you need it.

* What pops into your head — images or words — sometimes feels channelled.

* You may find your niche in art, music, writing, dance, craft or the theatre.

THE SEVENTIES OX

* You're worth a lot of money, or your particular talents are priceless.

* Some partners or lovers will see you as the gold at the end of the rainbow.

* You're a rich and rewarding character to be around and spell good news.

* You'll acquire property, jewellery or antiques which always hold their value.

THE EIGHTIES OX

* You're warm and always nice to come home to, even when times are tough.

* You have issues to face on the home front: moving a lot or family disruption.

* People want to get close to you, because you give them what they need.

* You generate a lot of heat through the sheer force of your personality.

THE NINETIES OX

* Your inner child is alive and well, and will be with you right into your old age.

* You are a natural mother, godmother, aunt or teacher/nanny/babysitter.

* You represent comfort and safety to people; they can relax around you.

* You know how to have fun and amuse yourself, but you need rules too.

THE TIGER

February 17 1950–February 5 1951
February 5 1962–January 24 1963
January 23 1974–February 10 1975
February 9 1986–January 28 1987
January 28 1998–February 15 1999

THE FIFTIES TIGER

★ You're good at visualising something and then slowly making it come to life.

★ You do well in careers which involve moulding ideas, animals or people.

★ You're prepared to work slowly and patiently to get the results you want.

★ Perfection is always out of reach for you, but try not to sweat on it.

THE SIXTIES TIGER

★ There is a light, restless quality about you — you have many different sides.

★ It's hard to pin you down as you are so multi-faceted and colourful.

★ You have lots to say or communicate — you're a natural singer/actor/talker.

★ You find it hard to come up with one point of view, as you have so many.

THE SEVENTIES TIGER

★ You're secretive and private and you don't like the world looking in.

★ You're a sensual person who gets a lot from her own private pleasures.

★ You're a non-conformist who goes her own way and does her own thing.

★ You don't have time for conservative opinions about how women should be.

THE EIGHTIES TIGER

* You're nostalgic by nature and love connecting people from your own past.

* You believe in the values of friendship and camaraderie — the group!

* You're highly sociable and appreciate good restaurants, food or cookbooks.

* You love swapping stories and sharing memories with people around you.

THE NINETIES TIGER

* You are a glorious, mysterious woman who makes a huge impact on people.

* You are a riddle wrapped inside an enigma and you're hard to decode.

* Expect a connection with marketing, tax, finance or the building business.

* Nobody ever forgets you — you're the eighth wonder of the world, and more.

THE RABBIT

February 6 1951–January 26 1952
January 25 1963–February 12 1964
February 11 1975–January 30 1976
January 29 1987–February 16 1988
February 16 1999–February 4 2000

THE FIFTIES RABBIT

* You carry deep secrets which are well-buried and take a lot of excavation.

* Nobody is ever sure if you're going to explode or not, and neither are you!

* One major incident in your life could have triggered disaster . . . it didn't.

* Part of you is pure dynamite, but that's a part that nobody will ever find.

THE SIXTIES RABBIT

* Part of you is wild, fiery and out of control; another part wants to stop it!

* Your energy can run away with you and cause problems, and you know it.

* You're good at damage control with others, as you practise it on yourself.

* People or ideas light your fire, but be careful what/who you say yes to.

THE SEVENTIES RABBIT

* You deal with life by fooling around, having fun and playing 'let's pretend'.

* You have difficulty seeing situations and people the same way others do.

* People find you amusing, cute — or just impossible to deal with/understand.

* Drugs or alcohol can confuse you enormously, as you may have discovered!

THE EIGHTIES RABBIT

* You are a spiritual person with a strong sense of mission, or a big cause.

* You understand that your chosen job/role will take a major sacrifice.

* Sexuality, virginity and fidelity are big issues for you to tackle and explore.
* There is a part of you which longs for solitude, peace, quiet . . . and God.

THE NINETIES RABBIT
* You believe in people power and love events which unite the crowd.
* You are community minded and get involved with local functions/fundraisers.
* You have a natural flair for buying, selling, bargaining and serious trading.
* You are the kind of person who brings people together from all walks of life.

THE DRAGON

January 27 1952–February 13 1953
February 13 1964–February 1 1965
January 31 1976–February 17 1977
February 17 1988–February 5 1989

THE FIFTIES DRAGON
* You are a religious or spiritual person whose faith gets you through life.
* Destiny says you will often fly solo in your life, or spend much time alone.
* You are hard to ignore or forget and your influence goes wide and far.
* You've suffered, but your life is always a monument to your total belief.

THE SIXTIES DRAGON

* You're a work in progress, and you'll always be striving for perfection.

* You're potentially gorgeous — stunning, even — but you know it takes effort!

* The closer you get to perfecting your abilities, the more others invest in you.

* You're drawn to further education, self-development . . . and DIY makeovers.

THE SEVENTIES DRAGON

* You're always changing, on the deepest level — you never stay the same.

* Anyone who thinks they know you has no idea; you're a true chameleon.

* The key to your real personality can only be found by a therapist or psychic.

* You're big on transformation for yourself and for other people around you.

THE EIGHTIES DRAGON

* In a previous life — or even earlier in this one — you were known as a fighter.

* You have a 'been there, done that' attitude to conflict of any kind.

* Stresses from your childhood or adolescence are history, but you can't forget.

* You know a lot about the art of attack and defence — and others see it too.

THE SNAKE

February 14 1953–February 2 1954
February 2 1965–January 20 1966
February 18 1977–February 6 1978
February 6 1989–January 26 1990

THE FIFTIES SNAKE

★ You're sweet, generous and kind and believe even the small things help.

★ You have a natural feeling for birds and animals, and people who are needy.

★ There is something innocent and childlike about you, whatever your age.

★ You're generous by nature, and are well-known for giving a little . . . or a lot.

THE SIXTIES SNAKE

★ Born in the tumultuous Sixties, you have a wild and uncontrollable side.

★ Destiny will link you to valuable real estate, wealth or luxurious lifestyles.

★ Part of you is rock-solid, but part of you is unpredictable, fast and furious.

★ Sometimes you're the storm; sometimes you have to withstand the storms!

THE SEVENTIES SNAKE

★ You're a born teacher, and pass on wisdom based on your own experience.

★ You've got a passionate side, just like the Sixties snake — but do you need it?

- ★ There will be two distinct phases in your life — wild woman and wise woman.
- ★ You know how to let go of what, or who, you once desired and truly mature.

THE EIGHTIES/NINETIES SNAKE
- ★ You believe in friends, groups and anything which brings people together.
- ★ You may be musical, a good singer, or just a fan of downloading/live bands.
- ★ You believe in giving for the sake of it, without any expectation of reward.
- ★ You're incredibly sociable, naturally giving, and turn anything into a party.

THE HORSE

February 3 1954–January 23 1955
January 21 1966–February 8 1967
February 7 1978–January 27 1979
January 27 1990–February 14 1991

THE FIFTIES HORSE
- ★ There is something magical, wonderful and not quite real about you!
- ★ You're helpful by nature and believe in lending a hand whenever you can.
- ★ You feel most comfortable when you're around women just like you.
- ★ You're born to party — you love socialising, dancing and dressing up.

THE SIXTIES HORSE

* You're an independent person and could easily choose single parenthood.

* You believe in doing things yourself — you don't need to rely on men.

* There have been times in your life when you've been totally self-sufficient.

* You are confident, have a strong sense of identity, and are a born coper.

THE SEVENTIES HORSE

* Destiny says you'll have to defend your life choices more than most people.

* You know that everything depends on persuading people to see your views.

* If you are at odds with the rest of the world, you'll have to face the world!

* When you win others over on a point of principle, the rules have to change.

THE NINETIES HORSE

* You're capable of incredible focus and concentration when you choose.

* You look deeply into situations and people and pick up what others miss.

* You may be psychic, intuitive, mediumistic or have a natural sixth sense.

* Your professional life, or your interests, will involve peering into the future.

THE RAM

January 24 1955–February 11 1956
February 9 1967–January 29 1968
January 28 1979–February 15 1980
February 15 1991–February 3 1992

THE FIFTIES RAM

*   You are electrifying company and are always exciting to be around.

*   You light up people and situations so that others can see them clearly.

*   The spirit of rock'n'roll is inside you; you're a livewire and a challenge.

*   You're the wake-up call people don't ask for . . . but you make a difference.

THE SIXTIES RAM

*   You're always aware of where you are on the social or professional ladder.

*   You can't help considering who's ahead of you, and who's far below you!

*   If you're the spiritual type, then your soul's advancement will be crucial.

*   Ambition is in your DNA — it's in your nature to climb higher and higher.

THE SEVENTIES/EIGHTIES RAM

*   Some of your biggest inspiration comes from meditating or hibernating.

*   Sometimes the smallest things change your life — like an 'aha!' moment.

* It's only when you take time out from other people that you see the light.

* If you're one of the creative rams, you rely on sudden ideas and insights.

THE NINETIES RAM

* You understand any person, creature or situation which needs rebuilding.

* Occasional storms in your life always trigger a process of slow rebirth.

* You know how to transform yourself, and how to let others transform you.

* Your life goes in cycles of endings, followed by positive new beginnings.

THE MONKEY

February 12 1956–January 30 1957
January 30 1968–February 16 1969
February 16 1980–February 4 1981
February 4 1992–January 22 1993

THE FIFTIES MONKEY

* Freedom is always a mixed blessing for you — there's usually a price to pay.

* Your lifestyle, choices and ideas frequently run into opposition 'out there'.

* Money is an ongoing issue for you and you really know the cost/price of things.

* No matter what happens in your life, you always have hope for the future.

THE SIXTIES MONKEY

★   You are soft, attractive and in touch with your female side — it's your purpose!

★   You are physically or just emotionally delicate and can be damaged rather easily.

★   Fashion, style or beautiful objects make up your world.

★   You're not really built for the tough stuff, but you know your true function.

THE EIGHTIES MONKEY

★   There is a purity and innocence about you that is rather rare and special.

★   Your family or ancestors have a direct link with your life and times now.

★   You have a natural feeling for ancient places, buildings and civilisations.

★   No matter how many changes you go through, your essence stays the same.

THE NINETIES MONKEY

★   You're a sensualist and have a big appetite for pleasure in almost any form.

★   You're a consumer by nature, and could be a gourmet or a shopaholic.

★   You're sociable and like the company of people who share your good times.

★   You may have food, spending or addiction issues unless you pull back.

THE ROOSTER

January 31 1957–February 17 1958
February 17 1969–February 5 1970
February 5 1981–January 24 1982
January 23 1993–February 9 1994

THE FIFTIES ROOSTER

★ You're a natural teacher, professor or 'wise woman' type in this lifetime.

★ People come into your life to learn from you — do you learn from them too?

★ You see the world in two different ways: via knowledge and via reality.

★ Your challenge is to acquire wisdom, but know how to truly transmit it.

THE SIXTIES/SEVENTIES ROOSTER

★ Your energy is direct, aggressive and needs an outlet — tennis or martial arts?

★ You'll learn a lot about who has power, and who doesn't, during your lifetime.

★ You'll do whatever it takes to ensure that you come first — and you survive!

★ Part of you knows what it's like to be vulnerable despite this; it's your karma.

THE EIGHTIES ROOSTER

★ You'll learn that relationships aren't the be-all and end-all in this lifetime!

★ You're naturally optimistic and positive and can always see a way forward.

* You know what it means to choose to be happy, and you do it well.

* You have a special kind of courage that other people can learn from.

THE NINETIES ROOSTER

* At heart, your ideals and values reflect those in your birthplace or country.

* You don't just hold beliefs, you actively follow them through in your life.

* Your life will be full of major transformations as you evolve and change.

* There is something spiritual and special about what you have allegiance to.

THE DOG

February 18 1958–February 7 1959
February 6 1970–January 26 1971
January 25 1982–February 12 1983
February 10 1994–January 30 1995

THE FIFTIES DOG

* You have innate style, even when life is tough and you're battling it out.

* You're not afraid of anything, and have the ability to keep ploughing forward.

* You'd rather have silk than nylon in your wardobe — clothes/accessories count!

* You know how to protect yourself well against all of life's varied possibilities.

THE SEVENTIES DOG

★ You understand the connection between the mind, body and spirit very well.

★ Your body's rhythms are important to you — but your soul counts too.

★ Fitness, gyms, yoga and alternative therapies/sport have a destiny link for you.

★ You know there's no point in worshipping the body without seeing the spirit.

THE EIGHTIES DOG

★ You're gifted at getting rid of the non-essentials, and may use this gift in your work.

★ You're not afraid of hard work and it's your karma to do what has to be done!

★ You like a neat garden, an orderly lifestyle and no excess/waste in your life.

★ You're very good at taking care of appearances — the look really matters.

THE NINETIES DOG

★ You come alive when you're by the beach, or in other natural and open spaces.

★ You understand why the simple pleasures in life are often the best of all.

★ You're always open to sharing the fun in life, or making new connections.

★ The whole point of living for you is relaxing, having fun and letting go.

THE PIG

February 8 1959–January 27 1960
January 27 1971–February 14 1972
February 13 1983–February 1 1984
January 31 1995–February 18 1996

THE FIFTIES/SIXTIES PIG

* You don't take injustice lying down and will protest noisily if you have to.

* Your basic rights are an issue with you, in your personal life and at work.

* You believe in people power and have seen how a group can change things.

* You are prepared to take action against any exploitative person/firm.

THE SEVENTIES PIG

* Even when you try to keep things in, your emotions have a way of escaping.

* There is something sweet, feminine, heady and intoxicating about you!

* Your true self is usually revealed to others accidentally or unintentionally.

* People have no idea how powerful you are until you hit a crisis in your life.

THE EIGHTIES PIG

* Your brand of wisdom doesn't necessarily need a lot of education behind it.

* You're a natural philosopher and have a special way of seeing the world.

*   You're incredibly knowledgeable and have a lot to pass on to other people.

*   You may be academic, you may not, but you could give a lecture tomorrow.

THE NINETIES PIG

*   Your inner child is alive and well and always ready for grown-up playtime.

*   You are protected by the people around you, or by your work/home environment.

*   This protection makes it possible for you to do your own thing/have fun.

*   You may have issues with being mollycoddled or fussed over by others.

YOUR INDIAN
MOON SIGN

How are you seen in India? Vedic astrology is complex, but finding out your Indian Moon Sign, or Nakshatra, is a good place to begin. There are twenty-seven of them, and you can find yours at www.panchang.com, which is the best website I know to calculate your own Nakshatra at no cost. Click on Moon Sign Report and 'Try For Free' — it's run by Michael Geary, author of *Moon Astrology for Lovers* (Thorsons). The site as a whole is excellent and well worth exploring.

What follows is my own Western interpretation of Indian Moon Signs, based on personal research influenced by the work of Vedic expert and consultant Keven Barrett. Keven is the founder and national president of the Australian Council of Vedic Astrology, and a life member and accredited teacher at the American Council of Vedic Astrology.

If what you read about your Moon Sign inspires you to look for more, then either Michael Geary or Keven Barrett can help with a consultation.

At the end of this section, I have asked Keven to walk you through Indian (Vedic) astrology in more detail, so that you begin to get a feel for this crucial part of global spirituality and divination.

YOUR INDIAN MOON SIGN

ASHWINI — THE HORSEMAN

You are less interested in worrying about money than most people, and prefer to focus your time and energy on your next holiday. You are adventurous and love exploring new ideas on the internet, and new places on (and off) the map.

THE FEMALE ASHWINI

You are a free spirit and truly independent. Tradition says you may quit work after age fifty — the chances are good you will have enough money to retire early. Vedic astrology also states you could marry between twenty-three and twenty-six, but to commit before this age could result in a separation. You are more likely to have daughters than sons.

BHARANI — THE ELEPHANT

You're an important person in the grand scheme of things, and loom large on the landscape (just like a real elephant). This means other people can sometimes resent you. Your attitude to the good life is usually 'more, more, more'!

THE FEMALE BHARANI

Tradition says you will shine as a receptionist, guide, saleswoman or sportswoman. You may have problems with your in-laws, though! You could easily marry around your twenty-third year. In general, you are an optimist who makes her own opportunities in life — and then makes the most of them. You're attractive but your teeth may need attention.

KRITHIKA — THE RAZOR

You can cut people off quite easily if they interfere with what you want — particularly if someone in the family is trying to obstruct your plans. You can be quite sharp with people and start arguments — it may help to compromise!

THE FEMALE KRITHIKA

You could become a doctor, chemical engineer, administrator, tailor, leather worker or full-time wife with this Moon Sign. Tradition says you may have few children — or none at all. You need to look after your natural beauty with special care after you turn twenty-seven, so spend more time and money on yourself then. Your marriage will take work.

ROHINI — THE CHARIOT

Rohini people of both sexes are said to spend the first twenty-five years of their lives going backwards and forwards — just like a real chariot — in their business dealings. Anything which relates to the movement of stock or livestock may do well.

THE FEMALE ROHINI

If people push you too far, you may feel like running over them with your chariot wheels! You're good at making connections with people, and have a talent for repartee. If you do not overcome stubbornness and suspicion in your marriage, you may find yourself hitting the road — sooner rather than later. Self-control brings a happy partnership.

MRIGASIRA — THE DEER'S HEAD

Tradition says you are devoted to your mother, although you will live far apart from each other. Just like a real deer, you may have thin legs or seem tall and lean. You are alert, fast on your feet and can lock horns with others.

THE FEMALE MRIGASIRA

You like the finer things of life and are money-minded, and can end up with a pile of savings or assets if you manage your life correctly. You will always have a lot going on in your life, even after you are married. You could do well in electronics, communication, engineering and any job which is normally seen as male territory — it won't put you off.

ARUDRA — THE HEAD

You are hot-headed and can quickly lose your temper and be slow to forgive people. Avoid black magic as it is bad karma for you. You are beautiful, and your eyes are your best feature — although you have a noticeably strong nose.

THE FEMALE ARUDRA

You live in your head and can be very critical of people. It's possible you'll have a stepfather or stepmother, depending on your full personal Indian horoscope. You could do well in educational and scientific fields, or be a consultant. You're a good talker. According to tradition, you may marry late in life. Be careful with coughs and colds at all times.

PUNARVASU — THE BOW AND ARROW

Sexually, you know exactly how to hit the spot. However, you could do it more than once, and end up with more than one marriage. You like music and are a good dancer, and if you are lucky may be able to incorporate this into your job.

THE FEMALE PUNARVASU

Just like a real bow and arrow, your purpose can be positive or negative. You always have an intense impact on other people, though. You do not suit business partnerships particularly well, so be careful. Tradition says that before the age of thirty-two you may not get the business results you want, either. You're a big water drinker as well!

PUSHYA — THE FLOWER
You are easy on the eye, and may even be beautiful. You are spiritual, and possibly religious, and understand your part in the scheme of things. You could easily make money from land or property. Success tends to follow you around.

THE FEMALE PUSHYA
Tradition says you could become a private secretary, or work in places where you must keep a lot of secrets and have the trust of other people (like the CIA, MI5 or ASIO!). You are shy by nature, just like a flower which closes its buds, but do learn to express your feelings to your partner and family or they may mistakenly think you don't care.

ASHLESHA — THE SERPENT
Like the serpent, you shed your skin periodically and renew yourself. Your life is full of relaunches, and each time you reveal a new side of yourself, your life force increases. You are a magnetic person — people are compelled by you.

THE FEMALE ASHLESHA
Tradition says you could lose financially at age thirty-five or thirty-six, but gain unexpectedly at forty. Up until the age of twenty-five you need to be careful of underhand dealings or dirty business or trade deeds, as your snake-in-the-grass behaviour could cause you trouble. Keep an eye on your in-laws as there is a chance they could hatch a plot to create husband trouble!

MAGHA — THE ANCESTORS

You have a huge respect for tradition and the past. You see the community as your family and make plenty of contributions, giving whatever you can. You may have to take on responsibility for one or more brothers and sisters.

THE FEMALE MAGHA

You will have full control over the household. Expect a comfortable lifestyle fit for a princess. Thanks to your karma, you could easily become a boss, manager or CEO. Children look good and, according to tradition, you are likely to have a son and then daughters. You could run an office as expertly as you run your domestic life/routine.

PURVA PHALGUNI — THE FRONT LEGS OF THE MARRIAGE BED

You have a big lust for life and an endless thirst for most sensual experiences, from music, to dance, to art. Tradition says you could easily deal in cotton, salt, honey, oil or government services! You're a good people person.

THE FEMALE PURVA PHALGUNI

You manage your family brilliantly; your partner is likely to be loving and your children will be obedient. You are prepared to make sacrifices for the marriage and for family life. Your partner may have a great job, which might inflate your ego a little — be careful that your neighbours and relatives don't begin to resent this.

UTTARA PHALGUNI — THE BACK LEGS OF THE MARRIAGE BED

Favours and help from powerful people will give you a big boost in your life and make you much more attractive to potential partners or lovers. You have a lot of affection for family. You can feel lonely if not in a true partnership.

THE FEMALE UTTARA PHALGUNI
You do well in jobs which deal with the public. Tradition says you have a talent for maths, astronomy, astrology, science, engineering and health. You could also become a model or actress, however! Your voice is very easy on the ear. Tradition says you may have a black mole on your face. You find it hard to keep any bad feeling for long.

HASTA — THE HAND
You will often end up in confrontations where you feel like saying 'Talk to the hand!', but each problem you face in your life will help you progress. Tradition says you can easily become addicted to alcohol — so be careful.

THE FEMALE HASTA
You have lovely eyes and ears. You are generally shy and not exactly motivated, but in between the slothfulness you have big bursts of energy. Your partner will be rich, and you may have a boy before you have daughters. Don't shoot your mouth off too much with the family and you should enjoy smooth relationships with them.

CHITRA — THE PEARL
You will go through many gritty situations in your life — some real ordeals or challenges with others — but each piece of grit will become a jewel of experience. Your appearance is distinctive; you stand out from a crowd.

THE FEMALE CHITRA
Tradition says that, like the male Chitra, you may spend the years between twenty-five and fifty living in another country.

From fifty to seventy-five you will become more interested in spiritual or religious matters. You are beautiful, with long hair, and love your freedom. You may have a talent for science, nursing, modelling or acting. You must work at marriage to make it happy.

SWATI — THE SPROUT
You are here to grow, prosper and flourish, and take the seeds of your early life and abilities and do something big with them. You are fond of pets, and have a strong sixth sense. You're always ready to learn or to educate yourself.

THE FEMALE SWATI
Your walk is memorable, as it's either noticeably slow or fast. You have a lot of friends, but you'd rather stay in than go out. You love religious rites and spiritual rituals. You could be promoted to an important position with lots of prestige, with travel thrown in. Your skin is sensitive, so look after it and always wear plenty of sunscreen.

VISHAKHA — THE GATEWAY
You're always ready to explore the next pathway, and the gate is always open for change in your life. Success tends to come in the second half of your life, not the first. You open up new subjects to very large numbers of people.

THE FEMALE VISHAKHA
People love your voice. You don't have ego problems as a rule, but may nevertheless attract envy from female friends or relatives. You could do very well in the arts, writing, publishing and literature. You could easily become close to your father-in-law, and look after distant relatives as well as those in your immediate family.

ANURADHA — THE LOTUS
You have to dig deeply inside yourself in this lifetime to find your roots — what is hidden beneath the surface! Until the age of twenty-five you could also put down roots in a new place, living far from the place of your birth.

THE FEMALE ANURADHA
Tradition says you have a great body and a slim waist. You respect people who are older and more experienced than you, and could be interested in politics, social work, music, fine arts and/or dance. Where health is concerned you are vulnerable to problems below the waist, so take care. You typically hold a central place with family and friends.

JYESHTA — THE UMBRELLA
Tradition says that between eighteen and twenty-six you will have financial challenges, but from twenty-seven to fifty you will have a stable life, with slow but steady progress, when you are able to put money aside for a rainy day in the future.

THE FEMALE JYESHTA
You have a muscular body with long arms, and short or curly hair could suit you extremely well. If you are not born into a rich family, don't worry: you could still become wealthy through your own efforts. You are good at sport. Watch out for the way you manage your children — they could rebel if you restrict them when they are young.

MOOLA — THE ROOT
You like to dig deeply and get to the root of any subject, which is why you do so well in herbalism, gardening, science, medicine, and any area where you must deal with the natural world. You like to get to the bottom of things.

THE FEMALE MOOLA

You may have gaps between your front teeth. You have a good heart, but can be extremely proud and stubborn which can land you with people problems. Marriage will take a lot of hard work and perseverance to be truly successful and happy. In health terms, your vulnerable points are your hips, thighs and sciatic nerves.

PURVASHADHA — THE FAN

You may have almond-shaped eyes, and eyelashes which fan out at the edges, along with a long nose and a fair complexion. You are a shopaholic or a window shopper by nature, and always dreaming about what you might have.

THE FEMALE PURVASHADHA

You fan the flames of enthusiasm in whatever you approach, as you are energetic and have a lot of vitality. You like pets, but your family is a different matter and you could be quite against your parents or brothers. You could do well in education, banking, writing, publishing or in religious organisations. Don't expect kids to help round the house.

UTTARASHADA — THE ELEPHANT'S TUSK

What happens between twenty-eight and thirty-one will change your life in important ways. Your teeth are beautifully shaped and well-cut. You could be attracted to teaching, banking or religion when it's time to choose your professional path.

THE FEMALE UTTARASHADA

Tradition says you may have wind problems — sorry about that! You are very spiritual and drawn to beliefs and ideas which speak to your soul. You're a sociable person, although you often speak before you think. Your eyes are one of your best features. Before the age of twenty-five music will draw you, and you could easily inherit something from the family.

SHRAVANA — THE THREE FOOTPRINTS

You put one foot in front of the other to reach your goals in life and can't afford to be distracted in the pursuit of your ambitions. You'll walk a broad path around your country, or the world, and could live or study overseas eventually.

THE FEMALE SHRAVANA

You are tall and lean with a big head and broad face, compared to other women. Your front teeth could be big and wide apart. You are a big charity giver and generous with friends and family too. You could be in entertainment or the performing arts, or office and administration work. You prefer a partner with good etiquette and manners.

DHANISTA — THE DRUM

You have a natural sense of rhythm in bed and need to make sure you don't over-indulge in sex. You are musically talented, which you might expect with this Indian Moon Sign. You have some knowledge or natural flair for the occult.

THE FEMALE DHANISTA

Even after the age of forty you continue to look younger than you really are — and you won't even need botox to do it. You have a soft spot for anyone who is weaker or more vulnerable than you. You are multi-talented and could teach, design, decorate, or be drawn towards the secret service, treasury, banking, literature or even science.

SHATA BHISHAJ — THE CIRCLE

You are a spiritual and mystical person. You have broad cheeks and full lips. You believe in the universality of all things and could be drawn to religion or a deep faith of some kind. Despite this you have a really hot temper.

THE FEMALE SHATA BHISHAJ
You have a natural ability in science and could become a doctor if you choose. Until the age of twenty-five your mother is a central person in your life. Between twenty-five and fifty you could take up astrology and even become professional. Tradition says you can expect one child from your marriage. Gambling will make you miserable, so steer clear of the casino!

PURVA BHADRA — THE TWO FACES
One face is self-sacrificing and works for the good of all, in the most unselfish way. The other face is rather materialistic and self-centred. Be careful which one you show to the world as it will totally dictate your destiny.

THE FEMALE PURVA BHADRA
You tend to be slim rather than porky and your body is usually beautifully proportioned. You are a born leader when you develop your honesty and sincerity with others, and can get staff to deliver good work. You are either from a rich family or will marry into wealth. You could be drawn to science, technology, education, statistics or astrology.

UTTARA BHADRAPADA — THE COT
You'll enjoy the children who enter your world and will always be drawn to them. You have big eyes, and may have a sturdy body rather than be reed slim. You are very good with people and are usually extremely well-respected.

THE FEMALE UTTARA BHADRAPADA
You could be a lawyer, doctor, nurse or astrologer. Your partner's family will bless the day you walked up the aisle, as

you bring luck to your in-laws. You may be constipated, according to tradition, so you can't have everything! However, you will have true soul growth in this lifetime. Like a baby in a cot, you are here to develop yourself.

REVATI — THE TIMING DRUM
You are a creative person who can beat out new rhythms in her life without any difficulty. Your life will be full of big turning points and major transformations. You have a natural talent for music, dance, drama and literature.

THE FEMALE REVATI
You stand out in a crowd because you are extremely attractive. You can be incredibly superstitious, and if you become attached to a particular religion, belief or spiritual pathway, you may be overly rigid with all the rules, rituals and regulations. You could work in the arts, mathematics, or be a telephone operator, typist, teacher or ambassador.

OVERVIEW OF NAKSHATRAS (INDIAN MOON SIGNS) AND VEDIC ASTROLOGY (INDIAN ASTROLOGY)

by Keven Barrett

Before the introduction (around 1500 BC) of seven days of the week and the twelve signs of the zodiac, the system of astrology/astronomy used dated from approximately 6000 BC, and particularly from 4000 BC when records from the past were recovered. A translation of all this in English (now out of print) was compiled in 1896 under the title *Bharatiya Joyotish Sastyra*. The 360-degree zodiac was divided into twenty-seven divisions called Nakshatras, Indian Moon Signs, or Moon Mansions in some books. These twenty-seven divisions were split up into three sets, equalling 120 degrees, of nine Nakshatras each, and each nine sections have different meanings which are ruled by nine planets: the Sun, Moon, Mercury, Venus, Mars, Jupiter, Saturn, including the North and South Nodes (Rahu and Ketu). This system is based on the sidereal (movable) zodiac, while the religious ceremonies and crop planting was based on the tropical zodiac (fixed).

For example, from 0 degrees to 13 degrees 20 minutes Aries is ruled by the South Node, and between 13 degrees 20 minutes and 26 degrees 40 minutes Aries is ruled by Venus, and between 26 degrees 40 minutes Aries to 10 degrees Taurus is ruled by the Sun etc. Notice that in these three sections at the end of the Aries Moon Nakshatra it covers a Taurus Moon. Then the Ancients divided each 13 degrees 20 minutes section into four parts, called Padas, giving a slightly different characteristic for those having the same Moon sign. As the Ancients did not use the twelve zodiac signs, thus the carry over.

Indian Vedic literature and poems starting from about 6000 BC recorded their astronomical observation and astrological predictions, especially the verses of the *Rig-Veda* and the *Yajur-Veda*, all based on the Vedanga Jyotish lunar–solar calendar. (All current work and computer programs have been adjusted from the Saka calendar to the modern calendar: seventy-eight years difference.) These books refer to planetary positions and eclipses, and when converted to our modern calendar are extremely accurate.

The Ancients also knew that the Earth is a round ball made up of five elements travelling around the Sun, together with the planets, and that our universe travels around the galactic centre at rate of 2130 years per zodiacal sign. Thus, the age cycle is currently Pisces. It started in 288 AD and finishes in about 2400-odd AD — so much for the so-called Aquarius age which will begin at the end of the Pisces period. (Age cycles travel backwards through the zodiac.) It is only in the last few centuries that the Flat Earth Society 'discovered' all of this information about how the universe works.

The ancient Nakshatras writings covered every aspect of a person's life, but were compiled mainly for kings, royal families, and to predict the outcome of wars. The astrologers added or subtracted comments through the Padas.

CONNECTIONS, CLICKS, CLASHES AND CLUNKS

If I could have a can of catfood every time someone asks 'Is he compatible with me?', I would never have to go to the supermarket again. When people ask 'Are we compatible?' though, what they really mean is 'Will we get married and stay married?' This is where I have to hand the catfood back. Astrology can tell you about the good times and the bad times, but not the outcome — that's your choice.

It's the same with finding flatmates, or bosses, or business partners. All astrology can do is show you the chemistry. The final outcome is up to you.

What this part of the book can do for you is identify some of the areas in which you click and connect with people, and the areas in which you may have some problems.

If you have any of these planets — the Sun, Moon, Mercury, Venus and/or Mars — in the same signs, then you'll click.

If these same planets are also making harmonious patterns with each other (called trines and sextiles in astrology), then you'll connect. Fire and Air signs tend to connect with each other — so various combinations of your planets in Aries, Gemini, Leo, Libra, Sagittarius and Aquarius will fit nicely.

Similarly, any combination of planets in Taurus, Cancer, Virgo, Scorpio, Capricorn and Pisces tends to work well, as a general rule.

Clunking comes from planets in signs which form tricky patterns with each other — known as squares in astrology. Thus:

Aries and Cancer
Aries and Capricorn
Taurus and Leo
Taurus and Aquarius
Gemini and Virgo
Gemini and Pisces
Cancer and Libra
Cancer and Aries
Leo and Scorpio
Leo and Taurus
Virgo and Sagittarius
Virgo and Gemini
Libra and Capricorn
Libra and Cancer
Scorpio and Aquarius
Scorpio and Leo
Sagittarius and Pisces
Sagittarius and Virgo
Capricorn and Aries
Capricorn and Libra
Aquarius and Taurus
Aquarius and Scorpio
Pisces and Gemini
Pisces and Sagittarius

The clashes come from planets in signs which are opposite each other in the zodiac. This opposition can feel like a wrestling match between people — you're in the red corner, while someone else is in the blue corner.

Aries and Libra
Taurus and Scorpio
Gemini and Sagittarius
Cancer and Capricorn
Leo and Aquarius
Virgo and Pisces
Libra and Aries
Scorpio and Taurus
Sagittarius and Gemini
Capricorn and Cancer
Aquarius and Leo
Pisces and Virgo

As a general rule, the more two people's planets click and connect, across the board, the easier things will be. If you have a majority of clashes and clunks, though, being together will be extremely hard work — no matter if it's professional or personal.

Because most people are usually frantic to make a partnership or work association tick, they lean hard on the clicks and connections and try to ignore the rest. This is only natural, but sooner or later the clashes and clunks will have to be faced — otherwise, it's like editing out parts of your personality just for the sake of being part of a couple.

FAMILY AND FLATMATES

The most important planet to look at here is the Moon. Your Moon sign, and that of your flatmate or relative, has to click or connect with other planets if you're going to bond together or live together (without resorting to writing your name in pencil on the eggs in the fridge).

The Moon rules houses, flats, eating, comfort, security, the family and, above all, the situations and people which make you feel at home. So you can see why it's vital to have good clicks and connections for your Moon with their planets, and vice versa.

This also applies to a partner, if you move in with them. The sex might be great (especially if your Venus signs click or connect) but what about the nitty-gritty of domestic routine? It's really important that your Moon signs agree with as many of their planet signs as possible — otherwise you may feel rather uncomfortable.

WHO SHOULD YOU SHARE WITH?

You can't choose your family, but you can certainly choose who moves into your bed — or just your spare room.

Moon Sign Aries ~ Look for people with planets in Aries, Leo and Sagittarius first. Planets in Gemini and Aquarius are also good.

Moon Sign Taurus ~ Look for people with planets in Taurus, Virgo and Capricorn first. Planets in Cancer and Pisces are also good.

Moon Sign Gemini ~ Look for people with planets in Gemini, Libra and Aquarius first. Planets in Leo and Aries are also good.

Moon Sign Cancer ~ Look for people with planets in Cancer, Scorpio and Pisces first. Planets in Taurus and Virgo are also good.

Moon Sign Leo ~ Look for people with planets in Leo, Aries and Sagittarius first. Planets in Gemini and Libra are also good.

Moon Sign Virgo ~ Look for people with planets in Virgo, Capricorn and Taurus first. Planets in Cancer and Scorpio are also good.

Moon Sign Libra ~ Look for people with planets in Libra, Gemini and Aquarius first. Planets in Leo and Sagittarius are also good.

Moon Sign Scorpio ~ Look for people with planets in Scorpio, Cancer and Pisces first. Planets in Virgo and Capricorn are also good.

Moon Sign Sagittarius ~ Look for people with planets in Sagittarius, Aries and Leo first. Planets in Libra and Aquarius are also good.

Moon Sign Capricorn ~ Look for people with planets in Capricorn, Virgo and Taurus first. Planets in Scorpio and Pisces are also good.

Moon Sign Aquarius ~ Look for people with planets in Aquarius, Libra and Gemini first. Planets in Aries and Sagittarius are also good.

Moon Sign Pisces ~ Look for people with planets in Pisces, Scorpio and Cancer first. Planets in Taurus and Capricorn are also good.

WOMEN AND WOMEN

A whole book could be written on lesbian and bisexual relationships and astrology. It's an under-researched and under-represented part of the art. But there are some basic rules for women who prefer women.

Firstly, go back to your own Moon and Venus signs in the 'You' section of this book. The Moon describes what you need and what makes you feel comfortable. Venus describes what you love and take the most pleasure in. Somewhere between these two planet signs, you will find a little of what you want and need.

Some gay women have asked me about their masculine side, which they feel quite strongly. Astrologers always get into politically incorrect territory here, as even talking about 'masculine' and 'feminine' qualities can sound a little limiting.

Nevertheless, astrology is about ancient archetypes, and these just aren't politically correct. We still work with the idea that the Sun and Mars are masculine and describe the side of women that is more aggressive, more confident, more assertive, more authoritative and altogether tougher. If you are seeking something along these lines in your partner, check out your own Sun and Mars signs — and then hers — for insights.

If there really is strong chemistry between you, you will also find that your Moon, Mercury, Venus, Sun and Mars signs fall into the same groups, or come under the same signs.

Clicking Signs
These include Aries and Aries, Taurus and Taurus, Gemini and Gemini — and so on. For example, if your Mercury sign is Pisces, and her Moon sign is Pisces, you'll have one strong click in your relationship. You'll feel it from the first meeting too.

Connecting Signs
The more planet signs you share which fall into any of these groups, the easier it will be to live together and stay connected — despite any clashes and clunks.

One — Aries – Sagittarius – Leo
Two — Taurus – Capricorn – Virgo
Three — Gemini – Aquarius – Libra
Four — Cancer – Pisces – Scorpio

Clashing Signs
If you have a lot of planets in clashing signs, the relationship will be hard work. It doesn't mean it won't last, but you are

periodically going to have some massive differences of opinion!

Aries and Libra
Taurus and Scorpio
Gemini and Sagittarius
Cancer and Capricorn
Leo and Aquarius
Virgo and Pisces

Clunking Signs
Once again, if you have a lot of clunking planet signs between you, or just a majority of clashing signs and clunking signs, the relationship will be very demanding. In fact, it may not get off the ground in the first place!

Aries–Cancer–Capricorn
Taurus–Leo–Aquarius
Gemini–Virgo–Pisces
Cancer–Libra–Aries
Leo–Scorpio–Taurus
Virgo–Sagittarius–Gemini
Libra–Capricorn–Cancer
Scorpio–Aquarius–Leo
Sagittarius–Pisces–Virgo
Capricorn–Aries–Libra
Aquarius–Taurus–Scorpio
Pisces–Gemini–Sagittarius

WORKING TOGETHER

Even if you work on a farm, it's hard to avoid modern technology. Our working lives are dominated by e-mail, text messages, telephone calls and faxes. Even in a physical job, you also need to communicate. All of which makes your Mercury sign vital when it comes to judging who you should work for or with.

If you work in a profession where communication, information, education and/or transportation are central to the task, then your Mercury sign, and those of your employees, employers, clients and colleagues, becomes even more integral.

Studying or teaching? Once again, you'll need compatible Mercury signs. Mercury rules the written and spoken word.

Be you flight attendant, wheat farmer, politician or supermodel, you need lots of clicks and connections between your Mercury sign and the planet signs of other people to have workplace harmony.

Here's the score:

Mercury in Aries ~ Look for planets in Aries, Leo and Sagittarius first.

Mercury in Taurus ~ Look for planets in Taurus, Virgo and Capricorn first.

Mercury in Gemini ~ Look for planets in Gemini, Libra and Aquarius first.

Mercury in Cancer ~ Look for planets in Cancer, Scorpio and Pisces first.

Mercury in Leo ~ Look for planets in Leo, Aries and Sagittarius first.

Mercury in Virgo ~ Look for planets in Virgo, Taurus and Capricorn first.

Mercury in Libra ~ Look for planets in Libra, Aquarius and Gemini first.

Mercury in Scorpio ~ Look for planets in Scorpio, Pisces and Cancer first.

Mercury in Sagittarius ~ Look for planets in Sagittarius, Aries and Leo first.

Mercury in Capricorn ~ Look for planets in Capricorn, Taurus and Virgo first.

Mercury in Aquarius ~ Look for planets in Aquarius, Libra and Gemini first.

Mercury in Pisces ~ Look for planets in Pisces, Scorpio and Cancer first.

LOVE AND SEX

Venus is the planet of love and sex. In mythology, she is also known as Aphrodite. If a pure love and sex connection is going to last between you, then you really need a partner who has as many clicking and connecting planets as possible with your own Venus sign. Do the majority of your planets also click and connect with your partner's Venus sign? Then you could feel like soulmates.

The more clicks and connections you share, the easier it will be to seduce them, and also be seduced by them, over the course of a lifetime. Even if you break up, the heat will still be there when you run into each other on the high street with your Zimmer frames.

This part of your link does not cover communication. So if your Mercury sign clashes and clunks with lots of your partner's planets, you could be great in bed — but hopeless when it comes to talking about serious issues.

And there's more. Your Venus sign only describes how things are at candelit dinners and in bed — it says nothing about what a partner might do for your ego, your identity, and your sense of self. That's covered by your Sun sign, which we'll get to shortly.

In the meantime, though, it's fair to say that without a nicely supported Venus sign in your chart, it's going to be hard to keep the flame burning long-term. This is fine if you're together for the sake of the mortgage, the kids, or money. But without a partner whose planet signs click and connect with your Venus sign, you're unlikely to find too many wow factors on Valentine's Day!

For a repeated shot of love and romance over the course of a lifetime, look for this:

Venus in Aries ~ You need a partner with as many planets as possible in Aries, Leo, Sagittarius, Aquarius and/or Gemini.

Venus in Taurus ~ You need a partner with as many planets as possible in Taurus, Virgo, Capricorn, Cancer and/or Pisces.

Venus in Gemini ~ You need a partner with as many planets as possible in Gemini, Libra, Aquarius, Leo and/or Aries.

Venus in Cancer ~ You need a partner with as many planets as possible in Cancer, Scorpio, Pisces, Virgo and/or Taurus.

Venus in Leo ~ You need a partner with as many planets as possible in Leo, Sagittarius, Aries, Libra and/or Gemini.

Venus in Virgo ~ You need a partner with as many planets as possible in Virgo, Capricorn, Taurus, Scorpio and/or Cancer.

Venus in Libra ~ You need a partner with as many planets as possible in Libra, Aquarius, Gemini, Sagittarius and/or Leo.

Venus in Scorpio ~ You need a partner with as many planets as possible in Scorpio, Pisces, Cancer, Capricorn and/or Virgo.

Venus in Sagittarius ~ You need a partner with as many planets as possible in Sagittarius, Aries, Leo, Aquarius and/or Libra.

Venus in Capricorn ~ You need a partner with as many planets as possible in Capricorn, Taurus, Virgo, Pisces and/or Scorpio.

Venus in Aquarius ~ You need a partner with as many planets as possible in Aquarius, Gemini, Libra, Aries and/or Sagittarius.

Venus in Pisces ~ You need a partner with as many planets as possible in Pisces, Cancer, Scorpio, Taurus and/or Capricorn.

FIRE, EARTH, AIR OR WATER?

Some of your friends, family or partners may have an overload of Fire, Earth, Air or Water in their chart. This makes them rather extreme characters, and they will get on extremely well with just a few people, but find a large chunk of the population leaves them cold!

Are you dominated by Fire, Earth, air or Water in your chart? Here's the list:

FIRE — Planets in Aries, Leo, Sagittarius

EARTH — Planets in Taurus, Virgo, Capricorn

AIR — Planets in Gemini, Libra, Aquarius

WATER — Planets in Cancer, Scorpio, Pisces

AIR-DOMINANT PEOPLE

They have a big dose of Libra, Aquarius or Gemini in their chart. Think people with glasses — John Lennon and Grahame Garden from *The Goodies*, or Yoko Ono with those huge black shades.

This is what Air is all about:

Theories ★ Ideas ★ Mental energy ★ Communication ★ Wordplay ★ Analysis ★ Detachment ★ Fairness ★ Logic ★ Reasonableness ★ Cynicism ★ Intellectually weighing ★ Connecting — on an information level ★ Articulating ★ The internet ★ Shallowness ★ Superficiality ★ Coolness.

★   Air feeds the Fire signs without even trying.

★   Air can't bear Earth — too boring.

★   Air loves more Air — let's talk!

★   Air gets uncomfortable with too much Water around.

Still, the whole point of the elements is that they have to be balanced. If you suspect the airy type in your life is way too out of touch with the real world, suggest this exercise:

1. Take off shoes and socks.
2. Lie on the grass.
3. Imagine roots growing out of the body and into the soil.
4. Repeat after me, 'I am earthed'.
5. Then go and do something sensible, like putting up shelves.

FIRE-DOMINANT PEOPLE

Anyone with the majority of their planets in Aries, Leo and/or Sagittarius is Fire dominant. Think Madonna with her rallying cries, her air-punching and her general oomphiness. Think Tarzan or Napoleon. Tension or anger is never far from the surface with Fire — it's partly what seems to energise them.

This is what it's all about:

Enthusiasm ★ Leadership ★ Confidence ★ Optimism ★ Energy ★ Intuition ★ The future ★ Adventurousness ★ Gambling/risk-taking ★ Initiating ★ Driving ★ Pushing ★ Questing ★ Pep talks ★ Enterprise ★ Entrepreneurship ★ Belief ★ Just-do-it philosophies ★ Blazing ★ Roaring ★ Impressing ★ Warming

★   Fire needs Air — it hangs around people with Aquarius, Gemini or Libra in their charts because it needs the oxgyen.
★   Fire can't spend too long hanging around Water — it's the wet blanket effect. Drip, drip, drip!
★   Fire relates to Fire, and sparks fly.
★   Fire feels distinctly ill at ease around too much Earth.

Sometimes Fire types need to get back in touch with their emotions, and stop huffing and puffing, or running around like Tigger. Here's the formula:

1. Remove all clothes.
2. Get into a lake.
3. Float. And feel something!

EARTH-DOMINANT PEOPLE

If someone has a large dose of Taurus, Virgo or Capricorn in his/her chart then that person is Earth-bound. Think normal, down-to-earth and REAL PERSON. Think sensible, grounded and totally unpretentious. It's pure Charlie Brown from *Peanuts* — or, if you prefer, Her Majesty the Queen.

Here's what it's all about:

Practicality * Down-to-earth * Material * Financial * Realistic * Work-oriented * Building * Securing * Stabilising * Owning * Structures * Growth * Common sense * Normality * Endurance * Long-term planning * Reality * Anti-crackpot * Anti-fantasy * Pro-values * The collector * The builder * The solid earner.

* Earth provides a solid, rock-like holding facility for Water, so people with Pisces, Scorpio and Cancer bits are reassured and attracted.

* Earth just doesn't get Fire.

* Earth feels quite at home with other doses of Earth.

* Earth prefers to get a bit of distance between itself and Air.

If someone is too Earthed for his/her own good (plodding, becoming boring, becoming a breadhead, or slowing down) this is quite a good antidote:

1. Apply overalls.
2. Purchase one pot of red paint, one pot of yellow paint, one pot of orange paint.
3. Throw it at a canvas to loud rock'n'roll music.
4. Burn canvas and scream.

WATER-DOMINANT PEOPLE

This person has an overload of Cancer, Scorpio and Pisces in his/her chart. Chaos is often a trademark of Water — so is a total lack of rationality. Without Water signs, we wouldn't have photography or prose, though. Or *The Lord of the Rings*.

Here are the key concepts:

Sensitive ★ Emotional ★ Feelings ★ Irrational instincts ★ Vulnerability ★ Empathy ★ Sympathy ★ Tuning in ★ Unreasonableness ★ Anti-logic ★ Women's intuition ★ Therapeutic ★ Cathartic ★ Depth ★ Dreamers ★ Imaginative ★ Altered states ★ Consuming ★ Drowning ★ Mothers — and mother figures ★ Tears ★ Swimming ★ Surfing.

★ Water needs Earth to prop it up, so it looks for Taurus, Capricorn, Virgo.

★ Water and Fire just don't work that well.

★ Water and Water cruise together.

★ Water and Air aren't remotely complementary!

Sometimes people can be too Watery — in fact, you may wonder where precisely the real world seems to have gone. Here's a possible solution for the overly-Watery person:

1. Purchase gardening gloves.
2. Plant potatoes using a step-by-step instruction book.

3. When ready, pick potatoes and make potato soup, once again using a step-by-step instruction book.
4. Serve at a dinner party — on time.

YOUR CIRCLE OF FRIENDS

Which circle of friends has really lasted in your life? Which pub quiz team, football team, yoga group or yummy mummy network could you not live without? The chances are, everyone has the majority of their planets in the same sign group.

Which one do you and your friends fall into?

PLANETS IN FIRE: ARIES, LEO, SAGITTARIUS

A Fire group connection describes people who are mutually enthusiastic and fired up about life. You help each other to take awfully big adventures. When people with Fire links get together in a group, there will always be plenty of big ideas and big plans under discussion. Fire links also mean you boost each other's confidence.

The future is always extremely important to all of you, and sometimes the thought of what you will achieve tomorrow is more exciting than what is actually going on in the present. This is a high-energy connection — lots of immediate feedback, lots of bounced ideas, and a huge amount of lust for life.

PLANETS IN EARTH: TAURUS, VIRGO, CAPRICORN

An Earth group connection describes people who share a down-to-earth approach to life. You'll help each other out in practical ways if you share a link here. When Earth people get together there's a very solid feel — best described as 'We Shall Not Be Moved'.

Problems may occur when one of you feels the others are being impossibly stubborn. There may be differences related to money or values as well. This is a particularly mature and stable set of relationships, which may have a great deal of focus on the material — capitalising on life's rewards together. This would make a great investment group, or you'll just get into home renovations or property purchases together.

PLANETS IN AIR: GEMINI, LIBRA, AQUARIUS

An Air group connection is notorious for helping those who have it to run up enormous phone bills. Conversation and the flow of ideas — or gossip — are what keep Air-connected people interested. If you share links here, you can be a little cool with each other (this is not a touchy-feely connection by itself) but the rapport will be based on a meeting of minds. You'll value each other's intelligence.

There's a great deal of electricity between you, but it may not really ignite physically unless the mental energy is there first. This is a classic combination for an internet news group, by the way, or a network of people who do a lot of travelling or moving, but keep it together through e-mails. You don't really cry on each other's shoulders much, but you're never bored either.

PLANETS IN WATER: CANCER, SCORPIO, PISCES

A Water group connection is a very emotional, sensitive link between people. This can occasionally get mushy — or even teary-eyed — but those who have it often feel a 'soul' connection going on. Sharing feelings — by talking about them or by transmitting them silently — is an important part of a Water-based relationship.

When you clash, you'll accuse each other of being irrationally emotional! Passions run high in Water-based relationships. Jealousy and possessiveness, dependency and freedom–intimacy issues, are inevitably going to be extremely important. Sometimes it can feel more like a family than a bunch of friends. You'd die for each other. You like the same music, books or poetry too. And you love going swimming or surfing together — or meditating. Sometimes getting drunk does it for you too!

PLANETS IN FIRE–AIR: ARIES, GEMINI, LEO, LIBRA, SAGITTARIUS, AQUARIUS

If you share planets here, you'll be an intensely sociable bunch of friends, invited out individually and together. Air–Fire friends entertain themselves and others, and there is usually a strong feeling that you are on display, or providing some kind of social teamwork. The Air people — with Gemini, Libra or Aquarius planets — will appear to be the more logical in the group. The Fire-dominant friends will find that they feel more enthusiastic about life, and more charged up with ideas and plans for the future, when the Air friends are around them. In return, the Air people will feel needed and wanted. This network is notable for its go-getter quality. When you all get together it's like a film director calling 'Action!' One or two of you are bound to be a little famous or well-known too — for your talent, or sporting ability.

PLANETS IN EARTH–WATER: TAURUS, CANCER, VIRGO, SCORPIO, CAPRICORN, PISCES

As friends, you'll have no trouble getting your mortgages approved, sorting out the practical details of life and creating security together. You'll build your futures together, on solid concrete foundations. It's a practical network of people who can use their professional or business talents as a kind of free advisory service for each other. One or two of you in this group will end up rich through real estate investment or small business schemes. It wouldn't be surprising if one or two of you are also in marriages or relationships within this group of friends. Alternatively, in time, you may find that some of the friends in this network of people pair off. Cooking and eating out are two activities you all love, and people love being invited round when you all get together in the kitchen.

GAMES PEOPLE PLAY

We all play different games with each other — no matter if we are married, sharing a house with a group, working together, or doing the school run. People often play games based on their planet interaction.

You may repeatedly play out the link between your Moon sign and your husband's Mars sign, for example. Or you may act out your Venus sign against your mother's Sun sign.

If you feel stuck in a relationship, change the game. The typical connection between people contains several possibilities for relating. Here are some difficult patterns which are easy to fall into — are you stuck in any of them, with a person in your world?

GAMES PEOPLE PLAY: CLASHING AND CLUNKING

The connections you make at work, with friends, with family, in bed, in business or at work . . .

The Aries–Cancer planet game

One of you — the Cancer-planet person — is a great deal more needy, emotional and sensitive. The other — the Aries-planet person — is far more energetic, enthusiastic and independent. The Cancer-planet person will instinctively want to protect the Aries-planet partner, and aim for a close family feel. The Cancerian person may need to learn not to cling or lean — or shepherd — and the Arian person will have to stop cringing at all the emotion.

The Aries–Capricorn planet game

This is a significant difference. The Aries-influenced person tends to live for the future, in a fairly hyped-up and enthusiastic way. This is all somewhat dubious for the Capricorn-influenced person, who is far more practical and much more cautious about life. There is also a basic timing problem here. Capricorn planets respect patience and long-term effort. Aries planets simply can't be bothered and want everything yesterday.

The Aries–Libra planet game

This is a tricky one. The basic conflict will be between 'we' and 'me', and the Aries-influenced person needs to work extra hard to understand the Libran type's essential concern for harmony. There will always be tension here, no matter how hard the Libran type works to make sure that balance is maintained. It's nobody's fault (unless the Arian type is being particularly provocative or aggressive); it's just the chemistry of the planets involved. The Libran-influenced person will go to extraordinary lengths to make sure it all hangs together, despite feeling it's all rather unfair.

The Taurus–Leo planet game

The Taurus-influenced person will find the Leo planets belonging to the other person too dramatic. The Leonine person, meanwhile, is exasperated by what they see as the boring practicality of Taurus. One of you is full of faith, enthusiasm, self-interest and ideas. The other is rather more concerned with the practical details. Money, income and the personal values of both people based on these factors may become a hard issue. One thought balloon might say 'God you're boring', while the other one says 'You're such a diva!'.

The Taurus–Aquarius planet game

This will only make sense if the Taurus-influenced person has learned to put other values above money and material possessions. If not, then the Aquarian person will have a real problem with the Taurean person's values. One of you is interested in change, the other is not — and one of you is far more radical than the other. Taurus planets in a chart instinctively hang on and hang in. Aquarius planets cannot wait for an exciting new future to begin. The Aquarian type must draw on his/her humanitarian instincts to try and understand the Taurus type's anxieties.

The Taurus–Scorpio planet game

A clash over money, property or possessions (anything from hard cash to joint ownership of a television set) is just one possibility if you play this game hard and fast. A difference in values is very likely; what either of you think is worth selling out for could be a sticking point. Political values may be another point of contention. The Scorpio type always gets involved with other people's money, houses or flats. The Taurus type always gets involved with the accumulation of wealth, or the total rejection of capitalism (one or the other). Issues which arrive around Full Moon time in May and November are tricky.

The Gemini–Virgo planet game

This is an interesting clash, because you are both intensely verbal or mind-led people, yet you will irritate each other too. The Gemini type will find the person with Virgo planets too pedantic and hung up on the details. The Gemini type gets the joke while the Virgo type is still looking up the thesaurus. The Virgo type would like everything to be perfect and believes in dotting i's and crossing t's. The Gemini type just wants to get the message across. You'll notice this game more if you work together, or if your relationship involves a lot of e-mails.

The Gemini–Pisces planet game

The Gemini-influenced person will be terribly witty and sharp, while the Pisces-influenced person seems to take most of the damage — for themselves and the other victims of the Geminian person's comments. The Gemini type will find Pisces drowns them — the atmosphere becomes very sticky and gluggy. The Gemini type is motivated by words; the Pisces type is motivated by feelings, and ideas which are hard to articulate. One of you wants to get on the bus and go; the other one wants to float in the pool.

The Gemini–Sagittarius planet game

The Sagittarian-influenced person is a philosopher and sees the big picture. The Geminian type can seem rather superficial by comparison. A lot depends on the Sagittarian type's personal belief system, which could be anything from a mixed-up version of Buddhism to a fervent faith in Sinn Fein. If the Geminian type gets it — great. But if s/he misses the point, the Sagittarian type will feel like lecturing. The same sense of humour is vital; as you are both funny people by nature, if you don't have it, you'll both feel a little lost.

The Cancer–Libra planet game

The Cancer-influenced person doesn't care what people look like when they're sick. The Libran type wants a stain-free dressing gown, please — and preferably with piping on the hem. Cancer worries more about what's in and on the plate than the quality of the guests or the dinner service. Libra would rather have the right social mix than the right soup mix. The Cancer type is drawn towards the family or some other kind of clan. If the Libran person finds anything ugly or discordant about that bunch of people, they'll struggle.

The Cancer–Capricorn planet game

This is another of those 'fatal attraction' combinations, and some astrologers even argue that they are karmic — in other words, you had a past life together with equal amounts of love and difficulty. Whatever the reason, there is a basic conflict here between the need for home and family security and the need for career, success and ambition. It may be played out by each of you in turn, or the nature of the relationship may make it uncomfortably obvious that every time the domestic side is okay, work will suffer. The Cancer type is driven by needs, moods and feelings; the Capricorn type is practical.

The Leo–Scorpio planet game

The Leo-influenced person will find Scorpio rather too intense and complicated. The Scorpio-planet person will not feel as if their emotional needs are being met. Every time the Scorpio type seeks sexual intimacy and real relationship 'heat', Leo will start to feel uncomfortable. The Leonine person may find Scorpio to be a confusing game-player at worst, and the Scorpionic type will resent the considerable Leonine pride and ego.

The Leo–Aquarius planet game

The Aquarian type will 'weird out' the Leonine type, while anyone with planets in Aquarius has little time for Leo's silly pride and occasional ego benders. Leo-planet people rather like the system, because they believe in social order, preferably with a Leo type at the top. Aquarius thinks it's a waste of time or actively rebels against it. The Aquarian type has fixed ways of living and working which the Leonine type finds quite batty. If things go downhill between these two types, there may be shocking acts of rebellion by the Aquarian-influenced person — or ego blow-outs from the Leo type!

The Virgo–Sagittarius planet game

This is an interesting clash between a person who very much likes ritual, daily routine and the practical, reliable elements of life — and someone who would rather see the big picture. The Virgoan person needs his or her funny little food and body things, and the Sagittarian type wants to do other, more adventurous things with his or her life. Sagittarius planet people run on an intuitive trust in the future, but Virgo types want to make a list and cross things off as they are confirmed.

The Virgo–Pisces planet game

The Pisces-planet person wants to escape, dream, emote and feel. The Virgo-planet person wants to remain grounded and practical and pick apart the logic of things. Virgo types keep a diary; Pisces types keep fish in the bath. The Virgo type likes to have a daily routine in place, in order to be really effective and efficient. That means everything from breakfast ingredients to computer downloads. The Pisces type surfs the waves of whatever comes his/her way, which will mess with the Virgo type's head. The Virgo type steadily makes things happen; the Pisces type dreams about them. This clash will take work.

The Libra–Capricorn planet game

There are some things in life which are not particularly useful and serve no real purpose — but are beautiful and entertaining anyway. There are some people like this too. The Libran planet person enjoys all of it, but the person with Capricornian planets can't see the point. It is in the Capricorn type's nature to aim high and be quite goal-driven. The Capricorn-influenced person has an endless fund of common sense, yet may feel Libra is unappreciative, and more drawn to romance and art than what is practical. The Libran type would do anything to save a relationship — but if his/her career or social status is at stake, the Capricornian type puts that first.

The Scorpio–Aquarius planet game

The Scorpionic type will not understand the Aquarian person's fixation with ideas and theories, or the fact that their beloved appears to be cut off from the basics of emotion, sweating, seething and all the other things that humans do. Aquarius types can seem terribly cold after a while, and the Scorpio type will seem worryingly dark, a little too intense and just a bit too overwhelming for the cool, thoughtful Aquarian side. One of you gets jealous or obsessive. The other one thinks, 'That's so twentieth century'.

The Sagittarius–Pisces planet game

The person with Piscean planets expresses themselves with a lot of feeling, sensitivity and unspoken emotion. The Sagittarius type really does not have time or energy for the world of feelings. A shared sense of humour is vital, as the Sagittarian planet person thrives on it — if the jokes are missing, you will have to work extremely hard to find other connections between you. What you both have in common is a longing for other destinations (the Pisces type wants an escape route; the Sagittarius type always wants to be somewhere else) and a strong sense of faith. The Pisces type may still be fantasising, though, while the Sagittarius type has padlocked the luggage.

FOCUS ON COMMITMENT

CLASSIC PARTNERSHIP CLICKS AND CONNECTIONS

What does your partner do for your ego, your identity and your sense of self? Does he or she massage your self-esteem? Your Sun sign describes who you really are, at heart. That's why love feels more authentic (as if you're being loved for yourself) when your partner has planets in signs which click.

You already know how your partner's chart works with your Venus sign. This defines the heart of the relationship.

Over the long-term, though, you'll need a partner whose planet signs work with your Sun sign, so that you remain true to yourself in the relationship. What's the point in faking your personality or losing your identity just so you can be part of a couple?

For a real commitment, think about someone whose planet signs work with your Sun sign — as follows:

ARIES SUN SIGN WOMAN PLUS . . .

A partner with Aries planets

Part of you is part of your other half. And vice versa. Read the section on planets in Aries, earlier in the book, to understand both of you.

A partner with Gemini planets

Your Gemini planet partner will fuel a lot of your energy and lust for life just by being around. Things will move quickly with this one, for better or for worse. People will eavesdrop when you are in restaurants together because you have conversations that wouldn't be out of place in a Hollywood comedy. The Gemini type will come up with clever ways for you to be number one in your life which you are sure to appreciate. The Gemini type is Air; you are Fire, so your partner will fan the flames. It's like watching a bonfire fed with oxygen.

A partner with Leo planets

When you rev each other up with enthusiasm you can be quite a dynamic couple. Do expect fights, as one of you is rather ego-driven and the other can't stand being dominated. The person with the Aries side will inspire the person with the Leo bits to go on to bigger and better things, but it's a fiery match. If you have battles at work, or in other areas of your life, the Leo type will energise you. You can be dramatic and attention-grabbing together, and really light up a party when you arrive. You'll create a lot in your life, from projects to (possibly) children.

A partner with Sagittarius planets

Travelling regionally or overseas together will make you or break you. If it makes you, you could be together forever. Humour is your great saving grace. Between you, you also have a classic Fire–Fire dose of enthusiasm. I wouldn't be surprised if one of you actually froths at the mouth occasionally. If you share the same philosophy or world view, and you believe it's worth fighting for, then the Sagittarius type will be your moral/spiritual compass point. There is nothing lazy, boring, over-settled or over-predictable about you two. No matter how long you've been together, the energy still crackles.

A partner with Aquarius planets

A lot of the issues in this relationship will revolve around space and freedom, but as long as one partner can control his or her temper, this looks quite exciting. The person with the Aquarian planet/s has what it takes to fan the flames of the Aries type's enthusiasm and lust for life — without trying. As you are prone to conflict in your life, it's essential to the Aquarius type that it happens for a good ethical or philosophical reason. If your contests have the Aquarian type's backing, you'll be happy. If you both get involved in some kind of cause or campaign, then you can be an unbeatable team. Having similar political or moral views about life is important.

TAURUS SUN SIGN WOMAN PLUS . . .

A partner with Taurus planets

Part of you is part of your other half. And vice versa. Read the section on planets in Taurus, earlier in the book, to understand both of you.

A partner with Cancer planets

You both like to know where you stand, and a nasty break-up with a totally unsuitable, restless type for one of you just makes the current match seem more reassuring. Inevitably, the talk will turn to life's fundamentals early on, as one person obviously has tabs on real estate or domestic issues. Babies could come up unnaturally early in the dating game, or there will be a discussion about property ambitions. You could both get what you want too. This is all about homemaking or home building, basically, and it will come naturally to a Taurus–Cancer influenced couple. You could make a mint on real estate.

A partner with Virgo planets

You two are the sort of couple everyone clings to in a crisis, because there is something solid and sensible about both of you. Big career questions for one partner dominate things. So much Earth between two people guarantees loads of common sense solutions and straight-down-the-line plans and ideas. You will both have very fixed ideas about what you put on the shopping list, or in the fridge. You know what to spend your money on or put in your digestive system and you won't waver! This is a productive combination, with the emphasis on what you can build or buy together — or make and mend. Lots of shed time will be required for one of you.

A partner with Capricorn planets

You are both builders by nature, good at putting down roots at work, through your home, or through anything money can buy. There's steadiness, seriousness and success here. A lot depends on the other signs which are at work between you. But this is a strong link between two people who value security enough to consider overlooking any partnership clashes. If you join forces on a business level, as well as an emotional one, then you truly could be a twenty-first century power couple. Together you can be an immovable force, and heaven help anyone who tries to get in your way.

A partner with Pisces planets

You'll notice a familiar pattern creeping in after a while, but it feels easy and comfortable enough. One of you simply becomes the practical, common sense anchor — while the other dreams. Despite this, the Taurus and Pisces points in both your charts click together, so there's a sense of flow. The Piscean type reminds you that there is more to life than money. If you share a common ideal or cause this could be magical. You'll help the Pisces type to turn his/her visions into solid reality. If you both turn your backs on money for personal or spiritual reasons, you could create an inspiring alternative lifestyle.

GEMINI SUN SIGN WOMAN PLUS . . .

A partner with Gemini planets

Part of you is part of your other half. And vice versa. Read the section on planets in Gemini, earlier in the book, to understand both of you.

A partner with Aries planets

Your Gemini side feeds the other person's enthusiasm. The more you talk, the more motivated s/he becomes. This is one of those relationships with lots of feedback, phone calls and private jokes. There's an awful lot of energy floating around between you, and even the fights are productive. You know you are more about words and the Aries type is more about action — but somehow it seems to work. If the Aries type needs a clever battle strategy at work, or in his/her personal life, you'll come up with it too.

A partner with Leo planets

Lots of marriages, de facto relationships and business partnerships are built on people with Gemini and Leo planets on both sides. As a couple you will either be popular entertainers or sought-after guests, because you supply the talk and the Leo type supplies the rest of the entertainment.

Your Gemini side energises the Leo person, and boosts his/her confidence or lust for life. Don't be surprised if you end up being the Leo type's unofficial PR person or messenger girl from time to time. You're naturally gifted at selling him/her to the world!

A partner with Libra planets

It's unlikely you'll fight at all — if you do, other clashing planet signs are to blame somewhere in both charts. You'll spend an awful lot of time talking about The Relationship though. Your Gemini side is pretty good at articulating things and asking questions. The other person's Libran side loves all the weighing up of pros and cons between you. The Libran type's natural sense of justice appeals to your intelligence; you are both good at analysing people and situations, either in the world or in your personal lives.

A partner with Aquarius planets

You two were made for e-mail, but if you're not hooked up to a computer you'll just talk long into the night. Grunty, gritty passion may be hard to find, but the love is real, it seems, as Aquarius and Gemini planets have an uncanny way of finding each other. A very new age relationship could be the result, and you'll make it up as you go along. Ideas are the oxygen for your partnership and your shared library will be full of books about the most amazing concepts, theories or philosophies. You'll never be bored.

THE CANCER SUN SIGN WOMAN AND . . .

A partner with Cancer planets

Part of you is part of your other half. And vice versa. Read the section on planets in Cancer, earlier in the book, to understand both of you.

A partner with Taurus planets

Favourite home-cooked dishes, or a particular restaurant, becomes a kind of secret couple's code for both of you. You are big on real estate, gardening, home improvements, children or babies (tick one box, or all of them). The Taurus type sympathises, because although passion is all very well, what's the point unless you have a family — or a wonderful home to call your own? As a couple, you often look after other people's life crises, and make solid, sensible friends. An amazing gift for property renovation or real estate investment is likely.

A partner with Virgo planets

Food issues — or health concerns for one of you — tend to anchor the relationship in the real world and make it work. You're good at caretaking and feeding the Virgo type's needs. Your partner has to have his or her life ordered in a particular way (not to mention the kitchen) so you come to the rescue. You care a great deal about your home renovations, upkeep or improvements, which is also where the Virgo type comes in handy, as he/she is here to serve ... even on Sunday mornings. Children and babies, if you have them, will revolutionise your life and one of you will be utterly devoted to them.

A partner with Scorpio planets

Music or poetry may be the only way one of you can express everything you really feel, as emotions run deep on one side in particular. Possessiveness — of each other or the kids — is a factor. There will be times when you feel as if your life is an opera (or a soap opera) but at least it makes you feel alive. The Scorpio type will take you on a fascinating sexual journey and educate you about passion with a capital P, and possibly jealousy with a capital J as well. This is real, raw love — and even if you clash as well, something will always sustain it.

A partner with Pisces planets

This relationship will bring out tremendous kindness, sympathy, softness and saintliness in one of you.

Tremendously strong feelings about people in the family circle (negative or positive) are part of the deal too. This is a highly emotional match, and logic will come second!

You'll feel inspired by the Piscean type, and amazed at how important the world of books, films, music and the imagination is to them. In turn, you make them feel safe and secure. The Piscean type is sensitive and can bruise easily. You tuck them under your wing and cherish them.

THE LEO SUN SIGN WOMAN AND . . .

A partner with Leo planets
Part of you is part of your other half. And vice versa. Read the section on planets in Leo, earlier in the book, to understand both of you.

A partner with Aries planets
You love it when they go into bat for you. In fact, if you become their cause célèbre, it will be enough to sustain the relationship over a lifetime, no matter how many clashes there are. You find the Aries type's preference for action extremely sexy — and, typically, this partnership will take off almost instantly, or in a wham-bam-thank-you-Leo way. You both get incredibly enthused about life when you are together, and even people sitting five tables away in a restaurant feel the heat. The only real issue is self-interest. Your ego is healthy. The Aries type is a little selfish. You'll make it up in bed, though.

A partner with Gemini planets
Your Gemini-influenced partner likes travelling or weekend exploration, and you like travelling in style — or at least showing off a stylish set of wheels. Some of your happiest times together will be on luxurious short breaks. Sometimes your conversation will incline towards 'Enough about me. Anyway — what do you think of me?', which will irritate the Gemini type. And there will be moments in the partnership

when you have to remind them that gossip — or certain kinds of jokes — are undignified. Nevertheless, the Gemini type gives you the relationship oxygen you need. The result? A warm, lively connection.

A partner with Libra planets

The Libra-influenced partner has brilliant interpersonal skills which make this partnership one of the easiest you've ever been in. No amount of ego or posturing from you will get in the way of coupledom, as it's their mission to create togetherness, and they have the diplomacy, the public relations skills and the tact to make it work. You have always seen the point of romance — there is something noble and dramatic about it — so you are happy to fall in love with love, in their company. If you appreciate their extraordinary taste and aesthetic sense — and they like your wardrobe too — this could run and run.

A partner with Sagittarius planets

Great. You've always been wary of people who are too small, too suburban and too dull. The Sagittarian type has enough vision and scope to make you justifiably proud of them. You will travel together, or even emigrate, as one of you wants the big picture, and the other wants a life less ordinary. You both believe that almost anything is possible in this world, and seldom tell each other to back off from anything. This can occasionally result in tremendous mistakes, but the glorious victories are the only things you both care about, which is why this partnership produces some bigger-than-big achievements.

THE VIRGO SUN SIGN WOMAN AND . . .

A partner with Virgo planets

Part of you is part of your other half. And vice versa. Read the section on planets in Virgo, earlier in the book, to understand both of you.

A partner with Taurus planets

One of you knows the value of a good accountant, and it's amazing how this will make a difference to things! Spend two years building the foundations of love and it could last forever if other horoscope factors agree. Other people find a wealth of common sense operating when they look at your partnership. You believe in routine, both for your body and your mind. You only truly find yourself when you end up with meaningful work, either in your profession or at home. The Taurean type respects productivity and happily accepts how crucial your sense of duty and service is to your psychological wellbeing. This Earth connection keeps things real.

A partner with Cancer planets

There's a natural understanding here, and you won't have to work at it. One of you expresses his or her love in practical ways — around the house, for example. When one person is ill, the whole relationship seems to come into its own. Mind you, that's not a reason for developing serial flu — just a bonus. The Cancer–Virgo connection frequently appears in partnerships where the health and wellbeing of one partner is an ongoing issue; through food intolerances, for example. This partnership will come alive when you move in together, as your house or flat is something you can both focus on for the rest of your lives. The garden, too, if you have one, will be enormously important as you grow older together.

A partner with Scorpio planets

For one person, the quality and duration of the sex will become a bit of a relationship barometer. Just make sure all the other things are weighed up between you too. One person will be noticeably more emotional than the other in this relationship, but there is something sweetly supportive about the blend. One of you is much more sensible; the other is far more madly passionate. This connection between you really works, though: the Virgo type keeps the wheels turning, while the Scorpio type takes the relationship to another level. The Virgo type needs to cut loose occasionally and forget about work or fridge contents. The Scorpio type can show them what love is really all about.

A partner with Capricorn planets

You both know work is the really important thing. The Virgo type does it from a sense of service and duty, while the Capricorn type does it because climbing higher in life is in their DNA. Together you could easily run a business together, but if not, the home front will be where all the wheels turn, and with two Earth signs like this blending in a partnership, you can expect a big focus on bricks, mortar and soil. You two are wonderful in emergencies, and flakier friends or family may turn to you for backing or support. You're both experts at living in the real world and you can be each other's rocks.

THE LIBRA SUN SIGN WOMAN AND . . .

A partner with Libra planets

Part of you is part of your other half. And vice versa. Read the section on planets in Libra, earlier in the book, to understand both of you.

A partner with Gemini planets

You have always identified with the most romantic books and films, but what you may not have realised is that all the greatest fictional lovers relied on one thing: good communication. With a Gemini type in your life, you'll have it, and you'll love the way s/he articulates everything so clearly. There will be lots of short trips to amuse you, and a tremendous sense of fun and energy when you go out together. This is an incredibly sociable combination and the Gemini type is a wonderful networker and people-connector, which suits you fine. E-mails will keep this one alive.

A partner with Leo planets

You'll know it's good when you catch your partner having a small boast about you at a party. This relationship is about pep talks and ego-feeding. One partner is also rather good at bending and flexing, which is just as well, as there will be the occasional two-act drama. You like the visual or aesthetic side of life — anything from DIY interior design, to thoughtful gardening, to a passion for architecture or art. The person with Leo planets also appreciates the creative spirit, so if your tastes coincide, you will have a spectacular home in the end — or just go museum hopping together.

A partner with Sagittarius planets

This could take off when one of you travels, leaving the other one behind, or when you both decide to buy a plane ticket together. You believe in partnership and the power of two — the Sagittarian type may not be quite so sure, but you have what it takes to make this work, as you are the arch diplomat and people-pleaser of the zodiac. It helps if you share your partner's fascination with one particular philosophy or getaway location, as s/he is bound to be a natural explorer, traveller or philosopher of some sort. A shared sense of humour completes the picture.

A partner with Aquarius planets

The big saving grace of this relationship is your mutual ability to stand back from very emotional or confronting situations and reason them out. There is a lot of Air in this combination, and Air is the element which prefers logical reason over big, dumb emotion. If you both share a cause or a political viewpoint, this could be a relationship which changes the world as much as it changes both your lives. You believe in justice and a fairer planet. The Aquarian type is also likely to have strong ideas and views. You're sociable too, and the Aquarian type has a big network to explore.

THE SCORPIO SUN SIGN WOMAN AND . . .

A partner with Scorpio planets

Part of you is part of your other half. And vice versa. Read the section on planets in Scorpio, earlier in the book, to understand both of you.

A partner with Cancer planets

This relationship will bring out more passion, tears and depth of feeling in one person involved than either of you have ever seen before, but if all the other factors agree in your horoscopes, it's Love. Common sense will go out of the window a million times, as feelings rule the day here. You get your sense of identity from all your passions and obsessions. If one of them includes the Cancerian type, then every time you look at him/her you will feel as if you have come home. Children, pregnancy, babies, adoption and fertility (and your yes/no decisions) will be absolutely pivotal to the commitment you make.

A partner with Virgo planets

Being together has an electrifying effect on one partner, who will start to think about their body more, use it more and care about it more. If the sex is great, the relationship will be too. If you have other plus factors working for you, then this could actually have staying power. Although you are obviously more emotional than the Virgo type in this relationship, you admire their commitment to hard work and efficiency, either at home or on the job. You are temperamentally quite different, but the Earth–Water connection between your Scorpio side and their Virgo side will result in a nice balance between grounded love and emotion.

A partner with Capricorn planets

Let's just say that this relationship will bring out an obsessive streak in one of you, and leave it at that. The obsession could be work-related or relationship-related. But it's passionate! If you have lots of other astrological plus factors on your side, then this partnership will have what it takes to last, as you fundamentally believe that passion can last a lifetime — and the Capricorn type believes in permanence, full stop. You are a true power couple at heart, and if you decide to join forces on a business, or on any kind of campaign, you will really rock the world.

A partner with Pisces planets

You both understand that there are some fated or mysterious aspects about life, love, death or sex that cannot be easily explained. The sex could be psychic. There is a massive amount of feeling and emotion between you, and one partner finds a release through music, art or books. This is all emotion, no common sense, but who cares? You identify with heroes and heroines (real or fictional) who are driven, deep and complicated. Somehow, the Pisces type releases these same qualities in yourself, so you end up feeling more at home in the world — and far more like the person you know you are, deep down. Expect a poetic wedding ceremony.

THE SAGITTARIUS SUN SIGN WOMAN AND . . .

A partner with Sagittarius planets

Part of you is part of your other half. And vice versa. Read the section on planets in Sagittarius, earlier in the book, to understand both of you.

A person with Aries planets

The theme song for this relationship should be like a Ramones song: 'Hey ho, let's go!' You want to get out there and explore the bigger picture, which is why so many people with foreign accents or passports end up in your life. The Aries type makes it all possible, and for once you will be with someone who actually enjoys your need to wander, explore, migrate and move. You are both Fire types, so the enthusiasm factor is doubled when you get together. The partnership will come into its own when you travel, as you will share an incredible sense of mission about the journey.

A person with Leo planets

The Leo type respects, and approves of, your need to travel, explore, learn, teach, or publish and be damned. All these passions of yours make you a class act in the Leo type's eyes. There is a Fire–Fire connection between you, which makes both of you come alive and generates phenomenal energy and enthusiasm. You can fizz like fireworks when you both get revved up about the same things. You like reporting back from whatever (or whoever) you have been exploring lately; the Leo type makes a good audience. A five-star travel experience will be one of your best memories.

A person with Libra planets

The Libran type believes in relationships so much that s/he will put up with almost anything from you — including your worst jokes. If you share the same sense of humour, you'll be amazed at how much it becomes the backbone of the relationship. You make a formidable combination when travelling, although you will resent too much coupledom, so the Libran type needs to learn how to back off. It's highly likely that your personal philosophy or beliefs dovetail with the Libran's view of the world, as you're both concerned with what's fair, right, just and true.

A person with Aquarius planets

If you are both curious about the same ideas, theories and philosophies, then you will find harmony through the books on your combined shelves. There's a tremendous amount of freedom and space — real oxygen — in this connection. You need someone who accommodates your need to travel (on weekends, or even around the world, over a period of years) and the Aquarius type can give you that. You also like the big picture, and can't stand narrow-minded, suburban attitudes.

The Aquarian type is sympathetic and can accommodate your need to explore bigger ideas.

THE CAPRICORN SUN SIGN WOMAN AND . . .

A partner with Capricorn planets

Part of you is part of your other half. And vice versa. Read the section on planets in Capricorn, earlier in the book, to understand both of you.

A person with Taurus planets

If you're both typical, then a combined bank account will be an incredible motivator in the relationship. Real wealth is possible, as you know what it takes to get to the top professionally, and your Taurus-influenced partner has a nose for business, investment or finance. Seeing your investments go up in value is an aphrodisiac. The exception to this is the Capricorn/Taurus couple who have rejected capitalism altogether, in which case you'll be like a real-life version of the '70s sitcom *The Good Life*, as you dig and plant your way to hippie heaven.

A person with Virgo planets

When you first get together, plant a tree somewhere. Growing gardens, animals or children will be a happy cornerstone of this relationship. If your other astropackage signs agree, it's a hit. There's a tremendous focus on becoming solid home or land owners, and no matter if you do it on the cheap or you spend a lot of money, it's the productive, practical side of this partnership which will most excite you. You both know the value of hard work too. You do it for different reasons, but you genuinely know why job-related venting matters — and you listen!

A person with Scorpio planets

You are drawn to powerful people with impressive CVs or business cards, and the Scorpio type probably has quite a career, or at least a huge amount of social status. This suits you fine — you've never seen the point of falling in love with a total nobody. The Scorpio type will also supply the sexual passion, on a level which you may not have experienced before. You are proud of your ambition, your position and your staying power. The Scorpio type massages your ego beautifully, as his/her astrological connection to you is supportive and encouraging.

A person with Pisces planets

Just in case you forget to stop and smell the roses (or visit the aquarium) the Pisces type will be there to guide you gently by the hand. It's so easy for you to get caught up with climbing to the top that the arrival of a Pisces type in your life can feel like a holiday. Their occasional flakiness is expertly managed by you — in return, the Pisces-influenced person can bring a bit of imagination, magic, faith and wonder into your world. S/he is intuitive, and that can surprise and impress you. At the same time, the Pisces type's fantasies and daydreams can become realities, with help from you.

THE AQUARIUS SUN SIGN WOMAN AND . . .

A partner with Aquarius planets

Part of you is part of your other half. And vice versa. Read the section on planets in Aquarius, earlier in the book, to understand both of you.

A person with Aries planets

This is a definite plus factor. One of you seems prepared to try absolutely anything, which leaves the other partner full of admiration. There's some manic energy in here occasionally, so channel it into sex or mutual goals, not fighting. The other person's life outside your relationship gives you space, which you definitely need. You 'feed' the Aries type on some level, and they feel more like themselves when they are with you. In turn, just being around them seems to energise you. This makes all your brilliant plans or unique, offbeat ideas seem actually viable.

A person with Gemini planets

You've always identified with the outsiders, the rebels, the misfits, the renegades and the brilliant innovators in our world. You've never really related to people who are too ordinary or dull. Along comes the Gemini type, whose gift for asking the right questions, and sending the right e-mails, finally makes you feel understood. Never underestimate how comforting this is for you! The Gemini type knows how to probe and prod you, until even your weirdest views or opinions begin to seem viable. At heart, this is what you always wanted — permission to be yourself. The Gemini type's incredible curiosity and clever mind helps you be yourself as never before.

A person with Libra planets

Of course, the Libran type would rather have united coupledom — but his/her relationship skills are advanced enough to enable them to let you have your freedom. You need independence in a partnership, or you begin to feel distinctly strange. The Libran type is flexible enough to allow it. You are both influenced by the element of Air, which is light, breezy and free. Just being around the Libran type can make you feel as if someone has opened a window. The more planets s/he has in Libra, the more comfortable you will feel. They tolerate your weirdness too. Rejoice!

A person with Sagittarius planets

You do bring out the best in each other. Sure, one of you is a lot weirder by the other person's standards, but there's a similarity in outlooks or interests too. You could surf island beaches or just the internet together, decide to change the world or change yourselves. The combination of Sagittarius and Aquarius planets between you signals ongoing changes (never a dull moment) and plenty of ideas, exploration, travel and midnight conversations. Neither of you want a small, suburban life. Both of you want a bigger picture, or a more fascinating planet to live on. If you share a cause or campaign you'll change the world.

THE PISCES SUN SIGN WOMAN AND . . .

A partner with Pisces planets

Part of you is part of your other half. And vice versa. Read the section on planets in Pisces, earlier in the book, to understand both of you.

A person with Taurus planets

This could be fabulous if your other signs agree. Some wonderful experiences, indulgences and escapes lie ahead for you as a couple. Only money limits imagination here. There's bound to be a big emphasis on the sensual pleasures of being together — wine, spas, good music and other indulgences. So much depends on how rich or poor you are, or how your value system (your attitude towards money) is constructed. If you're hell-bent on a million bucks, your shared life could be like a Hollywood fantasy. If you're into alternative lifestyles or eco-consciousness, though, it will be skinny-dipping in the river at dawn for you.

A person with Cancer planets

If your personal charts are also in sync, this will be a classic love match, full of healing, self-sacrifice, and destined to bring out something saintly and special in you. You make each other feel as if you matter, and that you have something important to offer. If other factors agree, it's love. Children, babies, pregnancy, adoption or fertility issues will be a huge concern once the relationship gets going — your greatest source of joy, or your biggest source of bonding. This connection between you is emotional, irrational and like a real-life film.

A person with Scorpio planets

You've always identified with the poets, the saints, the artists and the musicians. The person with Scorpio planets will remind you of this, and allow you to move closer to your goal of a more imaginative or spiritual life. You psychically understand their obsessions and their passions, as well as their darker and more twisted emotions. Together you are dominated by feelings, not common sense, and although that makes for a partnership that can sometimes be utterly chaotic, you'll also see more sexual heat and romantic passion than other couples see in a lifetime.

A person with Capricorn planets

The Capricorn type builds the foundations for your personal Disneyland or nirvana. S/he has that practical, grounded core that you need, if you're ever going to turn your fantasies into realities. You long to take the Capricorn type by the hand and show them a different world; you're always encouraging them to take weekends in strange, alluring destinations or experiences — or at least, putting *The Lord of the Rings* on the DVD player and parking a brandy in their hand. What you get from them is a wonderful message that it's okay to be sensitive and imaginative, and all those other things that the modern world rejects.

WHY YOU FIGHT

Do you have ongoing tension in a marriage or relationship? Or constant fighting in the family, or with friends or flatmates?

The culprit is often Mars, the planet of war. If your Mars sign clashes with the planet signs in someone else's chart, you could be playing a rather angry game over a period of years. Similarly, if their Mars sign clashes with your planet signs, you could be drawn into a repetitive pattern of attack and defence.

YOUR MARS SIGN IS . . .

ARIES ~ People with planets in Libra, Capricorn and Cancer challenge you.

TAURUS ~ People with planets in Scorpio, Aquarius and Leo challenge you.

GEMINI ~ People with planets in Sagittarius, Pisces and Virgo challenge you.

CANCER ~ People with planets in Capricorn, Aries and Libra challenge you.

LEO ~ People with planets in Aquarius, Taurus and Scorpio challenge you.

VIRGO ~ People with planets in Pisces, Gemini and Sagittarius challenge you.

LIBRA ~ People with planets in Aries, Cancer and Capricorn challenge you.

SCORPIO ~ People with planets in Taurus, Leo and Aquarius challenge you.

SAGITTARIUS ~ People with planets in Gemini, Virgo and Pisces challenge you.

CAPRICORN ~ People with planets in Cancer, Libra and Aries challenge you.

AQUARIUS ~ People with planets in Leo, Scorpio and Taurus challenge you.

PISCES ~ People with planets in Virgo, Sagittarius and Gemini challenge you.

Annual 'Angry' Cycles

When the Sun passes through the same sign as your Mars sign, you can expect the heat to increase. Physical tension rises at this time, and your instinct for the kill (or your natural defensiveness) is more obvious. It's a good time to manage and monitor your reactions and refuse to be too swayed by other people's momentary madness . . .

Mars in Aries ~ Late March–late April
Mars in Taurus ~ Late April–late May
Mars in Gemini ~ Late May–late June
Mars in Cancer ~ Late June–late July
Mars in Leo ~ Late July–late August
Mars in Virgo ~ Late August–late September
Mars in Libra ~ Late September–late October
Mars in Scorpio ~ Late October–late November
Mars in Sagittarius ~ Late November–late December
Mars in Capricorn ~ Late December–late January
Mars in Aquarius ~ Late January–late February
Mars in Pisces ~ Late February–late March

SIGNS WHICH REPEAT IN YOUR LIFE

Do you ever have a 'run' on a particular sign? I have an Aries friend who spent a whole year going out with Librans, and then doing business deals with them. Another friend shudders at the thought of dealing with Virgoans — it's never worked out for her in the five years they've been coming into her life! If you keep bumping into the same signs, though, the universe might be trying to tell you something . . .

You Keep Meeting Arians

They're going to teach you about the fine line between being selfish and self-interested. They're going to show you that anger in itself isn't a bad thing, it depends on how you deal with it. They're going to instruct you in the fine art of being first in the queue. You'll learn about your own capacity to be self-assertive, and how to push without being pushy.

You Keep Meeting Taureans

They're going to teach you about your own value system — money versus everything else. They're going to show you how wonderful beautiful objects and possessions can be. They're going to instruct you about money management, one way or another. You'll learn a great lesson about what you will — and definitely won't — sell out for.

You Keep Meeting Geminis
They're going to teach you how to be a good and appreciative listener, but also how to talk — or write. They're going to show you that life actually makes sense if you analyse it, discuss it and read about it. They're going to instruct you in the art of short-distance travel. You'll learn a great lesson about what other people's siblings mean to them.

You Keep Meeting Cancerians
They're going to teach you that family really does matter, one way or another. They're going to show you what it means to completely identify with one's roots, origins, heritage or nationality. They're here to put you in touch with mother issues, food issues and real estate matters. Every time a Cancerian arrives, so do questions about parenting, home or family.

You Keep Meeting Leos
They're going to teach you what it means to be proud of yourself — or, conversely, to lack self-esteem. They're going to show you how fantastic it is to express yourself, in personal ways, through creative ideas, hobbies, interests or projects. You'll learn a great lesson about pride and dignity — and how you can avoid taking it too far, as well.

You Keep Meeting Virgos
They're going to teach you about your body, your health and your well being. They're going to show you that the

body–mind connection can't be ignored. They're going to instruct you in the fine art of paying attention to detail. You'll learn a great lesson about perfectionism, and how doing a job well doesn't necessarily mean becoming manic about it.

You Keep Meeting Librans

They're going to teach you about the aesthetic pleasures in life — flowers, art, tone, texture, colour. They're going to show you how important it is to hang on to civilised human behaviour, even when things become tough. They're going to instruct you in diplomacy. You'll learn a great lesson about compromise, and why it's easy to take it too far.

You Keep Meeting Scorpios

They're going to teach you that living life on the surface really isn't living at all. They're going to show you what being human is really like — and that includes all the hidden, complex and 'unacceptable' stuff. They're going to instruct you in the fine art of focus. You'll learn a great lesson about what taboos actually mean — to yourself and other people.

You Keep Meeting Sagittarians

They're going to teach you that life is basically absurd, and consequently that even the worst things have a Woody Allen twist. They're going to show you how important it is to travel and see the world, or become far more global in your thinking. They're going to reveal how crucial it is to have something to believe in, and something to find meaning in. You'll learn why excess never works from them too.

You Keep Meeting Capricorns

They're going to teach you that climbing patiently to the top is not some ancient yuppie concept — it's actually the foundation on which all life is built. They're going to show you what it means to be professional — and unprofessional. You'll learn a lot about the fine line between pessimism and realism. You'll learn what it means to be mature.

You Keep Meeting Aquarians

They're going to teach you what individuality actually means. They're going to show you how important it is to live in the future first, the present second, and the past last. They're going to reveal how exciting and liberating it feels to be utterly yourself. You'll learn a lot about doing your own thing without doing other people down.

You Keep Meeting Pisceans

They're going to teach you about the joys of escaping reality. They're going to show you what it's like to live in a world where being real, sensible, normal and logical isn't actually the big priority. They're going to instruct you in the difference between fantasising and lying. You'll learn a lot about compassion and kindness and the art of self-sacrifice.

THE LOWDOWN ON MEN: EMPLOYEES, COLLEAGUES, FATHERS, BROTHERS, FRIENDS AND LOVERS

Once you know a man's Sun, Moon, Mercury, Venus and Mars signs, you'll have an accurate picture of his personality. Does he have two or more planets in the same sign? Then he'll project the qualities of that sign in an obvious way, even if his Sun sign is different. A Taurus Sun sign man, for example, might have the Moon and Mars in Gemini — in which case he'll remind you more of a typical Gemini type than a Taurean.

As you read on, you'll see how the man in your life is using his planet signs. Some men 'play' their Mercury sign extra loud, for example — or they might show their Venus sign more than any other horoscope factor.

Is the man in your life well-known, even famous? Does he have a position of leadership and authority? Does he have star quality? Chances are, his Sun sign will be the most striking thing about him.

Is the man in your life a dedicated father? Does cooking, homemaking and DIY really matter to him? Is his family a cornerstone of his life? Chances are, his Moon sign will be the most striking thing about him.

Is the man in your life a born communicator? Does he work in a profession where his ability to use the written or spoken word is paramount? Chances are, his Mercury sign will be the most striking thing about him.

Is the man in your life noticeably well-dressed? Does he have a natural feeling for art, photography, architecture or design? Is he diplomatic and tactful, a natural PR person? Chances are, his Venus sign will be the most striking thing about him.

Is the man in your life into sport, or does he have an action-man job? Is he noticeably masculine, in an old-fashioned way? Is he tough and energetic, with strong attack and defence mechanisms? Chances are, his Mars sign will be the most striking thing about him.

MEN WITH PLANETS IN ARIES

Sport often rules if the man in question has the Sun, Moon, Mercury, Venus and/or Mars in Aries. That means watching it or talking about it . . . never mind playing it. In the original Aries myth, Mars, the God of War, ruled this sign. In times of peace, the fighting spirit is channelled through competitive sport. Most Aries-influenced men like to see a bit of muscle definition. Some of them head for a yoga class or a thrashy session in the pool. Others aim straight for weekend passions and pursuits that are going to result in a defined bicep — or two.

I have known a few armchair-bound men with Aries planets, but they were always tuned to the football. Elton John is an Aries Sun. Biceps are not his thing, but managing a soccer club is. In truth, if the man in your life has a planet in Aries, he really should be out there, *doing* something sweaty. Otherwise, he'll be blocking off a whole side of his personality, and men with this sign in their charts really need a physical outlet for stress. If your Aries-influenced man is the sedentary type, you may want to lob a cricket ball at him occasionally in the interests of his psychological wellbeing (and his biceps). Some of them are athletic supporters; some of them just wear the gear. Call it the leopardskin underpants sign and leave it at that. But underpants with a built-in jockstrap.

Basic aggression is at the core of Aries, yet a lot depends on the life and times of the man in question — if it's not acceptable, or even remotely wonderful, to be aggressive in his world, then he'll cut this side of Aries off completely. Still, this core hostility has a strange way of leaking out. There are many men out there with an Aries Sun, Moon, Mercury, Venus or Mars who are unconsciously aggressive. So they needle you, then claim they don't know why you're upset — or find other ways to provoke. The evolved types play-act their warrior side through sport or a creative outlet. The less evolved types deny having this in-your-face Arian side at all, but end up leaving a trail of fuming people behind them. The most tragically troglodyte Arian types are bullies. Raised in an environment where they were told it was both acceptable and *masculine* to be an invader, raider, gun guru or lout, they end up feeling like men out of time.

Assertiveness skills are what it's all about. Many Arian types seem to have them automatically, but there are a few who still need to do a swift exchange and turn Mars, the God of War, into something a bit more constructive. A man with an Aries planet has a need to declare war on something, but there are worthwhile goals and wasteful goals, and there are any number of ways of handling a fight. Being born with an Aries planet is like having a Neolithic caveman chained to your leg. So how do men deal with it? Sport or yoga is often an outlet for the energy. Alternatively, a Bobo the Clown punching bag works well.

MEN WITH PLANETS IN TAURUS

What is the single most obvious thing about a man who has planets in Taurus? It has to be his passion for music. Any sign which turns up in the charts of members of the Beatles, the Who, the Beach Boys, the Ramones, Nirvana, the Jam, the Doors, U2, ABBA, the Sex Pistols, the Smiths *and* the Rolling Stones has to be worth a closer look.

The Taurean link with modern music — and the Libran link — are attributable to Venus, which rules both signs. Venus is about fashion, women, hair and love, love, love. For a man with Taurus planets to stay sane and happy, he needs music — still the only place in modern life where a man can dress up, sing about love, sex and beautiful women, and not have tomatoes thrown at him. If you consider that everything from rock'n'roll to heavy metal has been about love songs, gorgeous women and fabulous wardrobes, the Taurus–Venus–music connection suddenly starts to make a great deal of sense. The best accompaniment for a Taurean seduction? A superb set of speakers.

Here's another reason why so many Taurus-influenced men get into music: money! Lots of capitalists are born with planets in this sign. It all depends on his values, though. If he's left-wing or alternative, he will make radical career choices based on that, and leave cash rewards behind. It's not enough to say that a Taurus planet produces an astute businessman, a natural accountant or a stock market genius. Taurus planets do lend an amazing awareness of the *price* of things, but it may not always be in dollars and cents. There are many ethical business success stories represented by this sign — just as there are also a fair number of Taurean types paralysed by these questions: Am I selling out? Am I selling my soul?

If a Taurus-influenced man hits a financial crisis, destiny says that it will have an extreme effect on his value system, his philosophy of life and the price he puts on the *priceless* commodities of life. Having a lot of money achieves the same effect. Having the Sun, Moon, Mercury, Venus or Mars in Taurus is like having an accountant in one ear and your conscience in the other.

MEN WITH PLANETS IN GEMINI

Funny, ferociously intelligent and forever young just about sums up Gemini. Men with the Sun, Moon, Mercury, Venus or Mars in Gemini have a way with words, above all other things, and a set of neurons that appears to fire twice as quickly as everyone else's. If the man in your life is strongly Geminian, he will also have a nickname or an alter ego, a 'twin' figure or sibling issue to deal with, and an ageless quality. The Peter Pan syndrome may come from the fact that Gemini-influenced men can't hold a frown for longer than five minutes — or maybe it's just because all the things they love in life emerged when they were in their teens. Few Gemini-influenced men feel inclined to give them up!

In the Gemini myth, Castor and Pollux — the heavenly twins — had to play alternate parts. These Gemini-influenced men also live their life with alternative or 'twin' names, careers, identities, nationalities — even relationships. Some of them have even ended up with three different titles — their christened name, their working name and their unofficial nickname. If you know a man with Gemini planets, you may have noticed that nicknames just grow up around him. Like twins, Gemini presents two faces to different groups of people, which is why Gemini funerals can be such a confusing business, as friends and family often have different names or nicknames for the person in the coffin! The brother–brother or brother–sister relationship is key to the Gemini type too. Love them or hate them, they are powerfully influenced by their siblings. Some of them even lose a sibling (perhaps through an earlier miscarriage in the family) and find that the ghost of the brother or sister who never was also dramatically influences their own life.

In the original Castor and Pollux myth, sibling rivalry may be part of the package. But the sibling relationship can be productive as well. Don't be surprised if a conversation about a brother or sister is one of the first things that comes up as you get to know the Gemini type better. They define their own lives and personalities, for better or worse, through their siblings.

Here's another thing about a man with Gemini planets — he knows how to work the language. Even if your Geminian man never makes it to publication, he will still be: a) endlessly quotable; b) witty; c) well-informed; and d) inventive with language. Some of them speak at warp speed, like my friend Murray. Some, like my friend James, even know how to talk backwards. My other male Sun in Gemini friends Fergo and Peter actually invent words — and they're much better than anything I've found in the dictionary!

Without Gemini planets, the world would have no *Curb Your Enthusiasm*, *The Simpsons*, no Monty Python, no Goons, no *Seinfeld* and no *Blackadder*. The men behind these shows all have the Sun, Moon, Mercury, Venus and/or Mars in Gemini. Along with Sagittarius, it's the funniest sign.

MEN WITH PLANETS IN CANCER

I can imagine that men with Cancer planets might migrate to another country — but forget their accent, their roots, their heritage, their national anthem? It's unlikely. The man with a well-developed Cancerian side identifies, needs, thinks about or relishes the homeland far too much. In astrology, Cancer rules the Fourth House of the horoscope, which is where people develop their sense of history and trace their roots. Men with planets in this sign are often strongly identified with their national or cultural roots.

Something also seems to happen to strongly Cancerian men overseas — they develop a marked affinity for their homeland. They become *countrymen*. One thinks of them, and their nationality, in the same moment. Cancer-influenced Americans I have known in Australia really hit those NY or LA vowels, and the English contingent can emigrate to Australia and still sound like the cast of *Creature Comforts* fifty years later! Whether they are aware of it or not, Cancerian types are always flying the flag for their country — or their culture — on some level.

Cancer-influenced men are caring by nature and make fantastic nurses, doctors, cooks, babysitters and fathers, if this sign is positively developed in their charts. If the sign is not finding a proper place in their personalities, then there is probably a big problem to deal with, which you can trace way back to their family experiences. If something wasn't quite working in the family system of this man when he was a child, the Cancer planet energy may result in someone who seems needier than the rest — hungry for care, rather than able to give it. Most Cancerian types, though, have a fabulously sympathetic quality, which they like to express in a practical way.

Men strongly influenced by Cancer planets make expert home brewers, chefs, cooks, winemakers, cappuccino kings and bread bakers. Heavily Cancerian men feel quite comfortable with pots and pans, oils and potions. If your partner has Cancer planets he may also be a home-maker in the literal sense. This is the brick-laying, land-surveying, extension-building sign. They can rent, but they can't hide. Most men with a Cancer planet want to own their own place or build an empire.

Having a planet here is like a homing signal for men, as they often identify their sense of comfort and security with the physical familiarity and stability of a place to call their own. They can be classically house-proud too. They really need a base, if they are typical of their Sun, Moon, Mercury, Venus or Mars sign, and being rootless can have a hazardous effect on their whole way of life. Even if they are globetrotters, they need a place to return to, or a home to phone.

This is an emotional sign, strongly associated with the family. For that reason, family issues are deeply emotional issues, and the Cancer-influenced man can try to be logical or utterly rational about it, but feelings will rule the day. When this sign is being channelled easily and just flows through the chart, you will end up with the classic family man. He puts his clan and his children before everything. Even the permanent bachelors will find someone or something to adopt — usually someone else's child, or a lost soul in need of protection. Should you be in a relationship with a Cancer-influenced man whose family feelings are basically cut off, frozen out or alienated, think carefully about it. Something fairly painful must have happened to stop the male maternal instinct, and it is likely to be a super-sensitive subject with your Cancer-influenced partner. The *mother–son* relationship is absolutely crucial for men with a planet in Cancer too, and with some of them it's the key to everything that's right about them — as well as anything that's wrong. Some of them have clingy mothers; some of them have lost their mothers (and worship them). Some hate their mothers — aargh. All of them have mater issues.

MEN WITH PLANETS IN LEO

For a man with the Sun, Moon, Mercury, Venus or Mars in Leo, creative self-expression is vital. Fashion, planks of wood and tubes of glue? Paint and canvas? Camera and film? Pen and paper? It doesn't matter — they all need a shed. Plenty of them multi-task. All of them need a niche for their creativity and self-expression.

Nothing is sadder than a Leo-influenced man who has never tried to experiment with this side of himself. The Leo planet man who 'doesn't do anything really' is often battling depression, or so out of touch with himself that he appears quite lost to those around him. It is the Leo type's right and birthright to pour himself into something with confidence and style — even if he does save it for the weekends. For a Leo type who is really living his life, there is no such thing as 'just' a job, or 'just' an interest, hobby or enthusiasm. Once he has found the right space to be *himself* in, you may as well just let him go off and get on with it. It's a classy version of what he did as a boy — the old 'Hey, Mum! Hey, Dad! Look at me!' routine. But if Leonine talent, style and self-expression is a by-product of sophisticated showing off, then so be it.

There is also an incredible dignity which goes with this sign. It has no room for anything common, mean, embarrassingly petty or vulgar. There are certain things beneath a Leo type — and, in this day and age, Leo planet men simply glide over the trash and the cheapness as if these distasteful parts of their world did not exist. You can try to drag a Leo type down to a lower level, or make him part of a less gracious environment. He will never succumb. It's not his style. And he won't make a fuss about it — he'll just look the other way until the world has re-adjusted itself. It's what the Americans call class and the English call good breeding. Having the Sun, Moon, Mercury, Venus or Mars in this sign is a guarantee that at least one side of this man will be expressed in a courtly, good-mannered, practically medieval way.

It is not enough for a Leo-influenced man to be classy, inspired or commanding. He must have an audience. He can express himself to the bathroom mirror if he wants to, but Leo basically needs some kind of collective 'you' to impress. Awful Leos are showy and pompous for this reason: they grandstand even when there is nothing worthwhile to grandstand about. Leonine men who have developed in the right directions can be showstopping once they truly have something worthwhile to offer, display or give. Usually, it is a little of themselves. Sometimes, it is all of themselves. But nothing done in the name of creativity or self-expression really seems to count for the Leo-influenced man until he has the compliment confirmed, the feedback registered, or the sound of at least two hands clapping in his ears.

Leo-influenced men often have an instinctive feeling that they are the right man to take the reins, at the right time. It is not a decision motivated by vanity, although there may be a certain pride in their own accomplishments when their leading role has got them somewhere. Usually, it is the Leonine man's gut feeling about the need for someone, somewhere, to have the courage and the inner conviction to show others the way.

That constellation up there (the smaller and larger lion) could be strung together to mean *anything*. The Ancients associated planets passing through this sign with the lion — both a symbol of jungle supremacy and divine kingship. Even modern observation proves them right: planets in Leo incline their owners towards a leading role. It is the sign of the captain, king, prefect, chairman, chief, boss, head, director, manager, prime minister, frontman — the *old-school* style of leader, in fact. If he can't be at the top of his particular network, group, team, business or company, then he'll be head of his own one-man show. Very few of them can stand being second or third in command for long, no matter if it's work or play — and even if he has just one planet in Leo, it will show.

MEN WITH PLANETS IN VIRGO

Virgoan men can always give you intellectual arguments for vitamins, workouts, skipping nicotine or avoiding toxins. This does not, however, lead to the image of the Virgo-influenced male as a paragon of good health. Some are, and some aren't — but those who aren't spend a lot of time worrying about it!

There are many different ways a Virgo-influenced man can get in touch with his body. Some of them throw themselves at gyms and health-food shops. Others enter the health professions. Still more become dietary faddists or enjoy a lifelong cycle of neglect-and-purge. Virgo-influenced men are stuck with an uncomfortable situation — if they are seen to be too concerned with iron supplements and muscle definition, it delivers a message that the body is existing at the expense of the intellect.

The other extreme is equally wrong, though: cigarettes, sloth, alcohol, drugs, sugar and fat offend Virgo's sense of logic. For this reason, it can take a Virgo-influenced man quite a long time to sort out where he and his body fit into the scheme of things.

Illness — mild or serious — is the one time that Virgo planets tend to leap forward into full consciousness. The traditional quest for purity and perfection that is associated with this sign seems to take centre stage when the Virgo-influenced body falls down. Episodes of illness or poor health are frequently the stepping stones to the classic Virgoan lifestyle seen later on — one in which every day is dedicated to the understanding that the mind needs to be served by the body, and that the body requires intelligent handling by the mind.

He's a data, word or digit freak too. Few signs enjoy absorbing information as much as Virgo. If the man in your life has planets here, he will be a lifelong student, either formally or informally. It is not just the need to know, it is the need to know *exactly*. The Virgo Sun, Moon, Mercury, Venus or Mars man asks 'Is that the whole story?' every day of his life. Virgo planets make a researcher of every man, and anything — a recipe book, a magazine, a computer game, a philosophical treatise — becomes fair game for Virgo's mental microscope. This is a nitpicking, fact-checking, detail-loving, mistake-slashing, eye-straining, page-turning sign. Google is a Virgo — strange, but true.

Part of a Virgo planet's function is to communicate — and to make connections. Like Gemini, Virgo is associated with the written or spoken word. The mass media, computers, education and academia all have an overload of Virgo types in their ranks. This sign worships the right answer, the perfect definition and the best of all possible *words*. Virgo-influenced men enjoy working the language — but playing with it is equally important.

Virgo rules the Sixth House of the horoscope, associated with the work ethic, routine, ritual, responsibility and duty. If you know a man with planets in this sign, he will express part of his personality through work, which can make him wonderfully productive, but also burn him out in quite a spectacular way. Workaholism is where the famous mind–body split manifests itself first. If a man who has a strongly developed Virgoan side turns into a machine (endless lists of things to do, obligations to keep, weekends to 'use'), then the body will intervene. This sign can only live in the head for so long before the rest of the system starts yelling reminders. Virgo-influenced men can be prolific and productive beyond belief, but they need a balance in their lives too.

MEN WITH PLANETS IN LIBRA

Men with the Sun, Moon, Mercury, Venus or Mars in Libra believe in love. Some of them are marriage celebrants; some of them just celebrate marriage. The wilder Librans skip the ceremony, but like to think you were together in a past life. Ruled by Venus, the Goddess of Love and Beauty, men with a Libran side can be hopelessly romantic. They are also far more at peace when they've found their other half, or match. They see it in these terms too: Yin and Yang, black and white, quiet and noisy, male and female, Beauty and the Beast. Walt Disney had a Libra Moon. When he'd created Mickey, he had to create Minnie.

Whatever a Libra-influenced man believes that he lacks, he hopes to find it in you. The scales describe Libra: one set of qualities must always balance another, and in this symmetry these men find a kind of beauty and order.

Libran-influenced men enjoy the mythology and poetry of romantic love, and will either be traditional romantics ('Let me open that door for you', and 'Roses — for you', and 'God, you're beautiful without your glasses!') or . . . radical romantics.

Ruled by the Goddess of Love and Beauty, Libra also goes *looking* for Love and Beauty. This is the sigh sign. It's also the swoon sign. Some Libran types welcome feminism, some do not, but it is hard for them to exclude all that is intensely female and romantic from their vision of perfect womanhood. There's a lot of Romeo and Juliet tucked away in a Libran type, and lots of them are permanently affected by reading the play or seeing the film.

Libra planets give men an eye for design. Some of them express this professionally, and others express it in their houses and wardrobes. Libra-influenced men really *care* about the way things look. Architecture magazines make some of them drool, while others disappear inside art galleries and never come back. Strangely enough, their taste always comes back to Venusian principles: symmetry, harmony, curve, line, balance and shape. Let other men grow cabbages — Libran types want roses.

They also want a balanced set of scales. Equality. Justice. Peace. Harmony. All these issues are classically Libran, and inevitably this leads these men into all kinds of battlegrounds. The unpalatable truth for a man with a Libra Sun, Moon, Mercury, Venus or Mars is that in order to achieve peace, he must sometimes get involved in a fight. Unbalanced and unfair situations always throw the Libran type into a dilemma: argue the point, or walk away? Destiny says that occasionally he'll have no choice, and it doesn't matter if the issue is ideological or personal. His Libran side loathes aggression, but it equally detests any situation which is patently unfair or wrong. The preferred option? Always peaceful protest and skilful diplomacy.

Libra and Taurus are the most over-represented planet signs in the modern music industry. Both signs are ruled by Venus, a goddess who believed in love songs and dressing up. The man with Libra planets is either musically talented or just completely sold on music; without his iPod or Bose speakers, he'll typically feel lost.

MEN WITH PLANETS IN SCORPIO

Astrologers associate planets in Scorpio with a deep understanding of the darker side of life. Sooner or later, everything from sex and death to God, the devil, the occult, drugs, murder, Nazis, racism, sin, taboo, and every other cheerful Scorpionic topic will drift into his world. If the man in your life is heavily Scorpio then he may find a career, or a personal life, which is very dark indeed, and full of intrigue and complications.

This is not a trivial or a superficial sign. It lends a kind of depth and intensity to those who have it. A Scorpio-influenced man may have planets in other, lighter signs. But one part of him is intensely private and rather serious. If a large chunk of the Scorpio-influenced man seems to exist below the surface, it is usually because he knows certain things are not fit for public consumption.

Scorpio planets are concerned with taboo — what is forbidden or off limits. Death and dying is one area most people have a problem with, but this is precisely where Scorpio often goes exploring. This sometimes points the man in question to the supernatural; everything from vampires to mediums. Occasionally the death issue is just what it looks like — a life marked out by important bereavements and losses, all of which have a major effect on the Scorpio type's personality in later years.

If the man in your life has one or more Scorpio planets, then he has a huge capacity for understanding the most difficult human issues, and the twin passages of death and dying are high on the list. Many men working in professions tied to the law, or welfare, or medicine have a Scorpio planet expressing this side of them. It is not enough to politely look the other way and change the subject to something nicer, because Scorpio is not particularly interested in that. Perhaps for this reason, men with Scorpio planets often seem to attract intense situations, or intense people — or be drawn towards experiences which ask them to go more deeply into life.

Along with death, human sexuality — in all its manifestations — is part of the Scorpionic journey. Two friends of mine, both of whom are Scorpio Suns, work on soft porn magazines. Two more work in social services and deal with paedophiles. Opera is also full of Scorpionic types — perhaps because they are dealing in a medium where rape and death are part of a professional vocabulary!

I have also seen several charts with Scorpio planets belonging to men in the Catholic Church. Catholicism has been the best way they know to manage all the big sex, death and morality questions. Scorpio types make excellent amateur or professional psychologists too — everything from homosexuality to the Oedipus complex intrigues them.

They keep secrets too — their own, as well as other people's. And even if the man in your life has to be dragged screaming into a Catholic church, there is a part of him which instinctively understands the ritual of the confession box. Scorpio types are never afraid of peering into the murky depths of human existence, no matter how dark it becomes.

Having the Sun, Moon, Mercury, Venus or Mars in Scorpio produces an intense focus which can border on happy fanaticism. Scorpio types are never 'slightly interested' or 'quite into' things. This man dives in, totally oblivious to ringing telephones or other mundane distractions, and gets lost for hours. This sign is all about passion. If the Scorpio-influenced male doesn't burn for his work, he'll burn for something else on his days off — astrology is often on the list.

MEN WITH PLANETS IN SAGITTARIUS

I have yet to find a man with a strong Sagittarian side who isn't an explorer of some kind, be he surfer, swimmer, walker, rider, fisherman, diver, country daytripper or pilot. Even those men with a Sagittarius planet who stay glued to the television fantasise about having a rugged-looking four-wheel-drive parked outside the front door or a round-the-world ticket to exotic places.

The man with the Sun, Moon, Mercury, Venus or Mars in Sagittarius needs broad horizons. He may be fascinated by the endless 'out thereness' of it all. He can't resist thinking about life at the other end of the globe, or in the cosmos, and loves foreigners (or aliens) as much as he loathes small-town attitudes. Lots of them become drawn to other cultures, belief systems, philosophies or exotic religions as they become older. In other cases, they pick and mix from a whole range of global 'isms' and develop their own eclectic world view. Sagittarian types seldom end up believing in the things their families or schools taught them, though. It's their mission to explore further, educate themselves, and expand their spiritual or political horizons.

With Sagittarian men, you often have to put the adjective 'international' in front of most of the things they enjoy — or have a flair for. This sign likes to think big. It looks at reality as a map, not a corner of the street, and enjoys stretching out. To really see a measure of Sagittarian energy, visit the once secret underground War Cabinet rooms in London, where Sagittarius Sun Winston Churchill directed the strategies which were to win World War II. The 'think global, act local' philosophy that is so successful for Sagittarius is embodied in the rows of telephones and coloured pins on maps in these tiny rooms.

There are a lot of preachers, legal eagles, political animals, philosophers and true believers on the Sagittarian list. If the man in your life has the Sun, Moon, Mercury, Venus or Mars in Sagittarius, then he may have a little — or a lot — of the true believer in him. He can become preachy . . . occasionally. But a lot of what this man is about comes from the times of crisis that he lives through. From there, he develops his own particular view of the world, even of the planet. Whatever his particular brand of faith, he has to find a sense of meaning in it all, or life is not worth the exercise. He also needs a thought system or set of values to justify his decisions, as destiny says he'll often be put in ethically or morally challenging situations where he must lean, hard, on his beliefs.

And . . . just when you thought you'd heard it all about Sagittarian types — did you know that this sign is linked to comedy? Only Gemini types are more dominated by their sense of humour. If he's typical of his Sun, Moon, Mercury, Venus or Mars sign he'll either be an excellent amateur (or even professional) funnyman, or at the very least have a bookshelf or DVD collection which reflects what he thinks is most important in life — and, usually, it's the people who make him laugh.

MEN WITH PLANETS IN CAPRICORN

Men with the Sun, Moon, Mercury, Venus or Mars in Capricorn are hung up on time. They collect clocks, or they are intrigued by Stephen Hawking's theories in *A Brief History of Time*, or they make a point of buying the best watch they can afford. As children they are fascinated by the clock-swallowing crocodile in *Peter Pan*, and the watch-bearing rabbit in *Alice In Wonderland*.

Time, history, calendars, antiquity and age are their things. Men with a strongly developed Capricornian side often gravitate towards careers or social positions where they are expected to take an eternity to find success. They enjoy a distant mountain-top to climb to, and are often classic examples of a thirty-year crawl for overnight success!

They are builders by nature. Block by block, brick by brick, Capricorn Sun, Moon, Mercury, Venus or Mars men build. Their finest hour? Usually the one they gave up twenty years earlier, when everybody else was at a party. Developing discipline is part of what Capricorn is all about. Destiny says that remarkably few shortcuts will be available to them, and extraordinary ambition is necessary to fuel this long slog. If the ambition is realistic, then the Capricorn-influenced man will have an extraordinary life.

A man with the Sun, Moon, Mercury, Venus or Mars in Capricorn will typically have an 'old man' in his life who has a major effect on his development. It may be his own father. It may be a senior male authority figure, like a manager, a teacher, or just an influential relative.

Sometimes the link can be so intensely personal that the Capricornian type will not particularly want to discuss it. It is through this 'old man' figure, however, that a Capricorn-influenced man will come to terms with his own manhood. The star of the American men's movement, Robert Bly, places a great deal of emphasis on father figures and 'elder statesmen' in his ideas on manhood, as does the Australian psychologist and author Steve Biddulph. Who is the old man in your Capricorn type's life? Understand that, and you have the keys to a lot of mysteries about him.

If something goes wrong, a Capricornian type can find his 'old man' (literally) or a male authority figure becoming a burden, not a reward — as is the case with a dominating or abusive father, for example. One way for a Capricorn-influenced type to resolve this kind of problem is to seek out an older mentor, or wiser, experienced guide figure. This can be achieved through work, or other interests or activities. In this way, he'll earn his substitute father figure and get on with the business of being who he is — a serious, seasoned, savvy individual.

On some level, any man with a Capricorn planet is only asking this: 'Teach me . . .' Ultimately, with enough mentors and guides along the way, they themselves will become an 'old man' or a 'Father Time' figure for somebody else.

Turning twenty-eight, twenty-nine and thirty is a big deal for this man. It's his Saturn Return, and Saturn rules Capricorn. It marks the true entry into manhood, if he's typical of his sign, and serious decisions (marriage, mortgages, parenthood, divorce, new jobs) usually come with the territory.

Does he have a lot of planets in Capricorn? He'll be among the most serious men you've ever met — and unbelievably cautious as well. He'll also have made phenomenal professional or social progress in his life, usually ending up a whole social class or two above his parents — or making it to the top in his career. Capricorn is symbolised by the goat, which climbs steadily upwards. A man with one or more planets in Capricorn typically has this kind of upward trajectory in his life too.

Does Saturn make a lot of aspects (patterns) in his personal birth horoscope? You can tell at glance by entering his details at www.astro.com and looking for this symbol ♄ on the horoscope wheel. If it has plenty of lines stretching out from it, then he'll have a lot of Saturn influence in his chart.

If so, depression may be an issue for him. And if you're going to live with him over the long-term, understanding the planet Saturn, its cycles and its influence will be incredibly useful for you. Ask your astrologer to look at his chart with particular reference to Saturn and see where it takes you!

MEN WITH PLANETS IN AQUARIUS

Aquarian men can try to conform to other people's expectations if they want to, but it seldom works out. After a couple of crisis situations in their lives, they usually wake up to their own need to be different, and by their forties these men are typically living their own lives, in their own way. It can be extremely difficult to live as a man with the Sun, Moon, Mercury, Venus or Mars in Aquarius. Schoolboys are fed such rigid messages about what they can — and can't — do in this life that it takes a certain kind of bravery to depart from the rules if you were born male. Ironically, it is the departure from convention — or the norm — that Aquarius is all about. Plenty of mad geniuses and brilliant rebels come under this sign. So do men who are renowned for going their own way.

Aquarius-influenced men do not go quietly. They do not necessarily believe everything they are told. They are not particularly interested in being popular, and if they can avoid falling into line, they will. Just avoid getting them started on God, republicanism, the media, the existence of extra-terrestrials, the New Age, men's liberation or censorship. Unless, of course, you prefer all-night conversation to all-night sexual marathons.

Men with Aquarius planets are ahead of their time, partly because they are profoundly interested in tomorrow. They embrace technology, theories and inventions which seem unusual or 'difficult' in the present, but make remarkable sense several decades later. The Aquarian fascination with the future may manifest in a passion for science fiction, an obsession with science, or the pursuit of astrology.

Technology (computers, chips, bytes or satellites) are *huge* with Aquarian types. Give them the machine that goes *ping*, every time.

Aquarius planets promote an interest in change and innovation and 'the shock of the new', and men who have them are less interested in tradition and the status quo and far more excited by the idea of change and reform — new ways of doing the same things. Better ways of handling traditional ideas. Brand-new concepts to *completely replace* what was there before.

Aquarius gets its energy and its inspiration from a place so far out of most people's field of vision that the things the Aquarian type becomes passionate about are frequently missed or misunderstood. Transmat beam, anyone? The internet? Cable-fax-microwave-home-computers? The world before Aquarius and the world after Aquarius always looks like a radically different place.

Adolescence is an interesting time for Aquarian-influenced men. From this time into their early twenties, they are given more legitimate freedom by society than at any other stage of their lives. Rebellion and wildness is almost expected of young males then. And that may explain the unexpected images in the Aquarian man's photo albums: 'This is me running around naked on a desert island with a lampshade on my head', or 'This is me being dragged away on a protest march'.

Someone, somewhere, is always telling Aquarian types to settle down and do the right thing. But when they do, they are invariably unhappy. They don't want somebody else's idea of security or happiness. What they need is a lifestyle and career that will allow them the following things: friends, freedom, flexibility.

This last point — about the stubborn Aquarian insistence on freedom — is extremely important. Part of them wants it on an ideological, principled level. It gets dressed up as the quest for civil liberties — or free enterprise.

Friends and groups are his thing too. He'll either have a network of friends that is virtually a second family (or a substitute family), or involvement with at least one organisation, and possibly more.

How do you pick a man with the Sun, Moon, Mercury, Venus and/or Mars in Aquarius? Go through his wallet for all the membership cards, or look at his e-mail lists for his never-ending list of friends.

The friends are likely to be a mixed bunch too. Gay, straight, black, white, educated, uneducated, rich, unemployed . . . he typically knows an eclectic bunch of people. More than any other man, the Aquarian type is also gifted at being platonic friends with women. He's a forward-thinker, and consequently a natural feminist. Women pick up on it, and discover that his light touch makes it easy to do the just-good-friends thing.

Does he have two or more planets in Aquarius? Then he'll be noticeably cool and detatched about life. He does fine being single, or if he gets married he'll hang on to his single lifestyle longer, with plenty of time away from the marriage. Heavily Aquarian types are extraordinary to watch in times of emotional crisis or drama, as they have the ability to instantly remove themselves from the situation and analyse the whole thing from a distance. You want tears? Blood? You're unlikely to get it from a heavily Aquarian type.

MEN WITH PLANETS IN PISCES

Pisces is the sign most associated with what can be seen with the mind's eye — if your man has the Sun, Moon, Mercury, Venus and/or Mars in this sign, he'll be imaginative and highly visual. Put a canvas in front of a Piscean type and you'll see just how differently his vision functions from everyone else's. Give him a camera and he'll either produce a work of art, or something so unfocused it looks like art anyway. A blank notebook? An excuse for poetry . . .

Have you heard about the link between Pisces planets, drugs and alcohol? It's famous in astrology. It's down to this: most men with the Sun, Moon, Mercury, Venus or Mars in Pisces need to escape into an alternative reality. Certainly, hallucinogenic drugs or vodka can function like dressing-up boxes for the Piscean head, and many of them enjoy the blurring, or distortion, that occurs with them. However, lots of them figure out early on that drugs and alcohol have a stronger effect on them than most people, so sometimes they get into other escapes instead — like scuba-diving, an addiction to the cinema, or art, or meditation.

I have known vets and cancer therapists with Pisces planets, and a few modern-day saints and healers as well. Pisces is associated with sacrifice — sometimes on a daily level (time, energy or money goes out to others), or, occasionally, in a powerful, once-in-a-lifetime way. The wisest, most wonderful Piscean types always do this out of compassion. The ability to give something of themselves comes from this issue — in imagining how another person must feel. Many of the quiet achievers and forgotten saints in your town are probably Piscean types. Your man may have planets in other signs which are more self-interested, but his Piscean side basically wants to give it all up, and give of himself. On an ordinary, everyday level this produces the classic Piscean kindness and sensitivity.

Lopsided Piscean types take the concept of sacrifice to an extreme, and end up becoming martyrs who enjoy the moaning and the mooching that goes with the territory. Also, perhaps, planets here can produce the classically dazed and confused individual who believes his whole reason for existing is to be a human dartboard. Rescuing these rare, but lost Piscean types can end up being a life's mission for some women.

Pisces planets give a man a strong sense of the absurd too. I once interviewed Piscean type Kurt Cobain, and he spent the first five minutes trying to convince me that Nirvana were going to organise a gigantic hypnotic wheel on stage to mesmerise their audience. A whimsical imagination — and a happily overdeveloped sense of the ridiculous — are Piscean trademarks. Their sense of humour is particularly loopy — like Rolf Harris meets Dr Seuss, via Robin Williams.

Does Neptune influence his personal horoscope? Go to www.astro.com and type in his birth details to find out. If you see a lot of lines stretching out from the Neptune symbol Ψ in his horoscope, then he'll be a Neptunian, with plenty of aspects (patterns) involving this planet.

That means a massive dose of Pisces in his chart — because Neptune actually rules this sign too. So dazed and confused will often be his natural state, and his memory may be bad — or he may be unfocused. Put him in, or near, water! Neptune rules the ocean, but even if he's not lucky enough to live near the sea, a long bath with candles will do the trick.

A man who has the Sun, Moon, Mercury, Venus and/or Mars in Pisces, with Neptune aspects in his chart, needs to submerge himself in an alternative world in order to feel normal. This is why baths can work such amazing magic on him — or a few laps in the local swimming pool. He also needs poetry, fantasy and music more than a lot of other men if he is strongly Piscean and Neptunian. They ground him, and he'll be easier to live with if you let him disappear into these other worlds!

WHAT MEN WANT

Is your boss having a Pluto cycle in his career zone? Then he wants total control, and you need to know how to manage it. Is your father having a Saturn cycle in his home zone? Then don't try to sting him for a loan; his mortgage or home repair bills could be astronomical just now. Is your best Aries friend making new friends with drug problems? Why not show him the chapter about himself on these pages before it goes any further!

What men want, at any given time, depends on what the planets are doing in the heavens. The following information shows the biggest issues of all, for your male work/family/love/friendship connections into the early twenty-first century.

Note: If you are more interested in the women in your world than the men in your world, then the information applies equally. Just switch 'she' for 'he'. If your priority is learning how to understand what your mother/sister/girlfriend or female boss/colleague/client is experiencing, please feel free to gender-bend everything you see here, as the same life trends will apply.

As ninety-nine per cent of the questions to my website are from women asking about men, though, I thought it was time to supply some answers. Here, at length, is (I hope) what you want to know about what *he* wants.

THE ARIES FRIEND TO FEBRUARY 2012

His social life is dominated by one or more dreamers, drinkers, drug fiends, creatives and saints. Are you one of them? With Neptune in his zone of friendship and group involvements until 2012, his 'normal' friends will be few and far between.

One or two of them will have the Sun, Moon, Mercury, Venus and/or Mars in Pisces, or Pisces rising. They'll be in creative jobs, or heavily involved with charity, or religion — or in regular office jobs, but with an important weekend drinking/drug habit. Through his friends, Aries learns to escape — be they Buddhist meditators or party animals.

He's addicted to groups in these years, and if one doesn't work out, he'll join another one. It's through the group that he finds his ideals, his fantasies, his daydreams, and possibly even nirvana. That's why so many Aries men you know are channelling their imagination, as well as their spare time, through anything from a rock band to a political party.

Friendships can sometimes seem more like relationships in this cycle, as one person plays the rescuer/saint figure and the other person plays the victim. Aries needs to be careful that he isn't getting stuck into co-dependent, unhealthy friendships in these years.

There will also be one or two rather confused, chaotic friendships — which neither side is entirely clear about.

What does he want from you at this time? Firstly, he'll need you to understand that his escape route is via his friends, or the group he's a part of. That's where he's putting most of his wildest visions and ideals. Chasing the dream also means making sacrifices, though; so you need to understand what he's giving up, and why.

Aries needs to be extremely careful with the new friends and acquaintances he lets into his life in these years. Not everyone will be clear or honest about what they are really up to, so his radar needs to be switched on. When Neptune is making difficult patterns in the heavens in his zone of friends and groups, he could be deceived by someone who claims to be a friend or part of the group, but who has his/her own agenda. If at any point Aries catches a whiff of something strange — like the hint of a gas leak under the door — then he needs to stop what he is doing immediately and pay attention. The so-called friend in front of him may be anything but!

Genuinely altruistic, magical, miraculous and special people — and groups — will cross his path, though, and this is where he'll miss out if he doesn't get involved. Those who give unconditional compassion, energy and time for others will be among the highly influential new friends now making an impact. Some will have religious or spiritual connections too.

Once again, though, the Aries radar needs to be kept on. He needs to give new friendships and group involvements time before committing himself.

THE ARIES EMPLOYEE/CLIENT/COLLEAGUE/BOSS NOVEMBER 2008 TO JANUARY 2024

Be prepared for this: twice a year, around the New Moons and Full Moons in December/January and June/July, your workplace will be subject to change. Why? Because your Aries employee/client/colleague/boss will also be subject to change, and from 2008 to 2024 it will be powerful, steady and relentless.

Those New Moons and Full Moons, in the signs of Cancer and Capricorn, will trigger an ongoing transformation in the way he works, and the way he sees his role in the wider workplace. Often, there will be a power struggle involved, and the shift in workplace politics will create a domino effect which ends up affecting your life too.

Aries needs to crash and burn a few times in this period, so he can strip away the non-essentials from his life and work, and become more powerful. His occasional meltdown will actually help him to a) find the right career path, if he's on the wrong one, or b) restructure his slice of the company or business in order to ensure its survival into the twenty-first century.

The balance of power in his field or industry will concern him a lot more than usual. Pluto, the planet now affecting his career, will put him in a position where he can pull the strings or hold the controls — but, on occasion, it will also put him in a position where he becomes aware of just how much power other people have. Both situations will teach him a lot about the game of life.

Memo to the Aries boss in these years: on no account try to dominate or run the show, as the law of astrology says your actions will have a trickle-down effect, and you may not like what trickles down. Tempting though it will be to imagine that he is Master of the Universe in these years, it is a temptation best avoided. The cycles of Pluto have a funny way of levelling out the playing field after a few years.

Expect him to be more intense about his ambitions, his projects and his plans at this time. He may even become obsessive. This will often prove to be the making of him — but everything in moderation. If more than half his life is being turned over to company expansion, or ruthless ambition, then his Pluto cycle is clearly running out of control.

If a family member is also involved in his industry or business, then these years will be a particularly decisive time. The family relationship may change as the career situation also changes. If the link between close relatives and the business is not necessarily a productive one over the long-term, then it may change so much that it has to end. One thing is sure: if his family and working life are mixed up, this will be a particularly intense period in his life, when almost everything about the working relationship, as well as the family connection, has to be investigated at the deepest levels.

What does he want in this period? Most of all, he wants his promotion, his award, his record-breaking profit, or his stunning achievement. Just as he was obsessed with travelling, or doing business overseas, or studying, or exploring religion or publishing before, he will now be solely focused on his career.

Some Aries men will ignore their careers in this cycle in favour of a hobby or part-time pursuit which they see as their real vocation or calling. If so, the obsession will be squarely targeted at this extra-curricular activity or goal.

THE TAURUS EMPLOYEE/CLIENT/COLLEAGUE/BOSS TO FEBRUARY 2012

Martin Luther King famously said 'I have a dream' — and so does Taurus, in these years. You will come to recognise that slightly glazed, far-off look in his eye extremely well by 2012. Sometimes it will lead to his most impressive achievements. At other times, it will lead him straight up a gum tree, without a ladder. Time and experience will help him, and you, to understand the difference.

Neptune, the planet of fantasy, daydreams, visions and high ideals, is affecting his career to 2012. When inspiration strikes, reality may have nothing to do with it. Depending on how expensive or time-consuming his ideas are, this will either plunge him into career chaos, or take him to the giddiest heights of achievement, pulling off the kind of goals which genuinely inspire those around him as well.

What does he want to 2012? A job which is so much more than just a job! Rather like Walter Mitty, he will be fantasising about his life rather than living it — all of which means practical issues may often pass him by. If Taurus is your boss, he will need a grounded second-in-command to keep him on track.

Which brings us to the subject of staff and colleagues . . . hopefully he has already learned one difficult lesson about who to trust! Before this period is out there may be another one, but all Taurus has to do is use his radar a little better. The people who are most problematic in his career in these years will be those who have a problem living in the real world. They may have drug or alcohol issues, or alternatively be lifelong self-deceivers, blind to the true facts about people or situations. Professionally, if Taurus has not yet learned to screen people before opening himself up to them, it's time he did.

It goes without saying that he also needs to be more open, honest and upfront himself in these years, as Neptune often signals a time of dodgy tactics and self-deception for him, as well as his staff or colleagues . . . and even practical Taurus is not immune.

If he works for you, expect patches of heavy fog and low visibility from time to time. Chaos and confusion will probably occur on a regular basis. If you work for him, there will be times when your meetings will be as clear as mud.

The pay-off? Over the long-term, his achievements should do you credit. If he sticks to his highest ideals and his truest visions (the kind that benefit everybody, not just Taurus — and the kind that can actually become real), then you gain too. His reflected glory may be yours, or he may take your business to more inspiring places.

Plans or people in the workplace which are clearly dubious to sensible outsiders, are the first things he should jettison, though. There has never been a more important time in Taurus's history to cling to his Earth sign roots. That means both hooves on the ground!

One final note: it's possible that, during this cycle, Taurus will sacrifice his job, or walk away from a career, in order to pursue his dreams. Before doing so, he needs to talk to as many Aries men as he can, as they had this astrological career phase before him. Before he throws everything away for a vision, it might be useful to talk to people who've been there before, to find out what worked and what didn't.

THE TAURUS FINANCIAL/PROPERTY PARTNER TO NOVEMBER 2008

If you are married or de facto and share a mortgage or bank account, this cycle will also have an impact on your love life. In other cases, you may be in business with Taurus, or have some other kind of financial or property arrangement with him — involving anything from an investment to a car or home.

What you need to remember about this cycle is its intensity. In fact, if you think back to previous years, you'll probably notice a pattern: around the New Moons and Full Moons of June/July and November/December, there's a tendency for Taurus to either totally transform his financial position, or to sit back and deal with it as destiny does the transformation for him.

Here's one thing you don't want from your joint financial dealings with him — a power struggle. Yet, with Pluto in his zone of cash, property, business, possessions, shared resources (like talent) and investment, it's hard to avoid. The whole point of astrology, though, is to sidestep what doesn't serve us, and until 2008, it is Taurus's job to carefully and deliberately avoid any suggestion of a power play. This applies no matter if he feels he is on the top or the bottom.

Detachment is not easy for Taurus, especially if cash or a home is involved — or even a treasured possession. Nevertheless, there will be times between now and 2008 when he needs to stand back and count the true cost of his peace of mind, and the true value of being proven top dog. What's the actual financial stake, in any battle for control that might be going on?

Don't expect the status quo to remain the same between you in these years, and prepare yourself for the fact that he may want to clear out his financial management and business interests at regular intervals. He may voluntarily crash and burn, or there may be epic moments in his career or financial life which force him to begin a big money detox. Once again, it may be around the New and Full Moons of June/July and November/December in any year that it all starts to roll.

It will be hard for him to accept that power isn't money (or property) in this cycle. It may also be difficult for him to avoid becoming obsessed by two- or three-way agreements over cash, property and possessions. This is all part of Pluto's learning curve, though, and the longer this cycle runs, the easier it will be for Taurus to educate himself about which attitudes serve him and which don't. If moving into an all-powerful position financially costs him dearly in other areas of life, then where's the gain? Taurus will learn a lot about the true price of things in the years to 2008.

If you are one of the women who is splitting up with Taurus, or dealing with the aftermath of a divorce, then you may find yourself tempted, at several points, to enter into a complicated game that involves either outright shows of power and control or rather subtle and buried string-pulling. How do you get out of it? The old-fashioned solution of putting yourself in Taurus's shoes could work well for you. Try and work out precisely why he wants so much control, or why he feels so threatened by the idea of you having all the power, and then go from there. Above all, remember this is the sign which is here to work out its own value system, so it can teach the rest of us. A conversation with Taurus about the true price of peace (as opposed to ongoing stress) might be worth your time. Having trouble getting him to the table? Offer to bring the wine, and make it vintage.

THE GEMINI EMPLOYEE/CLIENT/COLLEAGUE/BOSS TO MARCH 2011

He wants to resign or retire. Alternatively, he wants to change the system and start a one-man revolution in his particular business, field or industry. If you're his boss, give him more freedom. If he feels trapped or confined, he is likely to rebel against you, and you will come back from lunch to find a cleared desk and a virus in your computer. You will need to be tolerant (within reason) in these years, as your Gemini employee will not be his normal self.

Is he your boss? Then he will be erratic and unpredictable. If he is also in his forties (experiencing his Uranus–Uranus opposition) then he will hit a mid-life crisis at the same time that he experiences a career crisis. You will need to learn how to 'surf' your job, on a daily basis. Sometimes he'll be at his desk; sometimes he won't. One day he'll install a new computer system; the next day it will crash.

Do not expect computers, fax machines, electronic security systems, high-tech fire detection systems or any other machine which goes 'ping' to work properly until 2011. And guess what? It's all his fault.

Here's the spooky explanation. Part of him is desperate for a break from routine. However, the responsible, career-minded part won't let him. Result? The technology misbehaves, so the routine is thrown out of the window. Unconsciously, it's what he wanted all along.

He may be involved in strike action in these years, and quite a few of them will hit a 'power to the people' phase. Clenched fist optional.

Is he your client? Then his own business or company will be going through so many changes at this time that he may pay late or, alternatively, challenge your bills. Be prepared for the Gemini guys on your files to ask more questions.

Does your Gemini work connection also have planets in Aquarius? (Find out his birthday if you can.) Then by 2011 he may be one of the truly radical Geminis who chuck in their high-flying jobs to become house-husbands, or to save the planet.

Uranian industries and professions (weird, progressive, new age, cutting-edge, high-tech, scientific) will attract hordes of Gemini employees by 2011. Is that your field too? Has someone new just come on board with a serious e-mail habit or a cell phone obsession? Chances are he's born in May or June.

The smart Gemini men will become innovators, inventors and experimenters in this period. Their crazy ideas will not seem so crazy in 2024, and you will be glad you invested your time and energy in them.

You also need to be aware that sometimes the system genuinely needs to change. If so, let him have some space. If he's got a vision of the way employee–employer relations should run, at least listen; for every mad concept, there will be one genuinely progressive vision for your company.

Warning: if you employ Gemini teenagers from now to 2011 they will be extra-adolescent. Expect rebels without a cause, with a cause and sometimes without a clue as well.

Memo: don't think you've got the boss worked out in these years. You haven't. British Prime Minister Tony Blair had this cycle when he formed an alliance with American President George Bush and bombed Afghanistan, followed by Iraq. Who knew? If your boss is a Gemini, expect the unexpected in the first ten years of the twenty-first century.

THE GEMINI BOYFRIEND/HUSBAND TO NOVEMBER 2008

Are you still together? Congratulations. You have survived one of the most notoriously difficult love-life cycles in astrology. You only get this kind of cycle every two centuries or so, and a lot of people never get to experience it at all. However, it's not over yet. By 2008 you will need to accommodate even more changes in your marriage or relationship than you have already been through, as Gemini is doing *all* his changing through his love life.

Pluto, the planet which is dominating his relationship or marriage in these years, always makes a promise: what you end forever will automatically create a new balance of power between you. The process often feels unbearably intense, though, which is why you may find the period around May/June and November/December of any year rather extreme. And the ending? It may be the death of an old relationship pattern, the last chapter in an ongoing shared plan, or even the departure from an entire way of life. Pluto requires that Gemini kill something off, in his relationship or marriage, in order for it to survive. It's an odd bargain. But in the end, Pluto always serves the greater good; that is its function.

So . . . not exactly the picnic you expected! But despite the intensity and the extremes that Pluto brings, it also brings the most profound new beginnings, once the rubble of the past has been cleared away by the dump-truck of destiny. What finishes in the relationship or marriage now clears the way for new growth, and a whole new order. The balance of power, in particular, will be different after Pluto does its work.

That word *power* is not something that romantics normally like to associate with marriages or partnerships, but it's unavoidable during a Pluto Seventh House cycle, which is what Gemini is experiencing to 2008. The power may be financial (you're richer than him, or he's got the keys to the house) or it may be psychological (you're the mother of his children, or he's in charge of your medication). All sorts of scenarios are possible.

Gemini needs to examine power issues in the context of your marriage or relationship as openly and as honestly as possible. If he lets them build up underneath the floorboards, not only will his dreams become weird, his entire life may become weird.

Pluto also brings taboos with it. What is the taboo in your marriage or relationship? When I look at my Gemini files, I can find life-threatening illness, euthanasia and childlessness. In addition, there is the spectre of an ex-husband or ex-wife (who must Never Be Discussed) and serious drug addiction. Money or family can be up there too!

In short, if you can't talk about it openly, it's a Plutonian taboo. If any light is going to be shed on it at all, it will happen around New Moon and Full Moon time in May/June and November/December — just like those other love-life issues which are bound to come up. At those times, the Sun, Moon and Pluto weave important patterns in the heavens, which ensure that Gemini has to pay attention to what is just below the surface, in his private life.

By 2008, the balance of power in the partnership will have altered. What brings you both to that point will be a sequence of changes (final chapters, followed by new chapters) which totally transform the shape of what you have together.

Sometimes, a Pluto cycle like this one can also end a relationship or marriage, with the most intense final 'bang' before the lights go out. If so, it may help Gemini to remember that sometimes, if there is too much to detox or recycle, the only way through is the way out. Pluto's job is to help us focus on the rubbish in our partnerships, and in our attitudes to love, sex and relating — so that we can turn it into something better. If there is too much stacked up to work with, however, sometimes things have to end.

Like all astrological cycles, though, this one is just part of a larger sequence. In time, as other planets arrive in the sign of Sagittarius (which rules Gemini's love-life zone), there will be new seeds, new growth, and new beginnings too.

If you have read this far, by the way, primarily because you are interested in your Gemini ex-husband or ex-boyfriend, remember that Pluto can sometimes resurrect a relationship or marriage and bring it back from the dead. This is not an absolute rule with this planet, but it happens often enough for it to be worth mentioning. If there is something in the dying embers of your long-gone marriage or affair that could possibly fuel a new, brilliant blaze — well, you can count on Pluto to help fan the flames again. If so, your new partnership is likely to have tremendous power, because it will be rather like a phoenix shooting out of the flames — apparently indestructible!

THE CANCER FINANCIAL/PROPERTY PARTNER TO FEBRUARY 2012

If you are married to Cancer, or living with him, and you share a mortgage, bank account, or other possessions and shared talents/resources, what follows will also affect your love life.

No matter if you are personally involved with Cancer, or just a business partner, you need to know all about Neptune's effects in his Eighth House of money, homes, possessions and resources until 2012.

If he hasn't already learned how to read the fine print on a contract, then he needs to. Some confusion, or even the occasional dodgy arrangement, may already have been an issue. Even if he's been free of this, though, the trends in his solar chart until 2012 make total clarity an absolute must in all paperwork that could cost him money (and make him money too).

If anything in his discussions with you about mortgages, shared bank accounts, mutual tax arrangements, wills, child support and other 'you/me/us' areas are unclear — or if he goes cross-eyed when you are talking with him — pay attention. Neptune is famous for spinning increasingly complicated threads of confusion from the smallest strand, so jump on problems before they can create real chaos.

Boundaries may also need to be defined with all parties involved in issues around property, money or possessions with him. You can see why this is particularly crucial in matters of inheritance or shared liability! He may already have struck this problem. However, even if he has escaped it, while this Neptune cycle is in operation, it's always best for Cancer to seek second, and, if necessary, third and fourth opinions. Classic financial messes can occur if Cancer does not clearly define what is his, and what is other people's. This applies to anything from joint possession of a CD collection to the responsibility for a child's school fees.

During these years, he needs to lose his illusions about people, or arrangements, which are misleading, or even deliberately deceptive. Equally, he needs to lose his illusions about what he is up to, if he is kidding himself that his own dodgy cash, business or property tactics are somehow 'okay'.

Getting real is vital in this cycle. And the first place to begin is with the facts and figures. Cancer also needs to be aware that although some business offers or financial choices now being put to him by others may be genuinely inspiring — and, on occasion, lead to the miracle he has been dreaming about — there will be a decent percentage which should be left well alone.

People who have drug or alcohol issues, or reality dysfunction, are the first individuals he should be cautious about!

It's so easy for the terms of any agreement or arrangement to be poorly defined in this cycle that he really will need outside advice, especially if large amounts or substantial properties (or valuable possessions) are involved. Vagueness can be charming, but not when cash is involved, and certainly not in this cycle! If Cancer has any questions about this, incidentally, he should exchange notes with Gemini men, as they hit this cycle before him. Confusion can cost when Neptune is in the solar Eighth House.

Imagination can be a friend or enemy now. It can help if he needs to create a clever vision of how his lifestyle or financial position could be — and he genuinely needs inspiration. However, Neptune can hold him back if mad fantasies replace practical planning. Will he be able to tell the difference between a valid vision and a deluded hallucination now? It's unlikely. You may need to be his reality check, or at least point him in the direction of trusted advisors or friends who can act as down-to-earth sounding boards.

Cash and property, and business possibilities, will bring out his beautiful idealism now ('Let's give 10% of the profits to charity!') and also trigger his inner flake ('Let's invest in old cardboard boxes people have left by the side of the road, and make our fortune!'). There will be risk times, and gain times, depending on what patterns Neptune is making at the time; feel free to check the Astrologer's Diary at www.jessicaadams.com to see what's happening in the heavens at the time!

Astrologically speaking, Neptune cycles are both mist and fog. The mist can be beautiful, like the smoke machines they use in *The Lord of the Rings*. It can add poetry, beauty, magic and wonder to the most boring situation. And the fog? Think driving along a treacherous road in the middle of the night, unable to see — this cycle can put Cancer on very shaky ground indeed.

You can marry or move in with Cancer in this cycle, or do a business deal with him (or even inherit his cash), and be amazed at how spiritual it all is. He might talk in terms of 'What's mine is yours' and seem to be above all that materialistic, capitalist stuff. Is he right or wrong? Are his motives pure or not? Will it end in bliss or in finger-pointing? These are questions you both need to ask, preferably with an accountant reading the fine print.

Reality should and must be his friend, wherever possible. The more he slips into an unreality (a fantasy land or a happy daydream), the more it is likely to cost him, in all senses of the word, when the real world comes knocking. And it will, too, either during this cycle or immediately after it ends, when Neptune has gone and the beautiful mist has disappeared.

THE CANCER EMPLOYEE/CLIENT/COLLEAGUE/ BOSS MARCH 2011 TO MAY 2019

This long seven-year itch will not affect his marriage, but it will certainly affect his career. If he is bored stiff by his job, but too nervous to change, then he may find the universe delivers the changes anyway, and circumstances propel him into a whole new ball game.

If his job or position confines him, or unfairly pigeonholes him, then it may be Cancer who makes a bold move, and either resigns, retires, or reads the riot act to his employers. Smart Cancerians will form an exit strategy first, no matter how stifled or suffocated they might feel at the time.

Sometimes the bolts from the blue (if he is feeling confined) can be generous and surprisingly easy to take. He may be headhunted, or promoted, or his business may go through a takeover which changes all the rules of the game which have been restricting him to date. Uranus, the planet which now rules his career, can be benevolent when it hooks up with his chart the right way.

If he's your boss now, or your employee, or client, the rules are the same: there are no rules! Either destiny will have a weird way of constantly upsetting his normal routine, or he will become the most erratic employer or colleague you've ever known, changing his mind, changing his days, or changing his plans without warning.

Strange, brilliant ideas which he believes are ahead of their time, or on the cutting-edge, will excite him. Some of them will work. Some of them will not. Some will help society change and make the world a better place. Some will turn out to be so cracked that nobody gets them (except Cancer). As with all Uranian cycles, this one requires outside help. Cancer needs to find those who have also trodden an innovative path in life (and preferably succeeded with it) to learn if he is pursuing something crazed or something worthwhile.

Cancerians who are seriously out of touch with their need for a lively, exciting and authentic occupation may find themselves unemployed, redundant, or faced with changes they did not ask for, in their chosen business or industry.

This planet can be difficult and disruptive. But its function is to change all the channels at the same time, so that Cancer suddenly has multiple choice, even if he doesn't know what's going on any more. Uranus gets him off the sofa and into the raw, exciting, uncertain — but fulfilling — Real World again. No doubt his first thought will be for his mortgage or rent when and if it happens. But the cycle he is in, no matter how disruptive, has its rewards. Every shake-up is a wake-up, and it's only when he is finally wide awake that Cancer will be able to look back and see, once and for all, exactly why his job was killing him.

Be prepared for the end of 'same old, same old' in his professional life. It may happen within months of this cycle starting too. New jobs, new technology, new hours, new business locations — all these things could land in stages, or land simultaneously.

This cycle takes years, and will be characterised by sudden turning points which give him an incredible sense of release, as well as by disruptive periods, when people in the workplace rebel or he rebels against them. Cancer will get through it all far more easily if he accepts that fate will sometimes shake the snowdome in patterns which make no sense, and sometimes shake the snowdome into a far more exciting picture. It's the 'no sense' pictures which will take time to understand and deal with. And who knows — perhaps the whole point of the pictures that look messiest is that he takes control and keeps shaking, and re-shaking, until he sees something he likes!

Along the way, Cancer will pursue work choices, jobs, projects, plans and lifestyle options which are ahead of their time. What he pursues today, the rest of the world will pursue in twenty years. Maybe even two hundred years. And a job may not be a job, in this context. All the above information may apply to something better described as a vocation or life calling — like a weekend hobby, or a full-time life as a modern house-husband.

What he wants now is best described by listing what he doesn't want: Mondayitis, routine, predictable employer demands, boring work, meaningless work, conventional ambitions, conformist behaviour, your rules, society's rules, the union's rules, old ways/predictable ways of doing things . . . the list goes on.

And, by the way, if a ridiculous amount of problems turn up in connection with the technology, the equipment, the transportation or the building attached to his job, don't be surprised. When Cancer is truly out of touch with his need for a break in this cycle, the cosmos will have a weird way of altering his routine by making sure the computer crashes or the cars need repairs. Sometimes, colleagues, clients and employers can follow this erratic course 'around him' too — all of which shakes the snowdome up again.

Conscious living is what astrology is all about. So . . . if it keeps on happening to Cancer, show him this chapter. If there is a part of him which wants to break free and he's not giving it a voice, it may be time for a new job — or at least a radical twist on the old one.

THE LEO BOYFRIEND/HUSBAND TO FEBRUARY 2012

What he wants from you in these years? Easy. The dream. The vision. The fantasy. No egos! No boundaries! He is looking for the mysterious and the miraculous from his marriage or relationship in the early twenty-first century, and nothing less will do.

This will make a percentage of Leo men extremely fantasy-prone, and you can expect anything from a secret crush on a porn star to a full-blown affair with another woman. If it happens, it will be because he has become lost in an imaginary world. Only a few Leo men will give in, but if yours is one of them, show him this page. Tell him he's having a Neptune cycle in his love zone. And Neptune is the planet of impossible dreams and self-delusion. Wakey-wakey!

Most of them will remain faithful, of course — Leo men are usually too noble (and too terrified of what the neighbours will say) to have an affair. However, be prepared for him to idealise you, and idealise the relationship as well. Starry, starry eyes are very common with this kind of cycle. So is addictive behaviour.

Incidentally, if his eyesight becomes worse when he is with you (if he needs glasses or contact lenses for the first time, or if he needs a stronger prescription), you will notice a remarkable difference in the relationship. Before blindness and after blindness might be the right way to express it — and it's not just because he's stopped bumping into the furniture. The rather confusing patches in your marriage or relationship, when you weren't altogether sure if he was seeing things as they really are, will tally with the eyesight problems. Once the contacts or glasses arrive, voila! Magically, he'll finally appear to be seeing you, and the relationship, clearly again.

It's the same with alcohol and drugs (prescribed and non-prescribed). If he drinks too much, or too often — or if he is dependent on anything from marijuana to sleeping pills — he will have a poor idea of the reality of you, and the reality of the relationship or marriage. If he kicks the habit, then normal transmission will be resumed.

And here's another thing — weird photos. Have you gone through a period recently where none of his DVD or digital shots of you actually *look* like you? That's Neptune. The technology is symbolically telling you something: he's not seeing you straight.

This can be harmless fun. So he thinks you're an angel from heaven, or even more beautiful than the day you were married? Wonderful. Other women would kill for such compliments. Just prepare yourself, though — he'll come down eventually, probably some time around 2012.

Fantasies that you are saving or rescuing him, or that he is rescuing or saving you (they often swap), are another common outcome of this cycle. He'll either martyr himself for you like an Irish saint, or flap around in front of you like a beached whale, in the hope that you'll row out the dinghy.

Some common — but totally avoidable — pitfalls in these years:

* You're in love with a Leo alcoholic or drug user. He turns to you for help.

* You have a drink or drug problem. He says he will marry you, or move in with you, so that he can save you.

* He starts an online relationship with a woman he has never met, behind your back. Her photo is out of focus, or out of date, or it's not even her.

* He converts to a religious or spiritual cause which you (frankly) find rather dodgy, because it seems to extract so much money from its members, or because it's so nauseatingly tax-effective.
Nevertheless, he's seen the light and wants you to see the light too. Again, he is convinced he can save you.

Those are extreme examples, by the way. And, as with everything in astrology, consciousness is the way through. Know the pitfall and you will avoid it.

There can be moments of great truth and beauty in these years if he plays it the right way. If he believes in you and the marriage or relationship, he will make great sacrifices. A Leo husband and a wife who develops MS . . . A Leo boyfriend and a girlfriend who needs him to give it all up for her new job in Antarctica . . .

Nevertheless, it's important that he has total clarity about why he's doing it, what's involved, and who you/he really are as people (rather than fantasy humans). It is vital that he tries to see you as you really are in this cycle. Who are you, when you're not with him? He may be projecting bits of his own personality onto you, even if you've been together for years. Thus, communication becomes crucial. Honest conversations about what you're really thinking and feeling — and what you really want and need from life — will help. Otherwise your Leo partner may be making it all up in his head. And no matter how flattering compliments are, knowing that someone is not in love with the *real* you, but with a picture in his head, can be hideous!

Is your Leo creative? This can be an excellent cycle for creative inspiration. You will be his muse, or the marriage/relationship will trigger some amazing songs, scripts, short stories, poems, short films, photographs or other forms of art and entertainment. Your partnership will fire his imagination.

Is he living with you, but confused about getting married? Are you engaged, but in a permanent holding pattern? Beneath the dazed-and-confused state of mind, you may discover that the real problem is his idealised fantasy about what a marriage or wedding should be. Chances are, it's something so totally removed from reality that even Hollywood would have a problem making it. No wonder he can't say his vows. Chances are, he's either terrified that it won't be like the Disneyland fantasy and he'll be horribly disappointed — or he's worried that as a husband he won't be able to live up to it. Solution? Get him to talk to people who are actually married. That should help him to change the film he has running in his head.

Cancerian men had this cycle before him. Do you know any women who had Cancerian boyfriends or husbands in the 1990s? You could pick up some tips. Similarly, if you have any Cancerian male friends, now is the time to ask them what it was like to be born under the sign of the crab and in a relationship or marriage in the '90s. Seeing why/how it was so hard for them to see their love lives clearly will help you fathom what your Leo man is going through.

THE LEO FINANCIAL/PROPERTY PARTNER TO MARCH 2011

Three things will affect the predictability of his financial position until 2011 — other people, twists of fate, and the forces of nature. Leo will gain and lose while it is going on, so if your cash is tied up with his (or the home is in both your names) then get ready to surf.

If you are in business with Leo, or have some other connection to him through your house, flat, assets, talents, possessions or resources, then once again — remember he is operating under strangely erratic and unpredictable conditions until 2011.

As a rule of thumb, anything he signs at the moment should give him the freedom to release himself with a minimum of hassle or expense. Uranus, the wild card of astrology, will send him in all kinds of directions over the next few years, and even the best psychic in the world won't be able to keep tabs. Consequently, flexibility is a good policy. Any financial institution or business partner who insists that Leo functions like an immovable rock is not really a good idea — astrologically speaking, this cycle is about surprises, U-turns and sudden changes.

When Jupiter, the planet of abundance, joins forces with Uranus in this cycle, the surprises (and they may even be shocks) will benefit Leo. It is impossible to categorise what might happen, except to say that opportunities often come disguised as the last thing anyone expected. Each time it happens to Leo, it will remind him (and you) that the pot of gold at the end of the rainbow usually appears when rain has not been forecast.

It's not something Leo should rely on, though. But when Jupiter and Uranus join forces (check at www.jessicaadams.com for dates in the Astrologer's Diary) he will be better off, at very short notice and often for the most unlikely reasons.

What about the downside? Managing it is the key. Leo needs to learn how to take on board all the unexpected jolts, and turn them into a freedom strategy. That is, after all, what they are there for. With each 'What was that?' moment in his life, there is a buried clue that suggests an alternative way of earning, spending, saving or accounting, hidden below. Most of the time, that alternative way will also be the road to freedom.

What Leo wants from you at this time is an understanding of his mad financial position. Counting on him for everything, all the time, at an agreed time and date, may not be such a good idea with Uranus in charge of his security. Instead, like him, you will have to learn to go with the flow, even when the flow is like a whirlpool in the middle of a tsunami.

Leo needs to be open to offbeat, unusual or innovative ways of managing his financial arrangements in these years. As long as these do not make his life any more erratic (financially speaking) than it has to be, it may well be that he will find the independence he wants, through the last set-up he imagined.

New ways of doing things — even rather loopy ways of doing things — could benefit him, as long as he is not so far out on a limb that he falls off the tree into a patch of nettles. Nevertheless, being open to progressive, new and different ways of doing business is the whole point of this cycle.

What Leo experiments successfully with, even if he is making it up as he goes along, could be ahead of its time. So — even though you are saddled with a financial or business partner who is about as reliable and solid as a Catherine wheel in these years — don't give up. What comes out of this period may well be radical, but as a financial method, practice or concept, it will also set Leo free and, one day, enable others to do the same.

New two- or three-way business, property or financial deals will be offered to Leo in these years. They will be exciting, come from nowhere — and need careful assessment. They are likely to offer only the most unpredictable returns — and a sudden loss is not out of the picture either. With Uranus in charge of his cash zone, Leo needs to be ready for anything!

THE VIRGO BOYFRIEND/HUSBAND TO MARCH 2011

Often, men in this cycle start affairs with this kind of think balloon in their heads: 'It's mad. It's exciting. She's totally wrong for me. It's never going to work. And I don't caaaaaare!' It all depends on how trapped he feels in his marriage or relationship; if there are lots of rules and ancient patterns being played out, Virgo might just use this cycle in his life to go for the most unlikely relationship, with the most unlikely person.

Remember, this outcome depends on how restricted he feels, and how brave/mad he's being about beginning an affair. Infidelity is not the general outcome of the Uranus cycle he's in now, although it's a definite risk that you both need to be aware of.

Much better, in the long run, is a radical revamp of the marriage or relationship you are already in. If it has become stale or predictable — or even non-authentic, in the sense that you're going through the motions of love — then you may need to shake things up, in order to let some oxygen in. Sometimes fate does that for you anyway: sudden, surprising events which affect the marriage or relationship may come at you from the outside world, prompting a change.

If you are relatively new in his life — in other words, if you've become partners in the time this book has come out — then you are likely to be remarkably different from his other partners. There is also likely to be a gap in age, experience, lifestyle, class, looks (or anything else you care to name) between you, and part of the excitement he feels about you comes down to one thing: you're different!

However, for one reason or another, the relationship with you is likely to be quite unpredictable. It may be down to you, it may be down to him, or it may be down to circumstances. Virgo may find it all a bit of a rollercoaster, though, with random chills, as well as totally unexpected thrills and spills. Uranus functions like an electrical storm, complete with lightning forks. It is free entertainment in many ways, but it is also a constant reminder that everything in life, love and nature is a strange experiment. That includes your marriage or relationship while Virgo is in this cycle.

A conventional wedding, marriage, de facto arrangement or relationship is not what Virgo should wish for at this time. It just won't work with the cycle he is in. It's far more likely that his love life will reflect the cutting-edge of tomorrow's social change; the new ways of living and loving the rest of us adopt in 2020 may well have been pioneered by Virgo years before.

Perhaps you're experimenting with an open marriage or relationship, or a unique custody arrangement, or living in separate homes — these are just three examples of classic Uranian relationships. If he was born in the 1960s, with Uranus close to his Sun, then he may well be one of the first Virgos to stick his hand up and volunteer for the new ways of dating, mating and relating. Cyberspace could have a lot to do with it, for one reason or another.

Individuality, independence and space will matter enormously to Virgo at this time. Can he hang onto those, and bond with a woman too? As you are one half of the equation, you will have to make sure it's possible. Alternatively, you might find that it's you who craves selfhood and freedom, and Virgo who is left wondering what happened to the 1950s' rules. Either way, you both get to learn about the power of one, as well as the power of two.

What he wants at this time, whether he is aware of it or not, is a connection which is honest. No faking, no compromising. Sexually and emotionally, the partnership has to be truthful, or else changes will have to be made, or fate will have to pull the rug. Either way, Uranus will get Virgo to feel the electricity.

Acts of rebellion are likely along the way. You may cut loose and curl your lip like Billy Idol (or, if you prefer, Sid Vicious). Alternatively, it may be Virgo who says he's mad as hell and he's just not going to take it any more. Through rebellion, the old rules are forced to change, or are thrown out of the window. Virgo may even try to work towards a no-rules situation if his craving for freedom is big enough. If you both agree that all these acts of rebellion are justified, then that's fine. But Virgo also has to prepare for the possibility that he is simply being an adolescent — or that you are! As always with this planet, a completely honest examination of the facts is the way through.

Uranus, the planet dominating his love life in this cycle, is about wildness. It's also about the buzz you feel when something is changing your world. Like a heat-seeking missile, Virgo will chase every woman who can offer him this now (if he is single), and if he is with you, he will simply chase every situation in the relationship that might lead to that. Some of them will be white-hot arguments, others will be impulsive holidays, sudden (surprising) conversations in the bath, or weekends of sexual experimentation. Give him anything in this cycle, but don't give him what he's had for the last five years.

The more you avoid tricky issues about the marriage or relationship (or the more he does), the likelier it is that Uranus will pull the rug. If you're faking happiness for the sake of the mortgage, the children, or because you're frightened of being single again (or if he is guilty of the same things), then by all means risk a conversation about the lack of happiness. To bury your heads in the sand, in this cycle, is to ask for a big sandstorm to come and blow you away. And on no account lock him in to your style of living and loving. The act of rebellion, when it comes, is likely to leave you gasping like a goldfish.

The potential is there for Virgo to invent, or even re-invent, a twenty-first century (even a twenty-second century) style relationship or marriage at this time. Will he succeed? He who dares often wins. That means separated and divorced Virgos too, by the way; perhaps they will be the first generation of men to organise a new kind of post-marital personal life, involving all the participants, without the usual hassles, heartache and angst!

THE VIRGO RELATIVE/FAMILY MEMBER TO NOVEMBER 2008

He has already seen more than one final chapter in his family circle since this cycle began in the late 1990s. There may have been the loss of a parent or other close relative — or some other kind of final chapter, as people have moved away, divorced or separated. Other family changes, too numerous to mention here, may also have killed off the old pattern, the old system, or the old set-up. That's Pluto's job, in the Fourth House of Virgo's chart — it transforms everything by making sure new space is cleared for a new beginning.

By 2008, every Virgo will have experienced at least one of these ending/beginning cycles, and possibly more. It is important for him to let go too. Releasing control over how things 'should' be with family members is the first step to allowing Pluto to do its work. It is unlikely he will ever be able to go back to the old version of family life he knew before this cycle began — and it's much better that he doesn't! Looking back, or hanging onto the past, will just hold up a natural process of family change.

Sometimes it is not a death or a departure which transforms the family, it is another taboo issue (quite unmentionable, except in a diary) which seems to drastically change things forever. If it all seems intense beyond belief, then both of you will know — Pluto is at work. Occasionally, skeletons in the closet fall out. Or a strange branch of the family tree reveals itself. Often, that can be enough to ring the changes for the way things used to be between parents, offspring and related parties.

The advice all astrologers give about Pluto cycles is the same: let go, and co-operate with what is taking place. What is taking place in his family life now is a natural, organic process, and trying to stop it is like trying to stop an apple falling from the tree, rotting and returning to the soil — or the growth of new seedlings when the soil has been fertilised, and the rain and sun have come. It's important for Virgo to trust that whatever (or whoever) goes at this time, it has its own organic process and its own agenda to follow — set by Mother Nature. In time, a new order will follow. A new version of the old family, or a new family. It is much better that Virgo willingly throws himself into the journey, even if he does occasionally feel as if he is descending into hell — in the end, experiencing the whole thing deeply and fully will speed the process.

His house or flat situation will also be affected in this cycle. It may already have come up, as Virgo has moved or renovated (maybe more than once), or dramatically seen one phase of his lifestyle end, to be replaced with another. Some of them emigrate in this cycle; others reconstruct their flat from top to bottom. Other possibilities: an intense period with flatmates, involving lots of change and crisis — or a dramatic change (up or down) in his living circumstances which redefines him, in relation to his family.

Here's a definite risk in this period: a power struggle with a live-in partner, parent, sibling, cousin, aunt, uncle or other close relative. Virgo needs to remember that if he takes the first step towards it, it is unlikely to go away any time soon. Pluto, the planet which produces power struggles and secret game-playing (and string-pulling), is here to 2008. If you allow yourself to participate in this desire to dominate (or the refusal to be dominated) you may well be stuck there for a year or two longer than you expected!

Is there anything toxic hidden under the floorboards, or buried underneath the property? Is there anything beginning to smell funny, tucked away in the storehouse of family secrets? In all cases, Pluto is likely to see it rising to the surface, if it hasn't already done so. Best thing to do? Put on the gloves and deal with it, as fully and deeply as possible. There is no point in skimming the surface, or trying to pretend this toxic stuff isn't there! Only when Virgo goes into things — be they home repairs or family questions — with full intention, and total fearlessness, can he begin to clear the way for a whole new home life.

THE LIBRA BOYFRIEND/HUSBAND MARCH 2011 TO MAY 2019

As 2011 kicks in, it's important for both of you to remember that the way it was before is not the way it's going to be in future! That will make the changes ahead — all of which are designed to bring Libra more freedom — easier to manage. If you have been in the kind of marriage or relationship where you always knew what was coming next, then the next few years will ask you to change your expectations. Expect the unexpected, and make friends with the big dipper of love and life — that's the best tactic with this new, strange cycle.

Libra may want things to stay the same, or he may consciously want them to change, but either way, the planet Uranus (in charge of his partnerships now) will shake up the pieces of the jigsaw puzzle and force him to put everything back together again in a new way. Old patterns will not work. If he's been the breadwinner, and you always had sex three times a week, and you always agreed not to have children — get ready. Before you know it, you could be out-earning him, you may find yourself pregnant with twins, and sex may vanish from your lives! Libra needs to learn this mantra off by heart now: all things are possible . . . expect everything.

If Libra is feeling strangled by the marriage or relationship, then nothing is going to stop him breaking free. It is better to face this need honestly, together, for obvious reasons. The solution may be an adapted version of your old relationship or marriage, with some radical plot twists or a new setting. Alternatively, it may well be that Libra decides the only way forward for him is single life.

Facing any craving for freedom together is certainly Libra's best strategy. If he goes wild, on his own terms, then he is likely to create more disruption in his private life than even he could have anticipated. This is no time to be a rebel without a cause, particularly if a love triangle is involved; it's unlikely to be the breath of fresh air he is searching for, and may, in the end, feel more like an electric shock.

If you come into his life once this cycle begins, then you will be the woman fate has chosen to shake him out of his old relationship patterns and love-life prejudices/expectations. Your presence in his life is very likely to raise eyebrows — you will either be drastically different from him in some way, or just remarkably different from his ex-wife or ex-girlfriend. In any case, you are the excitement he has been looking for.

Remember this, though — Uranus is the planet which hates a routine and dislikes order. So if you are hoping for a relationship which follows a well-worn plot, forget it. Your love life with Libra will probably follow an eccentric course at this time. Needless to say, the more you are open to change and new experiences, the less stressful things will be. Handle this cycle as you would handle an electrical storm. Duck and dive when you have to, and enjoy the show. If he's clever, Libra will find a way to harness all the wild, crackling energy he finds in his partnership with you, and use it to invent a new way to love and live. Uranus is the planet astrologers link to radical social change. While it passes through Libra's marriage and love zone, it's only fitting that he should be among the first to come up with a new way to co-habit, share, breed, date, mate, relate or even separate!

Libra, in his most unevolved state, could be guilty of big dumb rebellion in these years. It will do him no favours. Awareness is the first step (leave this book lying around), but your willingness to avoid dominating his space with restrictive rules and regulations is also vital. If you give him nothing to rebel against, what is there to kick?

Libra also needs to let go in this cycle. If you are the first to leave, or to demand changes (this can happen too), then it will be easier for him if he allows you the space to do this — and learns to release everything that came with your presence, from the income, to the social status, to the dreams.

Ouch! Uranus can throw you — just like a mild electric shock — and Libra needs to be aware of this. But its reward is this: once it has done its work, there is typically an incredible feeling of being fully alive.

This is the hardest thing to grasp about this cycle. On the surface, Uranus in the Seventh House of marriage and love sounds like a negative. It brings uncertainty, possible rebellion, radical change, and nothing which remotely resembles a 'normal' domestic or love-life situation. Sometimes it is there when a partner dies or departs — these are the facts.

What it brings, as a kind of exchange, is an exhilarating sense of freedom. Suddenly, there seem to be fewer ties, fewer shackles; more possibility. Until Libra goes through this Uranian process (and it can take many forms), he may never fully realise just how trapped he was in the structure of his own marriage or relationship. It's a little like living in a nice, safe (but dull) house for too long; it's only when a cyclone forces you to live somewhere else for a while that you realise just how much those four walls were locking you in.

That's the trade-off with this planet. If it comes wrapped in what appears to be 'bad news', then Libra needs to remember this: just like Virgo men, who had this cycle before him, the faster he can learn to surf the crazy waves, the more quickly he will discover the game the universe wants him to play. That game is called raw, real, exciting, thrilling LIFE, and although it can be a tremendous shock at first, in time he will come to see that even this wildly unpredictable cycle has its benefits too.

In its mildest form, this cycle will typically bring along a U-turn in the marriage or relationship, which is the last thing Libra expected — and he may do and say things which even he admits surprise him. His love life will start to feel more experimental, more exciting, less predictable. What he 'never' did, or 'never' entertained before, may become the norm!

Again, in its mildest form, this cycle will produce a woman (you, perhaps?) who is not the first choice he would normally make, or the first person his friends would expect to see by his side. And even though the relationship itself will never really be conventional or predictable, it will make him feel alive.

The cleverest and coolest Libran men will use these years to honestly address the issues of freedom, individuality and independence within a relationship, and work with their partners to find new set-ups which will better accommodate these needs. Instead of chaos, in other words, he will have creative solutions. And that can help you, as well as Libra, invent a totally new kind of partnership together, which in turn will help move the rest of us forward!

THE LIBRA RELATIVE NOVEMBER 2008 TO JANUARY 2024

Pluto will break down the old family set-up in these years and reassemble the pieces into a brand new structure. It's like watching children taking apart Lego and putting it back together again, though, admittedly, it may not feel like a game when it is happening!

What causes this change, or breakdown, is classically the death of a family member, or the departure of somebody else — perhaps through a divorce, or some other change. In other cases, there may be another issue to face for the family (probably quite taboo or off-limits) which also permanently reshapes the way things are between Libra and his parents, siblings, cousins, or other relatives. There may be a power struggle between family members which results in a total change in the chemistry, for example. Or there may be some other development which is extremely hard to openly discuss, but nevertheless seems to permanently end what was there before, in terms of family structure.

Does this mean Libra should tiptoe into the future in fear? Absolutely not. The whole point of astrology is to bring understanding and empowerment. Weirdly, it is when this cycle is operating at full strength (some years will be more intense than others) that understanding and empowerment will come from letting go.

Whenever Pluto affects us, it tends to make us feel that we don't have control of a situation any more. Here's a tip for Libra — don't fight it. By giving in to what is essentially a process of nature, he stands to gain, long-term. A new chapter in Libra's family life is waiting to be written. It cannot begin, though, until the old chapter has been thrown onto the fire, or recycled into something new. Life is made up of new chapters. If it wasn't, we'd all give up on it. That is something which astrologers know very well about Pluto —

to resent the process of change it brings, or to try and fight it, is to get in the way of growth.

Pluto rules any word beginning with the prefix 're' — recycle, repair, renew, revolutionise, rethink. That's exactly what will happen to Libra's family in these years. He is an Air sign, so he is able to detach himself from emotional situations and observe them from a distance. This will be useful in these years; Libra needs to understand that the more fully and deeply he throws himself into the process of letting go, the faster the process of change will be, and the more quickly he can move into phase two of family life — the new beginning.

Pluto works slowly. Don't expect this process of change to be obvious, in an upfront way, every day that this cycle is operating. Events will build up, piece by piece, hit a peak, and then go through a sequence of reverberating waves, like a ripple effect, until the change is complete. Watch the life cycle of anything that lives, decays, dies — and spawns new life — and you will see Pluto at work. From the death (or ending) of everything in the world comes some kind of new beginning.

If there is anything in Libra's family which is like the bottom of Oscar the Grouch's trash can, it will certainly show itself in this cycle. Rubbish must be cleared, issues must be faced, the can must be emptied and cleaned out.

Just like real rubbish, anything which Pluto brings up which is ignored or buried again tends to create a whiff after a while. Thus, for Libra, it is better that he takes things on as they happen, rather than pushing them away. Pluto is affecting his family life for many years, and the whiff of unresolved questions will take just as long to disappear, unless he rolls up his sleeves and does something about it.

Libra's house or flat situation will also be subject to the most intense process of change in this cycle. He could move a lot, or begin dramatic renovations. He may emigrate, or shift neighbourhoods, in a way which completely changes everything, from his career to his social status.

If he's been in the same place, living the same way, forever — then this cycle will be quite dramatic. Anything which has built up about the house, or flat, which isn't going to serve him over the next couple of decades will have to be changed. Alternatively, it may leave his life completely.

THE SCORPIO FLING/PARTNER TO MARCH 2011

I mention the word 'fling' in this section, because so many single Scorpio men will be throwing themselves into one night, one week, one month encounters during these years. Not all of them, of course, but — according to astrology — a higher percentage than usual. Scorpio is having a Uranus cycle to 2011. That means sex is sudden, wild, exciting, and has absolutely no connection to the world of conventional relationships.

What if this is your regular partner? Is he more likely to have a one-night stand these days? The truthful answer is, yes — if he's feeling trapped, bored and confined by your relationship or marriage.

Sex is a particular issue here. If Scorpio feels he is compromising or faking, or if he feels that you are locked into a routine, he is far more likely to experiment with alternatives outside your relationship now. That means anything from internet porn to a real live mistress. So . . . what to do?

Scorpio needs to make an ally of you, and you need to address the reality of your sex life. The planet Uranus is at work in these years, and it won't let either of you get away with a relationship which isn't allowing him to feel fully alive. So if it's the missionary position on Monday night, and him babysitting on Sunday while you see your girlfriends — forget it. More than anything else, this cycle is about kicking over the structure and changing it (sometimes losing it altogether) so that real life is allowed to break in again and he can be a Wild Man (capital W, capital M, if you don't mind).

What restarts the electricity for Scorpio now? Total honesty. In fact, even though it is likely to give one or the other of you heart palpitations, even a frank discussion about what is/isn't working in the marriage or relationship might just help both of you reinvent it.

The sex may become eccentric. You may even be shocked by what he wants. But better out than in, so to speak. Covering up, burying or suppressing what (or who) really makes him come alive sexually is only going to cause problems later. That's the rule with Uranus, the planet of honesty. Admit what excites you, and own up to what bores you, and then . . . deal.

If you have come along recently, or if you turn up in his life from now to 2011, then you are likely to play out a different pattern with Scorpio. This relationship game is called 'What the %$£ now?' and it's all about the thrills, spills and uncertainty of a wildly exciting relationship based on no guarantees whatsoever, but a tremendous amount of electricity.

Whose fault is it? It may be his, because he's unable to make plans and stick to them, or because his life is so full of X factors that you can never pin the relationship down. It may be yours, because you're hardly ever there (maybe you're a flight attendant), or because you blow hot and cold, or because just when you think you've got time together, your ex rings up wanting you to take the kids . . . the possibilities are numerous. Any combination of factors could be keeping this relationship unstable.

One thing is sure. If you look more deeply into this strange world full of question marks, surprises — and occasional bolts from the blue — you will find that Scorpio is getting masses of emotional and sexual freedom from the deal. This applies even if he moans about the way things are, or sighs and shrugs his shoulders. Stand back from the relationship you both have and examine it, and you will see that — delightfully — this is one of the very few affairs or partnerships he has had which doesn't tie him up or rope him down.

The entire subject of pregnancy, fatherhood, terminations, miscarriages, adoptions, sons, daughters, stepchildren and fertility treatment also has to be addressed in this section. Once again, the unpredictable planet Uranus is at work in these years, so it is better for Scorpio that he abandons any expectation of a normal or conventional path.

Some practical rules apply, though. If he doesn't want a baby, then he should always wear a condom, and if it breaks, which it may, make sure he's got the number of a 24-hour chemist for emergency contraception. And if he is on the trail of fertility treatment or adoption, then it is better to expect the unexpected. Libran men, who had this cycle before him, may be good sources of advice and encouragement in surfing the crazy waves to fatherhood.

What if the kids are at school, or adults in their own right? Then Scorpio will also find a change of rules. If there is anything about the father–child structure which is limiting him, on any level, it will need to alter. He may be in charge of these changes himself, or they may just happen — as fate takes a hand, and the universe decides to shake up the snowdome.

The father–child relationship in these years is unlikely to be 'normal' or 'the way it used to be' and it will be much easier for Scorpio if he accepts this. The challenge here is to invent a new way to be a father — and to understand that even real disruption with a son or daughter (mad behaviour or total rebellion, for example) has its own function.

Anything which shakes it up at this time will also wake him up. That illuminating wake-up call can help to alert Scorpio to a whole new set of possibilities for parenthood. The golden rule? Forget the status quo, as everything and anything is now possible as a parent, and yet no matter how surprising, shocking or even chaotic life becomes, it will also ultimately lead to more freedom in the parent–child relationship.

Scorpio men who will experience the most disruption as parents, and/or partners, are those who have organised their personal lives into neat, orderly patterns — because it's safer that way. If Scorpio is totally out of touch with his life, then he may not be living as a lover or father at all; instead, he might just be going through the motions.

Cue instant shake-up! The famous 'whammo!' effect of this cycle is likely to have a much bigger impact if Scorpio is leading an artificial life, in the interests of not rocking the boat. And that's when the world of parenthood, or love and sex, is most likely to become . . . a little weird.

The key to this cycle? A willingness to forget what is normal, nice or 'expected' of him as a partner and/or parent; and the courage to face what is really going on in his heart, and in his underpants. In addition, the courage to experiment with life and love in a way that means his own freedom does not come at the expense of you — or the children. As with all Uranus cycles, this one is (to quote the Bee Gees) staying alive; in this case, a greater feeling of 'aliveness' for Scorpio will be his reward for courageously surfing the crazy emotional or sexual waves, without hurting those around him. If he accidentally invents a radical new way to be a parent or partner in these years, so much the better. His life experiments can show the rest of us how.

THE SCORPIO RELATIVE TO FEBRUARY 2012

If Scorpio is your father, your brother, your uncle, your cousin, your grandfather — or if he is the father of your own children — then you will already be familiar with his confusion about home and family issues.

This cycle has been in place for a few years as I write this book (in 2006), and it won't end until 2012, when Scorpio will be astonished at how clear everything becomes. In fact, it may feel as if he's finally got glasses with the right prescription. That's how dazzling life becomes, when Neptune finally moves on. When it happens at last, he may feel as if the scales have been whisked away from his eyes, and suddenly the world of home and family will be revealed as it really is, in sharp relief.

Neptune is the planet which is dominating his house, flat, family and flatmate zone at the moment. You'll notice it most in connection with real estate, decorating or renovating plans; everything is a dream, a vision or a wild fantasy. Reality may have very little to do with any of it. Scorpio will go from being inspired at this time to being utterly vague — and even totally dazed — about what is possible.

He is likely to idealise and glamorise the home of his dreams, or even the neighbourhood/region/country of his fantasies, in this period. Reality will not get a look-in. The closer he gets, the closer nirvana will seem . . . however, in this cycle, Scorpio will also have to deal with the process of losing his illusions. The place he obsessed about with rose-tinted glasses for so long may well turn out to have flaws after all, and the come-down may be hard.

Your concern about all this fantasising should primarily be practical and/or financial. Will his palace mean a mortgage that neither of you can really afford? Will the country of his dreams actually have a job for you, when you get there? It may help to have other people who act as a reality check at this time: mutual friends he respects, or others who've trodden the same path and learned.

He may be confused about where home actually is in this cycle — or what it really means. The confusion may come from too much moving around, or from the fact that his roots have become ill-defined after family changes. Once again, once this period is over, he'll be much clearer about where he belongs.

All in his family may not be as it appears during this time. Not only the world at large, but Scorpio himself, may be looking at a version of reality which is far from the truth. Will the mirage remain? It depends on his own personal chart and the other cycles he is experiencing. Sometimes, this cycle coincides with a real revelation about the truth surrounding a parent, aunt, uncle, grandparent, sibling or other close relative.

He will make a sacrifice for the family in this cycle, or a sacrifice for a specific family member. The nature of the sacrifice (exactly what it is he gives up) will depend on the situation — but there may be a sense that he is being something of a martyr. Neptune needs careful handling. If the sacrifice is made from pure love and compassion (no ulterior motives) and if the outcome can only be for the best, then this one act may well be the thing that takes him higher, spiritually, and ultimately lifts his soul.

Not every sacrifice is justified, though, and not every act of sainthood/martyrdom is necessarily wise or even necessary. In these years, it can be useful for Scorpio to find a wise friend or confidant/e to act as a sounding board.

Even the simplest aspects of domestic life — the rules of leases, mortgages, builders' contracts — need special attention in this cycle. Scorpio needs to be absolutely clear about what he is agreeing to, before he supplies a signature. The same advice applies to issues around emigration, citizenship or even passports — anything connected to his homeland needs cautious handling, so the famous Neptunian confusion does not set in.

On the plus side, Neptune is all about inspiration, and it can be an incredible, creative force in Scorpio's life now. His imagination could help to turn a drab flat into a real-life wonderland, and a parched garden into a luxurious tropical jungle. Once again, as long as the visions are attainable, he could actually get the real-estate nirvana he is looking for — or, perhaps, the cliched 'dream lifestyle' that glossy magazines are full of.

A sacrifice will be involved if reality is to approach his dreams. That's part of the deal with Neptune — it may be time, energy, money, or something even more personal and precious. Scorpio may turn the pictures in his mind into reality, but Neptune's cycle is unlikely to give him a free ride. Something, or someone, will always have to be given up!

Chaos is a predictable part of this cycle. It may be family chaos (foggy patches when nothing is clear) or domestic chaos (the disarray that results from chasing dreams, before the removalists have unpacked the boxes). What Scorpio wants from you now, though, is an understanding that he is channelling his highest ideals, visions, dreams and improbable fantasies through the home front. What he needs? A sensible second opinion, so that what he gives up for the family, or for his picture of a dream home, is actually reasonable, viable and achievable too.

THE SAGITTARIUS RELATIVE TO MARCH 2011

The changes which have been affecting his family to date — and will continue to affect Sagittarius until 2011 — are not the kind which are easy to adjust to. Is it the way they arrive? (So sudden, so unexpected.) Or, alternatively, it is the way they unfold? (Life sometimes appears to come without an instruction manual.)

The more fixed or routine the family situation was in the 1980s and/or '90s, the more extreme the changes have been. This is because Uranus, the planet now in charge of the Sagittarian home zone, is all about ending established patterns. If your brother, father, cousin, uncle or other close relative (even the father of your own children at home) was part of a very fixed family structure before, then the U-turns in his destiny will seem all the more remarkable.

Until 2011, any aspect of family life which traps or confines Sagittarius will be changed. It may be his choice, it may not — but destiny has a strange way of making sure that freedom rules now. What takes place is likely to be sudden, and maybe in circumstances which are unusual, odd or one-of-a-kind. Sometimes Sagittarius will adapt (there are likely to be a series of changes in this period), and sometimes he will feel as if he has just been given a series of mild electric shocks. The end result is always the same though — a radical departure from the old set-up, clearing the way for a new family life which gives him more room to move.

The more prepared he is for the family to change in these years, the easier the changes will be. That's where astrology can help. This cycle can only happen to Sagittarius every eighty years or so, and it's happening now. Being open, and flexible, is the best way to handle it.

There may be rebellion in the ranks in this period. He may rebel against a family member, or one of his close relatives may decide to speak out or act against the clan rules. Sometimes the rebellion will be justified, as it's clear that some rules are made to be broken. Sometimes it may not! Over time, Sagittarius will come to know the difference, both in his own reactions, and those of parents, siblings, cousins or other family connections.

The challenge with this planet is to invent a new way of operating — in a way which is creative and courageous. Whatever may affect the family circle in this cycle is there to guide Sagittarius towards a different kind of domestic or clan existence. Life as an original statement is what this period is all about.

Often, the process begins with disruption: departures, sometimes deaths, often the arrival of a situation affecting the family which nobody could have anticipated, which has its own weird shape! It is at the point at which the hand of fate is shaking up the snowdome most violently, though, that Sagittarius needs to understand he will feel most alive. Think about electricity (which Uranus rules). It turns everything upside down (night becomes day), it can shock people when they are least expecting it (when lightbulbs blow, or when electric fences are switched on), and yet it also gives us more life in our days. Without electricity, we would spend half our time on the planet living a kind of reduced existence.

For Sagittarius, this analogy with electricity might be useful in the years ahead. No matter what happens to shake up the family he has known all his life (or the family patterns) there will be a kind of free life-booster, along with all the unpredictability. The energy that pulses through Sagittarius when he has to deal with unexpected shake-ups will also give him a bigger sense of possibility. Another analogy — remember how it feels when you fly into a foreign city, late at night, and see all the lights? That mixture of excitement, weirdness, adrenaline and sudden aliveness is a blast of Uranian energy. And it will hit Sagittarius through family developments on many occasions in this cycle. The trick, for him, is to be ready for anything and everything, and to accept that it is change which keeps everything, including him, throbbing.

'It isn't in the plan' is a familiar complaint from Sagittarius in this cycle. What he had anticipated, in terms of the lease, the mortgage, the renovations, the decorators or the flatmates, is most unlikely to unfold. Instead, like a Monty Python foot, the cosmic forces are likely to crush cherished plans and expectations, and introduce new elements which even the most gifted psychic would have a problem predicting.

Clinging to anything about the home front in this cycle is not a great idea. What he 'always knew' would happen with the house or flat, what he 'always wanted' and 'what's always been there' are probably going to be the first things to be thrown out in the wake of inevitable change.

Sagittarius may also start his own revolution in this cycle. So, if he's feeling confined or restricted by the place where he's living, or the region where he's put down roots, you may have to deal with upheaval, as he either converts the attic into an office, or carts you off to the nearest foreign embassy for a residency visa.

If you live with him, it should now be obvious that you need to be ready for almost anything. His domestic status quo will also be yours, to some extent, so no matter if he's knocking down walls in the middle of the night, or dealing with a sudden family 'situation', you will have to be there, be tolerant, and be open to the possibility of constant change.

As always with Uranian cycles, the way to cope is to surf. Watch the way professional surfers take the waves and come up smiling. Not knowing what is coming next — but making the most of it when it arrives — is the key to the kind of life force that only this planet can deliver.

THE SAGITTARIUS FLING/PARTNER MARCH 2011 TO MAY 2019

His sex life will be unique in these years. He doesn't want what the other men in the restaurant are having, and he certainly won't want the same dish you've been enjoying — yes, even enjoying — since the 1990s. Is this shocking news? Shortly after 2011 comes into view, it won't surprise him at all. Typically, the planet Uranus (which dominates his sex life now) is felt several months before it actually changes signs and starts to do its work.

How unique will the fling, affair or marriage be at this time? If he has planets in Aquarius, then prepare for something you haven't even read about. It may involve anything from extended orgasm to protracted periods of celibacy. What other people find eccentric now is what excites Sagittarius most. What he's after, most of all, is freedom — and whatever gives him freedom will be first on his menu, even if it also disrupts what was there before.

Rebellious acts may be common now. You may rebel against what you do in bed, or when you do it, or how often you do it — thus acting out the plot that will change the way you make love. Alternatively, it may be Sagittarius who suddenly says things can't go on as they are. Either way, the version of bedtime you have from 2011 to 2019, compared to the way it used to be, will be remarkably, radically different.

Is his private life stifling his self-expression on any level? This is such a difficult question, but it must be faced now. If he's going through the motions, following the rules, doing what he thinks he's supposed to do, not what he feels — then the snowdome of his life will definitely be shaken up.

If your relationship or marriage is a structure that has been created for financial, mortgage, social status or 'family' reasons, and if it has become hollow inside, or stale on any level, this cycle will be dramatic. Knowing it is coming will help Sagittarius, as rather than opening and shutting his mouth like a stranded goldfish, he will be able to proactively handle the changes.

The first change? Total honesty. Uranus is the planet that likes to keep things real. Without it, we would all feel half-dead, or be living our lives in darkness. So, no matter how much of a zap factor Sagittarius may experience once 2011 is underway, he needs to remember this: it's all about facing himself in the mirror without any cover-ups, and about facing you too. From this honesty, real progress can come.

What happens if a relationship or affair is really dead in the water? Sagittarius needs to do one of two things — either radically change it, or leave it altogether. Trying to stop this process is rather like trying to stop a storm. It's impossible. And in his love life, as in nature, storms are necessary and natural.

Children, babies, pregnancy, abortion, adoption, fertility treatment, stepchildren, sons, daughters and other people's kids (godchildren, for example) also come under the Uranian influence at this time. He may well change his mind about being a father, to a degree which stuns you and shocks him. Or he may follow the general aims he had, in relation to kids, before this cycle started — but find fate takes him on an unpredictable pathway.

Once again, freedom is what Uranus is all about. So even if the changes are disruptive in this cycle, freedom is ultimately what Sagittarius will gain. If the parent–child relationship is false on any level, or if his version of being a dad is stifling his soul, you can bet that something will happen. A son or daughter may rebel, or face major life changes. Or Sagittarius may throw out the old rules, or find that destiny intervenes and presents him with a life-changing situation where the rules have to change anyway.

Astrologers are unlikely to tell any Sagittarian in this period that the path of parenthood will be predictable. This strongly applies to adoption and fertility treatment. Surprise pregnancy is a common result of Uranian cycles through the solar Fifth House; if he doesn't want unplanned parenthood, then his bedroom drawers should become a veritable palace of condoms, both flavoured and unflavoured.

Kids and babies are the key to surprises — both okay and not so okay — in this cycle. Being ready to surf with the wildest of waves will help him. So will your tolerance and openness to change if you are the mother of his children, or the lover in his life. Sometimes the children will not be his own at all — they may be part of work-related issues, or just nieces/nephews/godchildren. Young people are the key to shaking it all up for him, though — and particularly in any area of his psyche where he has closed down to life's possibilities.

Boredom is just not possible in this cycle. Sexually, emotionally, and where children are concerned, life will be somewhere between the strangest fireworks display he has ever seen (nobody knows what the start time is, or the finish time) or a series of electric shocks. The famous jolting effect of Uranus is not designed to disrupt our lives without a good reason, though; through him, and his life choices, the rest of us will (in time) learn how to handle life and love in a truly twenty-first century way. What Sagittarius makes up on the spot, in his inventive handling of new challenges, will help the rest of us (particularly Capricorns, who get this cycle next) to work out new, impressively modern and progressive ways of managing relationships.

THE CAPRICORN RELATIVE MARCH 2011 TO MAY 2019

Capricorn will experience Uranus in his Fourth House of family in these years. The American astrologer Caroline W. Casey says that Uranus 'plucks us from what is not our life in order to cast us into what is really our life'. The British astrologer Patric Walker used to describe Uranus cycles as the winds of change. Either way, in your family, Capricorn will be at the centre of something which will occasionally blow at gale-force strength.

The issue about what is not his life is worth following up. If there is anything about Capricorn's family circle which is deadening his life force — even if he is apparently quite comfortable with it — then the universe will have a strange way of shaking it all up. The universe will re-route him if there is anything limiting, false or somehow not truly *authentic* about the way things are with the family. If the way things are with parents, siblings, cousins, aunts, uncles or other relatives is preventing Capricorn from truly moving forward in his life, then change will have to take place. Sometimes, that change can seem disruptive. It all depends on how ready Capricorn is to accept the flow of life — in all its different currents.

A current is a good way to describe what is happening from 2011 to 2019, as it also describes electricity, which is a Uranian force. Some changes in the family circle will create a buzz now; others will definitely border on the unmistakeable 'kick' of an unexpected shock on a live wire. Flexibility is a great help at such times. It is not Capricorn's usual approach to life (he is cautious rather than bendy), but being a rubber-band man will get him through. Circumstances affecting the family will probably arrive out of the blue, like a lightning bolt on a golf course. Because the situation is such a one-off, it's unlikely that anything in Capricorn's experience will have prepared him for what is to come. Consequently, he needs to learn to bend, to sway, to 'take' the kick, and then to work his way around this new development. Inventing a new or different way to manage family life is part of what Capricorn's path will be about in these years.

There will be moments when everything will be shaken up in family life, to the point where almost every old rule or expectation has to be changed. As a rule, the more static or stale the family system has become to Capricorn (whether he is conscious of it or not), the greater the reshuffle will be. Anything, from a divorce, to a death, to a change in a family business, can prompt the change. With Uranus, life is wholly unpredictable, so not even an astrology book can predict the exact nature of the developments ahead.

At this point, Capricorn may already be looking over his shoulder. But all he really has to do is pretend he is whitewater rafting in his canoe of choice. Managing the currents as they arrive will take him on a journey which is part thrill, part spill — and no doubt utterly terrifying at times, as there is no map.

In astrology, though, this is a journey that many men can say they have already accepted, and survived. Scorpios and Sagittarians, for example, have taken this path before; when Capricorn needs advice, he should listen to their experiences.

Every family has its own dynamic. It might be a power structure (mum in charge, brother second-in-command) or a financial or class system (sister married up, aunt married down). The variations in each person's family system are endless, and Capricorn will have his own. Uranian changes in these years will profoundly alter the way the family functions, and the way he relates to those in his clan. Uranus may knock down one domino, and the resulting effect could tumble down across the generations; it really depends how ripe things are for change.

This cycle also affects his house or flat situation, and flatmate relationships. Capricorn may initiate change at this time, either by moving, decorating or renovating. If so, the change is likely to be radical, and surprise himself as much as it surprises other people — it may literally be the last property, or the last area, that he or anyone else would have predicted he might choose.

Once again, if Capricorn's house or flat situation is restricting him and the universe can see more exciting and life-enhancing possibilities for him elsewhere, the Monty Python foot of fate may descend, and he may find himself forced to move, or being pushed hard to knock down the kitchen wall by the new love of his life!

Liberation is the Uranian word to beat all other Uranian words. In this cycle, no matter what happens, there will be genuine moments of liberation and breakthrough for Capricorn, enlightening him fully about what had to change and why — even if (at the time) it may not be so clear. Being free to be truly yourself, and lead a life which is truly about you (and not about some fake or compromised version of what you feel you should be), is the challenge now. Capricorn will take this challenge on, as a tenant, home-owner, family man, son, brother, uncle or cousin. And although the trip will be a mystery tour, it will also lead to the liberation that Uranus always promises.

THE CAPRICORN FLING/PARTNER JUNE 2011 TO JUNE 2012

Even though this cycle lasts for just twelve months, it offers Capricorn opportunities to add babies or children to his world (his own or other people's) and to expand and improve his sex life. What's more, although this Jupiter cycle repeats around every twelve years, in this particular 2011–2012 period, it hooks up with a trine (the best possible pattern) to powerful Pluto, so those opportunities will be life-changing.

If he is single in this period, he will be presented with one, two or more opportunities to date, mate and relate in a way which makes him genuinely empowered. Capricorn's image or public face is changing in this period — somehow, those changes will also help him find lovers who can give him the sexual growth his soul requires. Classically, Jupiter in the solar Fifth House coincides with lots more shagging/lots more learning ... or just one spectacularly important relationship which allows the lucky lover in question (him) enough time, space and opportunity to take his sexual self-expression to the next level.

If he has been in a drought before this cycle begins, he will have few complaints once it is underway. The caveat, though, is simple: Jupiter will open the doors; it is up to Capricorn to take off his jeans and go through them. This planet only offers opportunities; it does not make a reluctant man begin a fling or relationship if he simply is not interested.

For the most part, though, this should be a time of booming possibilities for erotic exploration, either with one partner or several. And if an e-mail flirtation is all that's required, that may well be what Capricorn gets — but even cyber-sex in this cycle is likely to help him grow and evolve.

In a steady relationship or marriage, if there have been problems or obstacles to date (anything from impotence issues to child-related exhaustion) then Jupiter may clear these out of the way. It is what is called a benefic in traditional astrology, a word which is closely related to beneficial. It's commonly called the lucky planet, and Capricorn may simply find his luck is in with you in this twelve-month period; the sex just gets better without effort, or there is more of it, or you go to a tantric yoga course and come back like a cross between Madonna and Aphrodite.

Children (his own and other people's) and pregnancy are related to this cycle too. Every twelve years or so, Jupiter comes along to boost this area of his life, so the chances are he'll become a first-time father, a fourth-time father, or even an adoptive parent or stepdad. He may find a niece, nephew or godchild in his life, or become more involved with children through his work or hobbies. Where possible, Jupiter will find an opening in the fence and put itself through — this planet seeks out all options and possibilities in order to add a dose of children/childhood to a man's world whenever it passes through the Fifth House.

If he has a son or daughter and there have been problems, Jupiter will help clear them. If he's proactive, the planet's influence will act like a booster to his own efforts. No problems? Then a son or daughter will simply expand life's possibilities for him — by winning awards, bringing him grandchildren, marrying into a family he likes, or by bringing good luck by some other route. Again, Jupiter will find a gap in the fence wherever it can, to make sure a son or daughter brings benefits in this cycle.

Creativity also benefits hugely from this period. If Capricorn has always longed to learn guitar, stage his own art exhibition, learn how to act — or pursue any other form of professional play or weekend self-expression — then this is the time to say yes to all the opportunities that come his way.

Capricorns who are already in jobs where they turn fun into work, or where creativity is paramount, may find this to be an astonishingly productive period, full of breakthroughs and growth. Jupiter is the bigger and better planet — so his sphere of influence may increase, or his work/hobbies may earn him money, or he may just go from learning the banjo to playing lead guitar. It all depends on what he invites into his life, and what he is ready for. But one thing is sure: creatively, sexually and where children are concerned, his luck is in. Add the trine from Pluto in his own sign too, and it's likely to be luck that changes his life and brings him a greater sense of empowerment than he thought possible.

THE AQUARIUS FRIEND TO NOVEMBER 2008

He has already been involved in one long-running power struggle with your network of friends — or with some other group of people, like a rock band, a football team or a political party. Knowing Aquarius, he's been in and out of groups (formal or informal) for his entire life anyway. Since the '90s, any of these networks, from share accommodation households to astrology learning groups, has probably been the source of significant game-playing.

This is not his usual style. But there is something about a long-running Pluto cycle which raises questions about who pulls the strings, who has the ability to pull rank, and who ultimately controls the game or calls the shots. Typically, since Pluto moved in a few years ago, Aquarius will have either pitted his own survival techniques against the group as a whole, or found himself in a group scenario with one player who seems to be determined to dominate.

The episode may have been short and sharp, or it may have been a long, drawn-out scenario — for example, with a small group of people in the workplace. At this point in his destiny, though, Aquarius needs to remember the rules with Pluto: no matter how tempting (or totally compelling) a struggle for dominance or power may be, resist the game, or prepare to play it to the end.

Here's another typical Pluto experience in this period: a friendship ends, but is recycled later, in a different form — as a business partnership perhaps, or even as a relationship. Sometimes, the friendship just dies, to be reborn as a totally different kind of social connection.

What does he want now? A group or friendship which is intense enough, and deep enough, to allow him to transform it. There is no other way he can realistically change the people in the group, the nature of the group — or the friendship. As a result, if you happen to be the friend in the group, or involved, you will need to understand his need to wade in and make changes. No Aquarian likes to think of himself as controlling. Heaven forbid he should be accused of trying to mould or shape the way people naturally are; nevertheless, with Pluto around, there may be a hidden desire to do just that. It will help Aquarius enormously if he examines himself and his motives, and drags the whole issue out into the light where he can look at it properly!

Sometimes groups end in this cycle. Sometimes friends die, or go away for good. Whatever dies now will be resurrected though, as Pluto takes things to the next level. A friendship or group involvement which survives the crises that Pluto is famous for will become extremely powerful by the very fact that it has emerged, unscathed, from the ashes. Once a friendship or group has been dragged through the Plutonian tumble-drier of hell, it has a way of emerging with added fibre later on. That's the rule with this planet — what doesn't kill a group or friendship makes it stronger.

Aquarius will have some influential or powerful friends around him in this cycle. Real movers and shakers or string-pullers. People with Scorpio planets may also be around him, and he has a lot to learn from their depth, their intensity, their passion, their obsessions, and the way they play the power game. At a guess, if someone who was born late September through late December is in his life, s/he is very likely to have one or more planets in this sign, and could be a central figure in the endless changes which Pluto brings.

Life will often seem like a real-life episode of *Big Brother*, *Survivor* or other group-related television programmes in these years. Quite a few famous Aquarian types have already been on these shows too — from John Lydon to Germaine

Greer, they have all learned about people politics and survival from Pluto in their zone of groups.

What Aquarius stands to learn in this cycle is the Three Musketeers rule — 'One for all and all for one' — and the viability (or otherwise) of trying to play that game. Is he more powerful when he joins forces with a group or teams up with a friend, or will he find more control by dominating these people, beating them, or just trying to change them?

In any event, it is usually the group which changes Aquarius — even though it may take some time for him to realise what has actually happened. Certainly, the importance of team effort will be drummed into him in this cycle, along with the basics he needs to learn about group chemistry and the real dynamics of power between friends or a small network.

Any friend, or group commitment, which has too much garbage, or too much toxic history, will not survive this cycle. It will either have to change completely, or it will have to exit his life. This is a hard rule with Pluto, the great rubbish-collector and recycler, and yet by this stage of the twenty-first century, I suspect Aquarius is already coming to know it quite well!

One final point: if a friend dies in this cycle, then the friendship itself will transform and recycle as a purely spiritual connection for Aquarius. The role that the friend plays after s/he has passed on will be just as significant as the role taken up during his/her lifetime, and Aquarius may even find that the departed friend starts to play a more powerful part in his life. If Aquarius is open to life after death — and a high percentage of these men are — then a friend who leaves the planet at this time may well re-emerge on the other side, to make contact. Pluto is the planet of death and resurrection, and if Aquarius is open to this idea, anything is possible! Remember, its job is to recycle, renew and revolutionise whatever (or whoever) is in the departure lounge of life . . .

THE AQUARIUS RELATIVE JUNE 2011 TO JUNE 2012

Your Aquarian father, son, brother, uncle or cousin (or other clan connection) will make the most of the family in this cycle, boosted not only by Jupiter, the planet of opportunity, but also by Pluto, which changes whatever it touches and ultimately adds power to the mix.

If there have been problems for, or through, family members, then Jupiter will provide opportunities to fix the issues, or a stroke of luck may remove the source of the problem by a simple twist of fate.

Jupiter expands the area of life it influences, rather like a cosmic bicycle pump, so the Aquarian's family may grow at this time, or if he has some other kind of clan (like a collection of flatmates, or a partner and several animals) then there may be additions to the entourage. Jupiter's key words are bigger and better; in this cycle, Aquarius will find that things open up and increase in his clan or family circle.

There are usually real estate pay-offs now. He may find the rental (or house-sitting arrangement) of his dreams, with more room, better facilities, bigger views, or a better area to live in. His property, if he owns one, may soar in value, or he may be in a lucky position to renovate or decorate and get amazing deals.

Aquarius could acquire more room to move just by dating, or marrying, someone who has extra real estate to share. He could also find a genuine bargain at auction, or through word of mouth; this is one year when he should cruise slowly past every real estate agency window he sees, and scan all the property advertisements in the newspapers or online.

If his usual living space is too cramped or small, or just limits his options, that will change — if he takes the opportunity — in this cycle. Of course, nobody can force an Aquarian's hand (least of all you) but there will be some intriguing possibilities now, and if he refuses, he will not see them for another twelve years.

This is a classic cycle for home improvement. Trees blocking views will disappear, cluttered hallways will become open spaces, attics will become lofts, and dingy entrances may suddenly acquire extra steps. Aquarius may do all this himself, or, if he is renting, suddenly find his landlord wants to be generous.

Aquarius needs to watch opportunities around May in particular, when the Sun joins Jupiter in the Fourth House of his chart and some dazzling luck comes his way. This may be the period which confirms his plans, or meets his hopes — or something new may come along, which changes everything for him, and opens up the home front in a spectacular way.

If Aquarius is looking for luck or support in this period (a safety net, or an option) then he should turn to the home front first, as astrological tradition says that it's likely to come from a relative, a flatmate, or someone connected with his home in some way.

His homeland — the country he considers his own — could also be the source of some luck in this period, and for all sorts of reasons. Fate has a funny way of delivering when Jupiter is around, and this year it's time for Aquarius to collect his cosmic, karmic rewards.

THE PISCES FRIEND NOVEMBER 2008 TO JANUARY 2024

If your friendship with Pisces survives these years, it will change shape and transform on the deepest level, becoming far more powerful in the process. If it doesn't survive, it may be because it belongs to his past, not his future. If so, Pisces needs to learn to let go, rather than hang on.

His social life will revolutionise during this cycle, with his usual circle or network changing beyond belief. There may be departures, or big lifestyle changes (marriage or children, emigration or other passages) which alter the chemistry that he and his friends share. The group, the team, the gang which he knew so well before 2008 is unlikely to remain the same.

Of course, from 2008 to 2024 is a long time, and most people could be expected to hit significant passages, from divorce to redundancy, in this period. And if he's a Pisces already in middle age, the illness or even deaths of some friends could also be statistically thrown into the 'high chance' basket.

Something is different about this cycle, though, and it goes beyond the usual changes Pisces might expect to see among his friends. There will typically be an intensity and an emotional depth about what takes place that permanently transforms the social landscape. The domino effect which results from changes with one friend may go on to affect the whole circle.

Pisces will make new friends and join new groups in this cycle which invite power or control issues. Just as he learned so much about people politics in the workplace before 2008, he will now be asked to take what he has experienced and use it to navigate his social life or group commitments.

Groups, in this context, can be anything from work-related networks of people (usually working teams) to rock groups, language classes, book groups or sports teams. With Pluto around, escaping complex questions about who dominates whom, and who pulls the strings, will be hard. The idea is to allow a new balance of power to emerge from the remains of what was there before. Such a balance of power should, hopefully, assist not only Pisces, but also his friends — and the world around them. The new balance of

power should help the general good when Pluto is around —
if there is any suggestion that what transforms only does so
for Pisces' own purposes, it is unlikely to get him very far.

People with Scorpio planets may emerge as new friends
in these years, or existing friends with Scorpio planets may
take centre-stage. Through them, Pisces will learn all about
power and control, and how the game is played, and why it
matters. He will also experience, first-hand, what to do —
and what not to do — when there are questions about the
pecking order, or the politics of friendship.

Friendships or group involvements which have
accumulated too much psychological or practical 'rubbish' in
Pisces' life may have to be recycled after a critical period of
change. Otherwise, Pisces may leave them, or be left by
them. In all cases, the idea is to let go. Submitting to a
natural, organic process of change is always the best idea
when Pluto is at large, even if releasing the old set-up is
difficult.

This planet is intense in its effects. It requires Pisces to dig
as deeply as he can into the core issues involved — whatever
is buried inside him — in order to deal with what has to go,
or what has to change. To get through this cycle as painlessly
as possible, he can help himself by submitting rather than
fighting. Clinging on to the old ways, to his old versions of
various friendships or group commitments — or to his old
patterns — may feel like it is energising him or protecting
him. After a while, though, Pisces may have to learn what
Aquarius has learned before him: letting go is the best
pathway. Change is happening for a reason, and if the old
way was toxic, or not in his best long-term interests (or other
people's), then the old way has to be shelved.

Nobody changes (at least, not on the deep level required)
without a crisis to provoke the change. The Chinese famously
use the same word for crisis as they do for opportunity! If

Pisces can see his friendships or group commitments in the light of this, then accepting the inevitable will be easier.

Issues around this are more likely to emerge when New Moons and Full Moons occur in the sign of Capricorn, typically around the middle and end of the year. This is when Pisces will have to accept that if something is to survive, it has to change shape — and there has to be a total examination of every issue, no matter how deeply buried it is, or how murky it might be.

This is the path to progress and, ultimately, this is what Pluto wants — a friendship, a social circle or a group which is rubbish-free and in the best possible shape for Pisces' future plans.

One more point: Pluto can sometimes resuscitate an old friendship or group involvement at this time. What (or who) seemed to be dead and gone may re-emerge, with new possibilities. By dint of its survival in his life, this friendship or group commitment will be even more powerful. And accepting it back into his life will bring about a profound change in Pisces!

THE PISCES EMPLOYEE/CLIENT/COLLEAGUE/BOSS TO NOVEMBER 2008

He is probably over his big career crisis now. It involved a power struggle with other people in the company or business — or his industry rivals. Alternatively, he self-destructed, and resigned, or was sacked, or faced some other kind of crisis. Some Piscean men were made redundant in the late 1990s/early 2000s, for example, and a few were forced to take different jobs in a company reshuffle. It all amounts to the same thing: a Pluto cycle in his career zone, forcing him to crash and burn, and rise again.

In its most diluted form, Pluto has simply changed his course without changing his whole career. So Pisces might have become a full-time parent in this cycle, and made his job part-time. Or he may have changed roles or projects within the same field. In all cases, though, the change is unlikely to have been easy. Pluto never transforms anything without thoroughly killing off what was there before, and often in the most intense way.

People politics is not something astrologers associate with Pisceans, but the Pisces in your working life has certainly learned how to play the game in recent years. One thing he may have been forced to learn fast is the way the dynamics of power actually operate in his field. What appears on the surface, in terms of seniority or control, may not be the way things are at all — in fact, with Pluto in his life, it's likely that the real hands on the controls are very well-hidden, and that the game he is playing is far removed from the one that appears to be taking place on the surface.

If Pisces has already quit a job, or given up on what was obviously a naked battle for control, then he probably feels as if he has detoxed, purged, crashed, burned — and been resurrected — all in the space of a few years.

Here's the rule with Pluto to 2008: if Pisces 'dies' professionally, he will be reborn, and when it happens — watch out. He will be both empowered and powerful, as all survivors are.

That word survival, by the way, is highly relevant to his position and his place in the world at the moment. After 2008 when Pluto changes signs, life will be less intense, but for something which is, after all, just a job, his profession can certainly seem like a life and death matter.

Even if he sticks with the same role or position throughout this period, it is likely to change shape, and he will have to transform with it. The process that brings this change about is likely to be powerfully intense — Pluto seldom presents us with a picnic when there are changes to be made.

If you are around him professionally in this cycle, you will have to understand the power game he is playing, because all Pisceans will have to conduct themselves in one. If you feel it's too convoluted, too murky, or far too intense for your tastes, then you should not become involved. Alternatively, sometimes the voice of an objective outsider is just the one that Pisces needs to hear — why is the most sensitive man in the zodiac (or, at least, the one who is most proud of his sensitivity) being drawn into a real-life game of snakes and ladders?

The best way to handle a Pluto cycle in your career zone is to willingly co-operate with the universe in getting rid of the rot in your job, or the dead wood in your particular field or business — without hurting anybody. If you feel that you need to leave in order to get a life, then make plans to do so, but understand that it will feel like a revolution, and affect you (and your home situation) deeply.

Pisces needs to understand that there is something obsessive-compulsive about life when Pluto is around, and that may explain why he is so passionate about dominating, or refusing to be dominated. It may account for his need to manipulate — or his determination not to be manipulated. Rather than be swept along with the more obvious currents of Pluto, though, Pisces would gain a lot from distancing himself and asking for second opinions from those who have survived similar experiences (Aquarians, for example), or those who have a useful, detached viewpoint.

Every Piscean has accumulated a reasonable amount of rubbish in his professional life, no matter how recently he has joined the workforce, or how long he has been in a particular industry. Attitudes which do not serve him for the long-term are now ripe for discussion, re-examination — and maybe a thorough clean-out. Old prejudices, fears, hopes and dreams which might have become toxic are now prime targets for Pluto's reputation as the plumber of the heavens. This planet forces Pisces to peer into the depths, dredge up all the gunk — and then clean up afterwards.

Decay is also a Plutonian process. Have you ever been in a job where everything and everybody seems to be breaking down, slowly? The photocopier might have died in the corner, or vermin might have moved in, or the lavatories don't flush; staff may resign, be sacked or just take sick leave for long periods of time. If it all happens at once, in the space of a year, you can be sure that Pluto is at work. And from that slow process of decay will come either a dramatic turnaround (a revamp, a renovation, a revolution) or an even more dramatic ending (the business closes and people move on).

Pisces, in this cycle, is far more vulnerable to this kind of change than other signs. If he holds an important job in the grand scheme of things, he may even find that his own personal destiny is part of a much bigger cosmic plan; in other words, his path to professional change in these years might actually serve a much bigger change, affecting the business, field or industry which he is such a part of.

The rule in these years, if you work with him, alongside him or for him? Give him space to change, and if you can help stop him hurtling into a real-life game of snakes and ladders, then do so. Pisces does not need power plays in this cycle, but he does need some kind of transformation, and maybe a resurrection too. If you can assist him in letting go and submitting to the process, you'll be worth your weight in gold.

GLOBAL BUSINESS CONNECTIONS

National horoscopes (set up for the time that a nation is 'born' — like 4 July for the USA, or 26 January for Australia) can tell you all you need to know about doing global business, according to astrology. What pushes a nation's buttons most? What products or marketing campaigns are likely to work best in different places? How should you approach business? National horoscopes, even if you just look at the Sun sign and Moon sign, can give you all the secrets . . .

The data here is from *The Book of World Horoscopes* by Nicholas Campion. In cases where a country has a range of potential 'birth' charts, I have narrowed it down to one final choice, through historical research.

People think the idea of a country having a birth horoscope is mad — until they see what the horoscope presents. So . . . if you're selling to Madrid, or Melbourne, read on.

AUSTRALIA

26 January 1788
Australia has the Sun in Aquarius, the sign of weirdness and freedom. Your Sun sign describes what you become famous for — Australia is well-known for being upside-down, and for having peculiar animals: the kangaroo, the platypus and the Tasmanian devil.

The Sun sign also describes what is heroic about you, what kind of heroes and heroines a country produces. The majority of Australian stand-outs have been (or are) mavericks, activists, eccentrics, punks and rebels, in true Aquarian fashion.

* Dame Edna Everage (aka Barry Humphries, who is also Aquarian)

* Dr Germaine Greer (another Aquarian)

* Ned Kelly, the bushranger, who wore what appeared to be a metal bucket upside-down on his head

* Cathy Freeman, the Aboriginal Olympian gold medallist (another Aquarian)

* Nick Cave

* Patrick White

* Brett Whiteley

* Fictional eccentrics, from Crocodile Dundee to Mr Squiggle

* Dr Bob Brown

* Peter Garrett

* Chrissie Amphlett

* Pauline Hanson

The list goes on!

Aquarius is about rights for everyone and everything, from gay men to disabled women. Australia is famous for its Sydney Gay and Lesbian Mardi Gras, and the historic Sydney 2000 Olympics opening ceremony was dominated by women for the first time ever — black, white and in wheelchairs.

The Sun sign describes what a country honours and respects, what (and who) it identifies with, and how it stands out on the world stage. Tap into the Aquarian-ness of Australia and you are halfway there if you want to be a success in that country. Use these words a lot in your spiel: freedom, independence, choice, individuality, uniqueness.

Most importantly, make sure what you have to offer is original. Remember, this is the country that invented the wine cask.

Aquarius is ultimately about freedom and independence. The Australian national anthem starts 'Australians let us all rejoice, for we are young and *free*'. Independence from Great Britain was finally achieved with Federation in 1901, and the debate about leaving the British monarchy and becoming a republic continues. Australia voted to remain a monarchy recently, but according to its horoscope, another referendum will be held before the end of the twenty-first century, and this time we will see it becoming a republic, once and for all.

If you are trying to sell people what they really need or crave, look to a country's Moon sign. This shows what the nation must have to feel secure, and also what it eats. In the Aussie chart, the Moon is in Virgo. Australia needs Medicare, its taxpayer-funded health system, and it needs pure, organic, good-for-you food. It also needs its gyms and personal trainers, its swimming pools and beaches, and its bushwalker-friendly wilderness. Sell stuff to Australia by emphasising purity and health-giving qualities.

Virgo is about the work ethic too. Australians need hard work to feel secure. To win an election here, always focus on employment and health. Then look at policies which stress the country's independence on the world stage.

Are you trying to sell your product, brand, CV or business in Australia? Emphasise your point of difference, even if you're selling pink elephants — no, *especially* if you're selling pink elephants. Then pass the mineral water round. That takes care of Australia's Aquarius/Virgo side in one neat hit.

Who clicks with Australia? Aquarians and Virgos, and those who have other planets, like the Moon, Mercury, Venus and Mars, in those signs.

FRANCE

6 October 1958

The Fifth Republic of France was born when the Sun was in Libra. France is Libran — romantic, devoted to art and design, attached to fashion, and deeply concerned with equality and justice. The French turn anyone who fits the Libran archetype into a star: feminine women, thoughtfully dressed painters, and Karl Lagerfeld and his ponytail, even though he's German.

The First Republic of France was born on 26 September 1792, when the Sun was also in Libra. The France we know from the eighteenth century, as well as the twentieth century, has all the romance (Colette's books, Edith Piaf's ballads), all the art (Picasso's Cubism, Monet's Impressionism) and all the fashion (Marie Antoinette's hair, Yves St Laurent's suits) you could hope for.

Libra is about charm. Think Maurice Chevalier in *Gigi*, singing 'Thank Heaven For Little Girls'. The French are blessed with a language which makes even the most banal sentence — about plumbing, say, or pig breeding — sound deliciously seductive and romantic.

What does France need? What do French people always come back to, in order to feel at home in the world? The Moon is in Cancer. The French need their own traditional food. The nation needs croissants, Coquilles St Jacques, *moules marinières*, and a slice of Roquefort cheese. It's what mother used to make, and grandmother too, because Cancer is about the family. Paris doesn't like anything new or foreign, like McDonald's. *Sacrebleu* and *mon dieu*! The French find security in Cordon Bleu instead.

Cancer rules property too — a home to call your own, and real estate investment. It also rules history, and the past. Don't try to sell anything to the French on the basis that it is revolutionary. They might have had a revolution once, but they don't need anything else, thanks very much. They hunger for tradition instead — their ancestors, and their roots.

Are you doing business in Paris? Mix the Cancer Moon and the Libran Sun, and book a beautiful restaurant that has been there since the eighteenth century. Talk about your mother a lot, or your grandmother — and exchange family photos from your wallet when the aperitif arrives. Wear beautiful clothes and shoes (it goes without saying) and wear a French label. Talk about your love life, flirt with anyone and everyone, and on no account present a boring, photocopied corporate document. The French will note the colour, the cut, the design and the watermark on your proposal, and points will be scored.

Who clicks with France? Librans and Cancerians, and those who have other planets, like the Moon, Mercury, Venus and Mars, in those signs.

THE UNITED KINGDOM

25 December 1066

The UK is Capricorn. It is about history, tradition and a deep dislike of change. Its heroes and heroines are mostly very old, or very dead — walk around Westminster Abbey to see them. Londoners survived the Great War, the Blitz and the 7 July terrorist bombings alike by standing firm, being sensible, getting on with things and rolling up their collective sleeves — true Sun in Capricorn traits. The UK's collective stiff upper lip is pure Capricorn, and so is the famous British stoicism.

Capricorn Sun sign people set boundaries. So does the UK — an island surrounded by coastline defences, both ancient and modern. Foreigners find the British rather closed and hard to get to know. Don't worry, it's not personal. It's just that the island was born on Christmas Day, and it only feels confident when the walls are up. Moats, drawbridges, barbed wire and radar — whatever it takes, the British will keep you out, just as the land itself rejects too much intrusion. They shall fight you on the beaches, if you try to get too close to them.

And then what happens? The British get drunk, and they let you in; in fact they may even go to bed with you, or cry all over you. But you can blame the UK's Pisces Moon for that. It has no boundaries whatsoever.

With the Moon in flaky Pisces, despite its uptight Capricorn Sun, what the UK really craves and needs is alcohol, and poetry, and fantasy, and the occasional funny cigarette. Britain is famous for its respect for ancestry (breeding) and tradition, thanks to its Capricorn Sun — but it craves the Beatles, and beer, and Edward Lear, and J.R.R. Tolkien — and Harry Potter too. English people feel safer when there is a lot of silliness or surrealism around. They find Monty Python sketches deeply comforting.

Until 2005, English pubs closed earlier than their counterparts in other countries, clanging the bell well before midnight. The result, for decades, has been its world-famous national binge drinking — Moon in Pisces again.

The Moon in Pisces is also about religion. The UK is built on its churches. The Queen defends the faith. This island has been threatened with invasion so many times since 1066, faith is sometimes all it's had.

The Moon in Pisces is about blurred vision too. London pea-souper fogs were famous in Victorian times. Even now, when the pollution has lifted, the whole country can be covered in heavy mists during winter, closing the roads. The soft drizzle on autumn and winter days also makes it hard to see. Add two pints of beer before closing time, and you can see why dazed and confused is often the country's natural state. During strikes and snowstorms, the island is plunged into chaos — Moon in Pisces again.

For a long time in the UK, glasses were only available on the NHS — so they were cheap and hideous. People went without them rather than see straight; there is at least one generation of English people, and possibly more, who have spent large parts of their life unable to read timetables or stop signs as a result. Pisces is about partial or total blindness!

Pisces is also about compassion and the milk of human kindness. The UK invented Live Aid. Charity shops are on the high street, next to Marks and Spencer, Gap and Woolworths. Sometimes there are as many charity shops as there are big corporate global chains. London itself has the Sun in Pisces too. It is the birthplace of the *Big Issue*, and the spiritual home of famously charitable types, from Princess Diana to Charles Dickens.

To do business with the UK, get two bottles of wine at lunch, not one, so the Pisces Moon is accommodated. Veer effortlessly between being cautious, sensible, pessimistic and solid (Capricorn) and whimsical, vague and sloshed (Pisces).

Who clicks with the UK? Pisceans and Capricorns, and those who have other planets, like the Moon, Mercury, Venus and Mars, in those signs.

THE UNITED STATES

4 July 1776

The United States of America was born on Independence Day, 4 July, under the sign of Cancer. Welcome to the land of Mom and apple pie. America's mother country, of course, is Great Britain. Over two centuries later, the whole nation still has mother issues, and, despite the Boston Tea Party, America still hasn't cut Britain's secure apron strings. Who did Cancerian George W Bush turn to on 9/11? The mother country.

Cancer is about food. If you have the Sun in Cancer, then you become famous for your cooking. For better or worse, America is the international home of Kentucky Fried Chicken and McDonald's.

France has the Moon in Cancer — America has the Sun in Cancer. They have more in common than first appears, and it all begins with the stomach. Cancer is about family food too — what was in your mother's pantry, or your great-grandmother's. It's about the national dish, and local produce, and patriotic shopping. You can't get most Parisians to eat American fast food, and you will have difficulty asking even the most sophisticated New Yorker to eat *l'escargots*. The two countries mirror each other, for different reasons.

Doing business in America? Eat American. Compliment the chef and the farmer who grew the food, if you like. It will go down well with your hosts, just like the pumpkin pie.

Cancer is about patriotism. America is proud of being . . . *America*. That means the surfers in California, and the traders on Wall Street, and the cowboys in Texas, and the casinos in Vegas. The Stars and Stripes are everywhere. America is a flag-waver, like so many Sun in Cancer people.

Cancer is about the family and so is America. Functional or dysfunctional, Americans must always refer to their parents, siblings, cousins and grandparents before they think about anything else. It is the home of the TV family sitcom for this reason, and also the home of therapy.

America is matriarchal. Think Rose Kennedy! Like a lot of Sun in Cancer people, it is also hung up on domestic life, real estate and home sweet home. Only in the USA could Martha Stewart have become a national icon.

The Moon is in Aquarius. America also has more in common with Australia than most people might see —

Australia's Sun is in this sign too. Both countries are desperate for their freedom. One had a civil war, another had federation. Both have started military action in the name of freedom.

Aquarius is rebellious, eccentric, unique and highly unusual. With its Aquarian moon, America needs a large dose of this in its culture and politics to feel truly secure. *The Simpsons* is America's most successful television series of all time, because it is about a family (Sun in Cancer) populated by weirdos (Moon in Aquarius).

Do you want to make a fortune in America? Repeat the mad family theme — look what it did for the Osbournes. The USA is tremendously proud of the family unit, but also needs a huge dose of craziness. Just add water, or Ozzy Osbourne, and mix. America needs its eccentrics.

The cross between the Cancerian Sun and the Aquarian Moon in the American chart also results in another predictable fixation — totally weird food. Well, have you ever eaten a bowl of Lucky Charms?

To sell to Americans, respect their patriotism, their total identification with the food that they eat, and the way they always express themselves through the family unit. Understand their craving for strangeness too; give them tons of space and room to move. Never cramp an American's style — their Aquarian Moon won't like it.

To win an election in the US, turn up to photo calls with your entire family, including your mother and grandmother, if she is still alive. Americans relate to matriarchies. Emphasise family policy too. And be seen tucking into homegrown beef, or homegrown tomatoes, or homegrown *anything*.

Serve the Aquarian Moon by being eccentric. Play the saxophone, like Lisa Simpson — it worked for Bill Clinton. Show you're committed to freedom by employing staff on an equal-opportunities basis — male, female, black, white, old, young, gay, straight, disabled — and use the magic word — independence — as often as you can.

Who clicks with America? Cancerians and Aquarians, and those who have other planets, like the Moon, Mercury, Venus and Mars, in those signs.

IN BRIEF:

CANADA

1 July 1867
Sun in Cancer, Moon in Gemini.

The same Mother England hang-ups as America — and the same attachment to its own home cooking (do you want maple syrup with that?). The Moon in Gemini has helped to produce famous writers and comedians, though — like Mike Myers.

CHINA

1 January 1912
Sun in Capricorn, Moon in Taurus.

Thanks to its Capricorn sun, China, like England, is big on tradition, structure, boundaries and barriers — particularly the Great Wall of China. The Taurus Moon is about its communism, but also about its massive global industries.

INDIA

26 January 1950
Sun in Aquarius, Moon in Taurus.

Not surprisingly for a country which fought for independence from the British, India is Aquarian. Its superstars are offbeat Aquarian types — Deepak Chopra, all the Gandhis. The Taurus Moon? That's Lakshmi, the money goddess.

ITALY

17 March 1861
Sun in Pisces, Moon in Taurus.

Welcome to Piscean vino country. More chianti for you? A Pisces Sun is often religious — in this case, it is responsible for the Vatican. The Taurus Moon reflects Italy's shopaholic side. Gucci, Fiorucci, Benetton, Prada, *grazie*!

NEW ZEALAND

26 September 1907
Sun in Libra, Moon in Taurus.

Like the French, the Kiwis are proud of their fashion designers (what's not to like about Karen Walker?), their Maori art, and their romantic love songs (thank you, Crowded House). The Taurus Moon reflects shopaholic Auckland.

SINGAPORE

9 August 1965
Sun in Leo, Moon in Capricorn.

Leo Singapore is proud of its aristocratic founder, Sir Stamford Raffles. The hotel has been home to royals and celebrities too — very Leo! The fish-tailed lion is Singapore's symbol. And the Capricorn Moon shows its conservatism.

SPAIN

22 November 1975
Sun in Scorpio, Moon in Cancer.

Sexy flamenco dancers and passionate bullfights — to the death. What other sign could Spain be, except Scorpio? Secrecy is a heroic Spanish trait (the Spanish Inquisition). The Cancer Moon is about the food: *paella* and *tapas*.

PreDICtiNG
THE FUTURE

Astrology is like weather forecasting when it is used for predictive work. It's pretty general, fairly reliable and, depending on your state of mind, you'll either hang on every detail or ignore it completely. Astrologers use solar charts, natal charts or horary charts (the big three methods) to peer into the future. All of them work, although in different ways: a solar chart will give you the news headlines of your life; a natal chart will give you a deeper and more personal reading; and a horary chart is designed to answer one-off questions.

I have worked with solar charts for twenty years, and trust them completely. But still, the information you get from them is always drawn in the broadest terms.

When I write sentences like this in a column: 'Expect pressure on the home front', it's pretty much like the weather forecaster telling you there's a cloudy patch to the north of your home town. Just like a weather forecaster, an astrologer using the solar chart method can't tell you at what precise time the clouds will appear, what shape they will be, what colour they will be and over which suburb they will have the biggest effect — but you'll still have enough hard facts to work with when you're making decisions.

I'm concentrating on Sun, Pluto and Jupiter cycles in this section, as these dictate the rhythms of the year. The Sun builds your confidence, Pluto brings out the really big changes, and Jupiter delivers opportunities.

And I'll also take a look at your Saturn Return, which you'll definitely need to know about if you're heading for your thirtieth birthday at the moment — and Mercury retrograde too, which helps you predict the chaos in your life (and hopefully avoid it).

Finally, I've written about the global trends we can all expect to 2025. Some astrologers will agree with me, some will not. What I'm using here are the slow-moving outer planets, like Uranus, Neptune and Pluto, to judge the global mood as we pass through the twenty-first century.

Sun Cycles For Life

I use natal (birth) charts and solar (Sun sign) charts to predict the future. Both of them work really well, so I'm happy to give you some Sun sign predictions here, based on your solar chart — which is much easier and faster to work with in a book like this.

The people who created Stonehenge knew all about natural cycles and how to use them. Otherwise, why bother dragging all that stone all that way? Those rocks are an astrological clock.

You won't need any rocks for this, though, just a good memory. Because the Sun travels through the same zone of your chart at around the same time every year, once you've remembered this, you'll always know what's going on in your life, anywhere in the world.

CYCLE SPOTTING

Sun in your sign — Cycle One
Sun one sign from yours — Cycle Two

Sun two signs from yours — Cycle Three
Sun three signs from yours — Cycle Four
Sun four signs from yours — Cycle Five
Sun five signs from yours — Cycle Six
Sun six signs from yours — Cycle Seven
Sun seven signs from yours — Cycle Eight
Sun eight signs from yours — Cycle Nine
Sun nine signs from yours — Cycle Ten
Sun ten signs from yours — Cycle Eleven
Sun eleven signs from yours — Cycle Twelve

Example: An Aquarian looking at her life from late July through late August will find she is in Sun Cycle Seven, as the Sun is six signs along from her Sun Sign at that time — in Leo. A Leo looking at her life from late January through late February will find she is also in Sun Cycle Seven. The Sun is six signs along from her Sun Sign at that time — in Aquarius.

YOUR YEAR — ANY YEAR

Late January to late February — the Sun is in Aquarius
Late February to late March — the Sun is in Pisces
Late March to late April — the Sun is in Aries
Late April to late May — the Sun is in Taurus
Late May to late June — the Sun is in Gemini
Late June to late July — the Sun is in Cancer
Late July to late August — the Sun is in Leo
Late August to late September — the Sun is in Virgo
Late September to late October — the Sun is in Libra
Late October to late November — the Sun is in Scorpio
Late November to late December — the Sun is in Sagittarius
Late December to late January — the Sun is in Capricorn

Sun Cycle One
You'll be talked about, photographed, singled out for attention, publicised or shown off.

Make sure you're looking and sounding good as it will be hard to miss the spotlight now.

Sun Cycle Two
You need to focus hard on your cash, mortgage, rent, savings, debts, credit card and tax. Give more time and energy to number crunching as your personal financial year is now!

Sun Cycle Three
Your brother, sister or cousin will be the focus of your attention. So will a short trip away, which you will take or plan. A brilliant idea or course, using your way with words, is here.

Sun Cycle Four
Your house, flat, flatmates and family are in sharp focus now. You will examine how confident you feel about your current rental, mortgage, renovation or decoration set-up.

Sun Cycle Five
Your sexuality will be the focus now, possibly because of a new partner, or changes with an old one. Children (your own or other people's) are also in the spotlight. So is your talent.

Sun Cycle Six
Your health and wellbeing is the centre of your energy now — and so it should be. Your working life, and tasks you must complete, will also be in the spotlight. Pay attention!

Sun Cycle Seven

The spotlight swings onto your partner, your ex-partner, your future potential date — and even that person who's been such a pain in the arse. Put it all under the microscope now.

Sun Cycle Eight

Other people's money, houses, flats or possessions (like cars or computers) are now in focus. Scrutinise the facts, figures and agreements. Give it time and energy while you can.

Sun Cycle Nine

You could easily travel now, or find a long-distance person or place enters your life in other ways. The spotlight goes onto study, teaching, publishing and any location miles away.

Sun Cycle Ten

Your career is in the spotlight now — or your course, or other achievements. How confident do you feel about everything? And how do you feel about that boss/teacher/authority?

Sun Cycle Eleven

The group you are a part of, or your friend, will take up a lot of your time and attention. You could make new friends with a person who is well-known — or a high-profile group.

Sun Cycle Twelve

The spotlight swings on your secrets, and the most private and confidential matters. You may spend more time alone, or on the sidelines — because you choose it, or it just happens!

TuRNiNG THiRTy —
YOuR SaTUrN ReTUrN

Between twenty-eight and thirty, you will experience your
Saturn Return. Saturn, the planet known as the Great
Teacher, will swing around to exactly the same place it was
in on the day you were born. This is a big deal in astrology
because it is such a rare event — and an even bigger deal for
you, the person going through it. And because this planet is
associated with long, loathsome learning experiences it is
definitely more difficult than the others; at times you will
feel as if just about everything is being shaken, inspected and
held up to the light for flaws. Any of the cornerstones of your
life — relationships, health, career, home, family, money,
friendships — may be seriously affected.

Typically, anything that is meant to be for the long-term
will be firmed up and set in concrete. You will end up
committing yourself very seriously and in a way that makes
you feel like that wonderful thing, A Mature Woman Making
a Mature Decision. There may also be parts of your life that
you are familiar with, or even that you want very much —

but at Saturn Return time, they will go. You may cut away things that aren't right for you deliberately. Or, if you are not aware of how inappropriate things have been for you, it's likely you'll feel quite fearful or anxious about the fact that things are changing.

I have seen enough Saturn Returns in the lives of my clients to know that one piece of advice will always work: go with it. Saturn can feel quite relentless — and end up making you feel thoroughly miserable and depressed — if you hang on to the things it wants you to let go of.

Just as important at this time is the idea of making the Big Decision. Just as you will have to let some things pass, there is also every chance that you will be presented with a chance to seriously commit yourself to something that is right for you. It may well have been on your agenda for years. Saying yes to it in a serious way will make you feel terribly responsible and terribly adult. But the good, constructive things that get firmed up now will be with you for a long time to come.

People divorce and marry on their Saturn Return. They emigrate. They have children for the first time. They buy houses. They change jobs. I left a seven-year relationship at twenty-nine, and then left my job as a journalist to form an astrology company at thirty. Several friends of mine married on their Saturn Returns.

Another interesting thing happens just after you're recovering from the stresses of your twenty-eighth and twenty-ninth years. As you dive into your early thirties, the planet Jupiter makes the best possible pattern in your chart. Jupiter is associated with opportunities, optimism and expansion. Characteristically, women go through a chain of events that looks like this:

1. Anxiety over elements of life that seem to be fading or disappearing from your life. Difficult losses, and an

acknowledgement that some things in your life were never going to be realities.

2. A difficult, but potentially rewarding commitment to life changes which are going to affect you for years to come. A rather serious feeling that what you do now must take you forward into the future too. Typically, a conviction that you are getting older and that you now have to get real about life.

3. After a couple of years of feeling terribly mature, sensible — and, let's face it — older about things, you lighten up. Saturn's influence fades as you move between thirty and thirty-one, and now that you know where you stand in life (you've been building the foundations, after all) you can relax and take risks again. As you move into your early thirties you will have a strong sense of knowing 'who I am', and even though the very end of your twenties may have been difficult and exhausting at times, you are now ready to do amazing things.

Classic Saturn Return milestones can include: marriage, engagement, separation, divorce, adoption, babies, mortgages, resignations, redundancies, health changes, financial turning points, family losses, emigration, coming out as a lesbian, inheritances, overseas trips and therapy!

PreDicTing ChaoS — MercURy RetrOGraDe

Mercury is the planet of communication and travel. And every now and then, it does something quite bizarre — it appears to go backwards, or get stuck. When this happens, things go wrong. How wrong? Well, this is what happened in April 1998, just as an early edition of this book was going to the printer. World Cup soccer tickets went on sale in France — by phone. Some twenty million calls went through, the English phone lines jammed, and the Dutch system came crashing down. Author Will Self had all copies of his new book *Tough, Tough Toys for Tough, Tough Boys* taken out of the bookstores and pulped, following mistakes in computer typesetting for the book. In the same month, Antony Beevor's book *Stalingrad*, published by Viking, was pulled after software printing errors. And *The Eros Hunter*, by Russell Celyn Jones, featured a scramble of wrongly numbered pages. I lost my passport and the disc which contained all the copy for this book, and went temporarily insane. I've never forgotten it . . .

Don't ever do anything major which involves signatures, telephones, fax machines, the internet, public statements, cars, bicycles, motorbikes, aeroplanes or the whole business of information, transportation and communication when Mercury goes backwards.

I've kept notes on this stuff over the years, and inevitably everyone, from my local bank tellers to my editors in magazine-land, goes through chaos. In other years, Mercury going backwards has also coincided with big banking errors and computer-hacker chaos. Treaties, contracts and agreements produced while Mercury is off balance tend to come undone later. Strikes affect delivery of parcels and letters. Computers play up. Car parts don't arrive. Public transport schedules go offtrack. Lawyers leave their laptops in taxis. My friend, the astrologer, columnist and author Lynda Hill says 'Mercury retrograde makes you swear more'. My literary agents in Australia, Curtis Brown, have clients who just won't sign contracts when this planet is misbehaving, as they know too well how often such contracts have to go back to the drawing board!

Something else happens when Mercury backtracks. Long-lost documents and objects — sometimes even long-lost people — turn up. In 1986, a previously unknown Shakespeare poem turned up in Oxford during one of these periods. In August 1998, in a rather famous example of a Mercury retrograde period, missing pages from Anne Frank's diary turned up.

You can make your life easier by backing up documents and taking extra precautions with transportation, travel, communication and information when Mercury goes backwards.

Media enterprises which launch under mad Mercury periods tend to flop, go through staff chaos, or suffer phone problems. I signed a contract with a radio station under a Mercury retrograde period. Three months later, the radio station pulled the show. Whoops.

Robert Wilkinson, whose book title, *A New Look At Mercury Retrograde*, is rather wittily printed in backwards writing on the cover, has studied the planet in depth. He gives many more examples in his book, but admits that his own life has not been immune from Mercury madness. 'I bought a state-of-the-art answering machine just prior to a Mercury retrograde period,' he writes. 'It proceeded to malfunction three times in five weeks, each time needing repairs.'

For your information, then, here are the next periods of Mercury chaos. Allow a day or two either side of the start/end dates to allow for different time zones.

Mercury Madness

14 February – 7 March 2007
16 June – 9 July 2007
12 October – 1 November 2007
29 January – 18 February 2008
27 May – 19 June 2008
24 September – 16 October 2008
12 January – 2 February 2009
7 – 30 May 2009
7 – 29 September 2009
27 December 2009 – 15 January 2010
18 April – 11 May 2010
21 August – 12 September 2010
10 – 29 December 2010

For more dates as they come up, please visit www.jessicaadams.com

So . . . what can you do?

When Mercury goes backwards, it's a good time to re-file, review, re-organise. Anything with a 're' in front it, basically. Use your astro common sense. This is not the moment to take wild and crazy risks with airline tickets, train connections, the postal service or your computer. You shouldn't let it stop your life, though. As with eclipses and other strange planetary phenomena, it's just a gentle warning from the universe that you need to take more trouble with things than you normally do. If it involves communication, transportation or information, don't leave it to chance.

Some astrologers believe Mercury retrograde forces us to slow down, and that's a good thing. If you have the Sun, Moon, Mercury, Venus and/or Mars in Virgo and/or Gemini then this strongly applies to you. Otherwise, you'll just go nuts trying to get everything done when neither your computer, nor the world in general, is behaving!

WORLD TRENDS TO 2025

Why did *Charlie's Angels* take off in the 1970s? Why were the Beatles big in the 1960s? What makes kids salivate over Cabbage Patch Kids in one decade and Teletubbies in the next? What on earth is responsible for global Sudoko madness, the rise of sushi, or the ongoing boom in mineral water and trainers?

Pop culture and more serious global trends — like safe sex, or political conservatism — are indicated by the particular sign of the zodiac that Pluto happens to be passing through in any given decade.

At the close of the twentieth century, Pluto was in Scorpio, the sign ruling sex and death. The world got a French perfume called Poison and an English cigarette brand called Death. People were hooked on *Sex, Lies and Videotape*. Ellen DeGeneres became the world's first lesbian sitcom star. And, on a terrifying scale, sex and death became linked for the first time as AIDS took hold. Scorpios, or people with the Moon or other planets in that sign, completely fascinated us — k.d. lang, Oprah Winfrey, Julia Roberts, Hillary Rodham Clinton, Winona Ryder, Demi Moore, Whoopi Goldberg and Prince Charles!

Scorpio rules sewers — the world got Teenage Mutant Ninja Turtles. It rules black — the dominant late twentieth century fashion colour. It rules vampires, so Anne Rice mania took over Hollywood. It also rules obsession (just like the perfume) and bats (viva Batman) and sex (*Sex* by Madonna, of course).

In short, the mood of the times was *Melrose Place* meets Vincent Price.

And the early twenty-first century? It belonged (and will, until 2008) to Pluto in Sagittarius. Here are some old predictions from the 1996 edition of this book.

BETWEEN NOW AND 2007 YOU CAN EXPECT TO SEE THESE CHANGES:
*1. The New Comedy. Television and film producers will be capitalising on a completely different trend in comedy, and a global obsession with funny books, funny series, funny **anything** will take over. Comedy will tackle more taboo issues and go into riskier areas, and a new breed of television or film comedy will emerge . . .*

Sagittarius rules comedy and light entertainment. The world got Larry David's *Curb Your Enthusiasm*, which is performed without a script, and has subject matter ranging from porn stars to funerals-gone-wrong. In this period, two other comedy innovations arrived. Reality TV (particularly *Big Brother*) and mock-reality TV, in the shape of Ricky Gervais's *The Office*.

THE NEXT PREDICTION FROM THE 1996 VERSION OF THIS BOOK WAS:
2. A Travel Revolution. New ways of getting to foreign countries. A huge shake-up and crisis for world airlines. Different pricing, different airline attitudes, investigations into airline cover-ups and corruption. Don't expect to be flying the same way, to the same places, by 2007.

After September 11, of course, none of us ever flew the same way again. But in the 1996–2007 time frame we have also seen several airline collapses, the end of Concorde on 24 October, 2003, and major investigations into airport security (or lack of it) in the face of terrorism. Most of all, though, it is the internet which has revolutionised travel. Even hundreds of years ago, Sagittarius ruled long sea voyages. Today it rules major airlines!

PREDICTION NUMBER THREE FROM THE FIRST EDITION OF THIS BOOK? A CRISIS OF FAITH.

3. *Discoveries about the universe and other planets prompt a total re-think of the Creation myth. The established religions will go through a massive re-evaluation. By 2007, everyone's idea of God will have been transformed. A whole new generation of spiritual and religious obsessives will emerge as a result. Expect more crises involving cults and other belief systems. New discoveries and debate will change the image of God. Sexuality and the Afterlife — and the traditional Church's way of handling those areas — will come up for worldwide debate.*

Has the global idea of God changed? Pluto in Sagittarius has certainly produced the global phenomenon known as *The Da Vinci Code*, together with the boom in Scientology and Kabbalah. Civil partnership, also known as gay marriage, is now legal in several countries — despite the Christian church. Al Qaeda have emerged as the leading religious obsessives of the age. And even the Afterlife has come up for re-examination, following the boom in TV mediums like John Edwards.

PREDICTION NUMBER FOUR: EDUCATION BECOMES HIP.

4. *New ways of learning and a massive shift in the way the education system is working will create a rethink from*

*upcoming generations ... CD-Roms and the internet are
already contributing to a new kind of self-education.
Libraries will also be revolutionised. However, the changes
in the way we are educated will have to come after a few
shake-ups.*

Meanwhile, the global crisis for universities (and their
funding) continues. As does the internet revolution, not to
mention Google's plans for a worldwide virtual library.
Watch this space until 2008, when Pluto in Sagittarius has
finally finished its job!

The 'really big punt' prediction from the first edition was
'Hard evidence of aliens/UFOs'. Not so far. But hey, as this
book goes to print, we have a couple more years left with
Pluto in Sagittarius to find it!

Other predictions from the first edition? I thought we
might leave our mobile phones at work (wrong!) as
workaholism became uncool. And that a language
scrambler or translator would link people across the globe,
on the internet (right). And that the fashion industry would
install computers to create a new sizing system for clothes
(it's on the way) ... and that taboo body-size issues like
anorexia, bulimia and plastic surgery would dominate the
headlines (right). All of this was based on not just Pluto's
passage through Sagittarius, but also the journey of Uranus
through Aquarius.

OUR FUTURE TO 2025 — PLUTO IN CAPRICORN

As you've just seen, Pluto transforms areas of life ruled by the
sign it is passing through at the time. So if Sagittarius was
about flying, funny people and fundamentalist religion, what
is Capricorn about?

You get to make the predictions this time.

Pluto's processes:

* Frequently involve death, either symbolically (something dies away) or literally (for example, the mass deaths brought about by suicide bombers or AIDS)

* Usually bring organisations or individuals to their knees, before a dramatic process of total revolution can begin

* Influence what obsesses us and compels us

Capricorn rules:

* Old age

* Social structure — the class system

* Big corporations with a gap between those at the top and those at the bottom

* Time, and our measurement of it

* Senior citizens — our grandparents and great-grandparents

* Bones

Between 2006, when this edition is being printed, and 2025, we're bound to see the 'death' of old age. Advances in medicine and science, together with massive financial investment by those who can afford it, could produce the first super-race of 105-year-old-and-counting people! Equally, it looks as if we are up for a crisis where older people are concerned, and at time of writing that may well mean you. How does our society handle responsibility for senior citizens? Any whiff of corruption in the old-age industry (particularly where retirement homes are concerned) may be the first area that Pluto in Capricorn tackles, once it arrives around 2009. And how about this?

Because of extraordinary medical, scientific and surgical advances we'll see the 'death' of old age. Old people, as we know them, will disappear.

If you want to invest in something, look at the anti-ageing industries and products, as we'll all be utterly obsessed with that from 2008–2009 onwards. There will also be an entertainment industry fixation with people in their 60s–90s, ending the youth cult. Everything from music to TV should reflect that.

Sceptics will say that as baby boomers and Generation X people grow old, they will naturally become fascinated by their own age status. But astrology also predicts this very clearly as Capricorn is all about senior citizens.

Corporations will crumble and fall too. Anything with a big pyramid structure and massive skyscraper towers is vulnerable. Check where your pensions or superannuation funds are. A crisis involving retirement, old age and large corporations is extremely likely, astrologically speaking, as Pluto goes through Capricorn. Corporations as we know them in the first ten years of the twenty-first century may be unrecognisable after 2025. They are very likely to face class-action lawsuits for manslaughter or other serious crimes.

Here's the wild card bet: the ultimate social structure in much of the Western world is based on royalty at the top and commoners at the bottom. If there is any period in history when royal families are going to be completely restructured and re-examined, this is it. And the English class system, in particular, will hit the point of no return. Will England see the end of the House of Lords?

Okay, time to get the Madame Za Za earrings off. But what do you see for us all to 2025? Visit my website at www.jessicaadams.com and leave your thoughts.

PLUTO POWER IN YOUR LIFE 2008–2025

ARIES

Oh, the joy of Pluto passing over the midheaven of your solar chart. It's here to transform your goals and ambitions. Not overnight, naturally. This process will take several years. Save all your old CVs and then come back to them after this cycle is over. You will honestly have difficulty in accepting them when Pluto has finished doing its work. This planet has a habit of taking you further and further away from what you thought you were working towards.

As early as 2009, you may consider giving up what has seemed like a perfectly okay career or study path until now. You may have recently become obsessed with a brand new mission in life. Or perhaps there's just a twist in a time-honoured career path for you . . . Pluto can take the same basic goals and reinvent them.

The last group of people to go through this solar chart cycle before you were Pisceans. They spent the best part of the early twenty-first century throwing in jobs, reinventing their careers, switching courses, rethinking their ambitions and transforming their roles. Some of them hit career crashes, because they were stuck on the wrong path. If you are also on the wrong road — in terms of your general future — it is possible that Pluto will give you some hard choices after 2009. Try to live consciously at all times, and be aware that if you are shuffling along on a professional path that is inappropriate, wrong or even just plain toxic, you may well find yourself in the ejector seat!

Pluto is about focus, desire and burning intensity. Don't be too surprised if you find yourself becoming deeply fixated on a particular project, job, goal or ambition. Rely on your friends and family to tap you on the shoulder if you become too fixated, though.

Pluto is also about power, control and influence. You will test the water in these areas while this cycle is operating. If you can remember the basic universal rules about not abusing this power, or manipulating people and situations, then Pluto could end up doing you some favours.

Do avoid power struggles, though — no matter if they are heavily disguised and played under the surface, or right out there where everybody can see them. There can be something very compulsive about Plutonian game-playing. If you feel yourself being dragged into the web, concentrate just as hard on pulling yourself out again. Otherwise you may end up losing a lot of sleep. This Pluto cycle will put you in touch with classic issues like: 'Where am I going/What am I doing/What does it all mean?' This is not such a bad thing. Pluto is extreme by nature, and the process may feel unnecessarily intense. However, many astrologers say that Pluto never changes anything without a purpose. In other words, some bits and pieces of your life were never meant to be there for the long-term. So if something appears to be going, going, gone, then maybe you should take a philosophical approach. Conscious transformation is probably a good idea. This cycle will confront you, in a very direct way, about who you are and what you're supposed to be doing with your life. If it's not deep, profound and wholly involving, then either you — or the universe — will want to do a U-turn.

TAURUS

By the time Pluto has finished doing its stuff in 2025, you'll have a completely different way of looking at the world. It's possible that you'll have a period of obsession with some kind of belief system, philosophy or religion. Pluto will transform your view of the world, and, your understanding of heaven and hell, life and death — and, above all, why we're here and what it all means. When Pluto is working for you rather than against you, you'll probably find that your new ideas and beliefs about things give you a greater sense of control than you've had before. Psychologically, there could be a tremendous effect on how you feel, both about yourself and about the world. You'll receive both the positive and negative effects of Pluto over this period, though. In your search for something a bit deeper and more powerful from life, you may encounter people who are rather controlling or have an unhealthy interest in manipulating people and situations. Any local or international travel you undertake will have a deep and powerful effect on you. There may be one particular country, or town, which has an almost hypnotic effect. That's because Pluto never does anything by halves. You can never be a tourist when Pluto is around — you tend to get truly involved with the place and the people you are visiting. Some of you may even switch countries and emigrate. The locals, the buildings, the culture and the atmosphere of the places you visit will transform the way you think about yourself and the world. It's common for women going through this cycle to visit somewhere like India, for example, and come back with an entirely new angle on life.

GEMINI

You can expect your finances and lifestyle to undergo a complete change. There will be one particular episode when it feels as if everything is breaking down. A mortgage may undergo a complete restructure, for example, or a superannuation/pension policy you have held for years may be closed. Some of you — unfortunately — will find that you are involved in a separation or other kind of loss, involving a partner, lover, associate or relative who was bound up with your money, your house or flat, or your possessions. If this is the case, then you literally will have to start from scratch. You may switch banks. You may buy or sell property. You may marry, or move in with someone, bringing about a profound change in your week-to-week budgeting. The late, great astrologer Patric Walker used to say that this cycle was about 'other people's money'. The money in question may belong to your husband or lover, or to a relative who includes you in his or her will. It may belong to your business partner or backer. Typically, it will belong to a bank.

Any new beginnings made along these lines will have quite a strong effect on your understanding of issues like money, power and control. In other words, if you sign contracts with financial institutions or partners, then you will be much more sharply aware of who is actually in pole position. This may sound cynical (and very unromantic, if we are discussing your partner or lover). However, it may help to be aware of Pluto's typical emphasis on the balance of power. This is a good time to ask yourself who stands where, and to aim for something more moderate if the piece of paper you are signing actually gives one side an unhealthy ability to call every shot. On several occasions, you will be reborn (in terms of your finances or lifestyle) thanks to the powerful input of a second person, or larger organisation, which is prepared to go in with you in some way.

This cycle also has something strong to say about sex. Don't be surprised if you find yourself becoming obsessed with some aspect of your sexuality over the next few years. Pluto tends to fixate women on the areas of the horoscope it touches. Through some fairly intense and profound experiences, you are likely to enter the next big sexual era of your life. Pluto is such an X-rated planet that I have no wish to go into all the possibilities here!

Finally, death. (This cycle isn't exactly an episode of *Happy Days*, I'm telling you.) By 2025, your ideas on death and dying will have changed massively. This could happen for all sorts of reasons — you may attend a funeral, you may have a near-death experience yourself, you may lose someone close to you, or you may have some kind of spiritual or religious breakthrough which changes your mind on things.

CANCER

The effects of this new cycle in your life will vary, depending on where you are today — single or attached. If you are single, expect a new relationship of the deep, meaningful, profound and compelling type. An affair with more than a hint of obsession, perhaps, or a marriage with a depth and intensity that you can honestly say you haven't yet experienced. By 2025 you will have taken on something that will change your life — or even ended up in a series of intense new relationships. A relationship or marriage which forms in this cycle is also unlikely to stay still. Something about both your personalities in combination means that things will repeatedly be restructured, reworked and reorganised.

There is no point in glossing over Pluto's negative effects, either. This planet has a reputation for creating a whole range of operatic, or even soap-operatic, scenarios. Jealousy, sexual obsession, physical threats, stalking, obscene phone calls, blackmail . . . you name it, astrologers have blamed it on Pluto. On a less dramatic level, Pluto can manifest as game-playing, manipulation, controlling or jealous behaviour, or big power struggles. On the positive side, you get powerful, healing, transforming, deep, unforgettable, passionate, intense, sexy and erotic partnerships. It all depends on how skilled you are at sidestepping Pluto's landmines.

If you choose to remain single, then the same issues — power, control, intensity, passion — will be channelled through a Significant Other who has nothing to do with love and sex, but may be your partner in a business, work, financial or practical sense. This relationship, built for solid and rather unemotional reasons, is likely to have the kind of depth and complexity you might expect from a sexual relationship. Pluto rules taboos, the forbidden or unacceptable topics which are far too deep, sticky and dark for the pair of you to throw around in casual conversation. For some de facto Cancer couples, the subject of weddings or babies might in itself become a completely forbidden and dangerous topic! For others, a darker subject might come up in these years — but you will find that it deepens the bond you share.

The partnership itself will transform even if you stay together to 2025. Your partner may go through the most dramatic and profound changes and experiences, which in turn alter the tone of the relationship. Or it may be you who deals with some kind of transformation, which seems to filter down into the partnership and alter everything from the way you eat together to the way you have sex. One thing is sure. A partnership in these Pluto years will have to change in order to survive. If it can't transform from its very depths, it may come to a close. It's also very likely that you will reach a new, profound stage in the marriage or relationship which makes all those Plutonian phrases and songs — "Til death do us part' and 'I would die for you' resonate with extreme meaning and power.

LEO
Between now and 2025 Pluto will change the way you work. As the majority of women are now working full-time or part-time, you're most likely to experience Pluto's effects on the job. If you have always worked a certain way, or followed your professional routines and rituals in a specific manner,

you can expect that to completely transform. If you were the Queen of the BlackBerry before, you may find a new way to structure your days. If you've always been chaos on two legs, the introduction of new equipment, new training or other X factors is likely to force you to shape up.

It's extremely likely that your current job may end or take a new direction. There will be plenty of endings and beginnings before 2025. Some of these power-packed changes will be of your choosing; some will happen without any input from you. You will build certain work or business associations which go beyond the usual skin-deep level of these things — some may feel quite intense, or represent something quite profound to you. You are also going to have to deal with power and control issues in the workplace or business sector. Don't be surprised if you find yourself caught up in something which feels a lot more tangled, dark and difficult than the usual 'Good morning, Miss Jones' relationship.

If you work with computers, you'll get a more powerful computer. If you rely pretty much on contacts and networking to help your career, you'll get some really powerful and influential people backing you. You may join an organisation which has a lot more clout than anything you're used to. Or you may find yourself in a new work set-up where the boss, or some other co-worker, has an extraordinary amount of influence over people. That influence may not be obvious at first. Handle your relationship with them very carefully.

This cycle also rules your health and wellbeing. Pluto is likely to change the way you eat (or what you eat), the way you drink (or what you drink), the kind of health insurance you have, the sort of attitude you have towards fitness and exercise, and even your understanding of the way the mind influences the body. The American astrologer and psychic Gail Fairfield associates this cycle with 'health issues involving sexuality, genitals and the elimination system' in her book, *Choice Centered Astrology* (Weiser). As the last sign to get this cycle before you was Cancer, you may want to ask people born from late June to late July about their experiences. Health in general will become a bigger deal. You may decide to detox in a major way, because Pluto likes to get rid of rubbish, and the idea that you can get rid of the rubbish from your body may begin to fascinate you. Only one word of caution: Pluto can produce obsession, so if you find yourself fixating on the gym, or a particular diet, or a specific level of fitness, it may be time to pull back.

VIRGO

You have the most intense relationship forecast of all the signs, apart from Cancer, over the next few years. So if you're involved with a Cancerian, expect life-changing transformation!

No matter which sign you are involved with, or if you are single or attached, you'll find that Pluto, in your department of sex and babies, will bring about a total revolution in your ideas about parenting — or not parenting.

In short, expect this:

* A shedding of old attitudes or expectations about babies and kids, in general

* A new quality of intensity in your sex life

* A complete transformation of the way you handle the physical side of love

* Experimentation with what other people might call sexual taboos

* Deeper and more meaningful sex

* Sexual obsession, from you or your partner

Pluto is the X-rated planet. Consequently, unless the publishers decide to put this in a plastic wrapper, it's not possible for me to go into each and every permutation of this cycle. But I hope you get the general idea. If you've never really thought about sex much before, or if you've left it to trot along by itself, then this cycle will change that. By 2025, you will have taken several giant steps towards a new, restructured kind of sexuality. You could go to a therapist if sex has been a bit of an issue for you. You may experiment with women if you have always been heterosexual, or try anything from radical celibacy to threesomes if you have always been a strictly vanilla kind of woman in bed. Check back with Leo friends, as they went through this before you!

Don't be surprised if you go through periods of mild obsession and unusually intense emotion where babies, sons, daughters, other people's children, pregnancy or fertility/adoption are concerned. If you do give birth in this cycle, it's likely to be something enormously powerful and profound for you. Some women just churn babies out and go home. With Pluto in this cycle, you can't do that.

They call Pluto the 'shrink' planet in astrology, because it encourages you to look more deeply into what makes you tick, and then it tends to change you. By proceeding with a pregnancy in this cycle — or even by going through a termination or miscarriage — you are likely to experience the 'shrink' planet in an incredibly personal way.

It's common for mothers to face big issues about power and control in reference to their son or daughter in this cycle. Your child may involve you in one of those situations where you really have to decide where the boundaries are. If you're an older Virgo, there may be difficult questions about grandchildren — who has the control? You, your grandchild, or your own children, who gave birth to them? There may be power questions which involve the nanny, the babysitter or teachers. As usual, Pluto will try to confront you with the most basic human issues, and control is top of the list.

Finally, this cycle has a lot do with self-expression and creativity. It is associated with having a brainchild of some kind. Whatever you produce or pour yourself into during this cycle will probably bring out the obsessive-compulsive side of you. You may also find yourself becoming a control freak over certain aspects of the end product! On the positive side, Pluto will lend real power and depth to what you are producing, no matter if you're an artist, writer, dancer, film-maker or Queen of the Weekend Hobbies. As with any Pluto cycle, if you feel yourself frothing at the mouth, it's time to switch the obsession. Take the same compulsive energy and apply it to something which won't mess with your mind — like gardening!

LIBRA

During this long-running cycle, the way you see certain family members or relatives is likely to change quite profoundly. The family situation will be dramatically different by the end of it. Sometimes Pluto can bring a death in the family, or a divorce or separation — this is an obvious cause of the sweeping transformations which occur. As a result of this loss, the chemistry between all the members changes. There may be a domino effect — because one person passes away, or decides to leave the family circle, changes seem to flow on to everybody who is in the clan.

This is one possibility. There may also be some skeleton in the family closet which is released at this time. You don't go through the death, separation or divorce — but secrets which have been successfully buried for years may come out. Another possibility? A family member comes out of the closet in sexual terms. Then there are the families who find that one member survives a life-threatening illness, or one member goes to jail. You may find someone illegitimate in the family tree, or Great Uncle Bob may turn out to actually be Great Aunty Betty.

All of this is not meant to alarm, by the way. Your life is not about to become a soap opera. It's just that Pluto has to be discussed in a fairly upfront, unafraid way. For you, the family chemistry change may be for more subtle reasons. One of your parents may switch jobs, or find a new role in the community, thus changing his or her attitude — the domino effect will have an impact on the whole family eventually, as the standard parental roles alter. A family member may even win the lottery — it happens — and the money suddenly changes everything overnight, including the way certain relatives deal with each other!

Some astrologers have noted that women going through this cycle have some kind of power struggle with their parents or brothers and sisters. It may not always be an obvious thing, either. The actual dynamics of the game which is being played could be deeply buried, and not always conscious.

Pluto is the great revamper. It also achieves what the Americans call 'empowerment' which, although it sounds good, is a slightly confusing term. Basically, it means that if you were always low on the family power scale, you'll probably creep up. Even if you run the entire show, you may gain even more influence. None of this happens overnight, though. Pluto is a slow mover. It's possible that someone — hopefully not you — will turn into a total control freak in this cycle. These kinds of situations can be prevented in the first place if you (using your cunning astrology knowledge) can sniff out the potential for a problem before it begins.

This cycle also famously affects your house or flat situation. By 2025 you will have moved, renovated or decorated several times. It will be an intense process. You may even uproot altogether and emigrate. At the very least, some part of your current flat or house will be replaced or added onto. The usual 'power freak' rule applies to real estate and housing issues now. In other words, if you sense that you are dealing with a builder, decorator or real estate agent who has a definite dark side, you may want to keep things *very* flexible! One other point. If you dig up your garden, make sure the man with the machine doesn't dig into the earth's crust.

SCORPIO

Your last Pluto cycle involved your money, your lifestyle and your possessions. In the last few years, you've restructured your budget or your source of income. You've had crashing lows, and pretty powerful highs. In a more moderate way, you've probably also suffered losses or big changes you could have done without, affecting your money, your business interests, your security, your lifestyle or your possessions. In typical Pluto fashion, you've since restructured things, rebuilt things, or recycled the set-up you had before so that it becomes truly viable.

At this stage in your astrological destiny, you are allowed to put your calculator down. The big, sweeping transformation is over, and the next cycle is underway. It's going to change the way you communicate.

Here are some concrete examples:

* Learning HTML, the internet language

* Learning a foreign language

* Work or career changes ask you to add technical terms to your vocabulary

* If you're deaf, you may learn new signing skills

* If you're living with a disability, new technology may help you to 'speak'

* Your vocabulary or wordpower may increase

* You may discover a talent for poetry, fiction, or other forms of communication — ESP counts too

* You may learn public speaking
* If you can't read or write, you may join a literacy programme
* New technology — e-mail, mobile phones, faxes, language scramblers — will alter the way you stay in touch
* Learning different listening skills, thanks to a new course or interest

On an ordinary everyday level, you may just find that you become more powerful and effective when you are putting things in writing or getting your point across. As with all Pluto cycles, the only problem is the risk that you will become too intense for people. Watch the way you come across, ask people for feedback if you need to, and re-read what you put in writing. If you're too wild-eyed and worked up about everything, then that's a sure sign that Pluto's negative effects are operating, and you may have to pull back or chill out.

SAGITTARIUS

Pluto is going to spend several years in the area of your solar chart ruling money, possessions, income and property. Expect a transformation in stages, rather than one giant sweeping change. Typically, December/January will regularly present you with the same familiar issues. How much control do you have over your cashflow or lifestyle? Is there a power play going on in terms of money, property or possessions, no matter how well disguised?

The Second House of your chart also goes deeper than dollars and cents, pounds and pence, and all the things they can do for you. It's concerned with your value system — what you tend to personally put a cash value on, and the kinds of things which go beyond money or materialism.

Pluto could change you from a communist to a capitalist, or vice versa. It may show you, in quite a profound way, what it costs to 'sell out' or sell yourself short. Ultimately, this planet will pose one question to you — what do you most value?

Here are some other common manifestations of Pluto in this particular cycle:

* Obsessive spending creates a financial wipeout

* A fixation with your earning power distracts you from other things in your life which have their own (non-monetary) value

* Through intense encounters with others, you learn that money really is power

* Your value system, which may dictate everything from the sort of job or role you choose to the kind of lifestyle you adopt, changes forever

* A complete restructuring of your earning power and personal budgeting

Pluto can create a wipeout situation if you take things to extremes. However, it is also the planet of rebirth and resurrection. Even if you do hit a critical point with property, money or possessions, you can build everything up again, in a new form.

Pluto can actually give you control and power as a result of your assets, business position or finances too. You may come to see, in a very raw way, exactly what ownership and earning capacity can do for a person.

CAPRICORN

Pluto is in your sign from 2008 and you may already be feeling its effects by 2009. A revamp of your face, hair or body is an early sign that this planet is making its presence known. In the first house of your solar chart, Pluto influences your image, your physical appearance and your persona. The woman you seemed to be before this cycle began will not be the woman people see afterwards.

Pluto is opposing the descendant, or partnership, area of your chart at the same time. So the profound changes in your closest relationships and partnerships over these years will also alter the way you look, the way you act, the way the world sees you, and the way you see the world. If you are by yourself during this cycle, then expect some quite in-depth and transformative changes of attitude. You may transform your view of what marriage, commitment, partnership and singledom means. In the process, you will also change yourself.

January and December of any year are key times for these issues. In fact, after a few years you may begin to detect a pattern.

Here are some common manifestations of this kind of Pluto cycle:

* Dramatic weight loss or cosmetic surgery
* A deliberate attempt to project a different image to the world
* A change in personal style or wardrobe
* A noticeable change in the way people regard you, thanks to changed circumstances
* Intense one-on-one situations, probably in your love life, that alter you inside or out
* Inner work — therapy, self-help, self-education — transforms you

This Pluto cycle classically results in some kind of re-launch. Same person, different name. Same person, different clothes. And on it goes — but the outer changes are also a manifestation of deeper personality changes taking place within. After Pluto's out of Capricorn in a few years from now, you may even have relaunched or relabelled yourself a couple of times.

There may be an image crisis at this time. That's okay. You need to shed an old skin. Don't be surprised if your reputation or public face — your packaging — is unwrapped, and then refitted. People may have stereotyped you or pigeonholed you a certain way, but after 2008 and by 2025 you will have been given several chances to change their perception. Surviving various image or reputation issues in this year will actually make you more powerful too. You'll often feel like a phoenix rising from the flames!

AQUARIUS

This is the most complicated Pluto cycle of all. This planet is now passing through the most mysterious part of your solar chart — astrologers have all sorts of opinions on what it means. Some link it to hospitals, institutions, prisons and asylums. Eek! I don't necessarily agree, by the way. What it means more than anything else is this — time to yourself, time to think, time to reflect. You can see why this might mean a short stay with a psychiatrist, of course. But more typically, what will happen in this cycle is a profound change in your relationship with the inner you, or the hidden you. This can happen through a fascination with dreams and their meanings. It can happen because you take off to Bali for a month to gaze at your navel. It may happen through a profound spiritual experience, perhaps one where you are required to go on a retreat or spend more time praying or meditating alone. You may see a psychic or astrologer who reintroduces you to yourself.

I hope you get the drift. You can still pick up some astrology books which talk about the Twelfth House of the chart (where Pluto is from 2008) as some kind of doom and gloom place, full of people in white coats carrying clipboards. After years of looking at charts with a big Twelfth House emphasis, though, I'm more inclined to say that it's about self-discovery through retreat. Because Pluto is extreme, this may happen in an extreme way. But enough generalisation.

Here's a list of Plutonian possibilities:

* You buy a home, time-share or holiday home where you can take regular retreats — it ends up changing your life

* You become obsessed with a special pastime or pursuit which you must necessarily do alone, or privately; in the process you transform yourself at quite a deep level

* Destiny will set up circumstances which take you off the merry-go-round of life if you do not consciously choose to take time out occasionally

* Dreamwork, psychic experiences, astrology, psychology, psychiatry or other means of peering into the human psyche begin to have a strong effect on you

* Anything locked in the basement of your mind which you haven't consciously known about or chosen to face may now reappear, so be prepared

* Odd experiences — omens, coincidences, obvious pieces of synchronicity and spookiness — send strong messages. It's very likely that this is your unconscious trying to get through to you when nothing else is working

People who have been through this cycle before you report getting a lot of mileage from dream journals and notebooks. This cycle is linked to the unconscious mind, so a quick flip through the works of Freud or Jung may also be useful. Art is another way of releasing Pluto's energy in this period, but don't be surprised if your abstract painting turns out to be free therapy.

Pluto is linked to crisis and revolutionary change. Matters which are private, secret and utterly confidential will get you to that point in this cycle. You'll need a diary or a confidant/e, for sure. And you might just go through the deepest, most profound stripping back of layers that you've ever known! Don't even think about sharing your experiences, though. Pluto in this zone of your chart is all about deep secrets, held back from other people's gaze. It's about an intense relationship with your inner self — and the door has to be locked.

PISCES

Friends you've known forever will go through some incredible transformations during the few years that Pluto is in Capricorn. One of them may go through a crisis, only to be reborn at a later date. Another may change before your very eyes, in a way which means the friendship itself has to alter if it's going to survive.

Here are some other typical manifestations of this kind of Pluto cycle:

* You become intensely involved with a group of people and find that you just aren't the same person after it's all over

* Agreeing to a specific role within a group gives you more power or influence than you would ever have enjoyed alone — or even with a partner

* A friendship changes and becomes more like a convoluted game of snakes and ladders than the sociable bond you remember; if it's going to last, then it will have to alter

* For some reason, friends — and even casual social acquaintances — have a more profound and in-

depth effect on you; it's more than coffee and conversation, these people have the potential to bring about great changes in you

* New friends emerge in your life — passionate, complex, soulful, intense, driven people

* Through friends or group activities, you come face to face with some of life's most taboo subjects — death, sex, the occult — anything which is normally hidden or off-limits

* A move, relationship change or other dramatic lifestyle alteration results in you having to wave goodbye to some friendships, or even start from scratch with a whole new social network

Pluto can never leave anything the same. So when it's passing through an area of your solar chart which rules friends, your social acquaintances and your group involvements, you can expect a whole new set-up. The faces may remain, but the chemistry between you may be very different in the long run. New people will come along, and a completely different way of operating socially is the likely result.

Pluto is the planet of obsession too. You may become completely transfixed by some kind of group, team, club, association or network. And don't be surprised if you make friends who have a strong dose of Scorpio in their personal charts, or a profession or personality which seems typically Scorpionic or Plutonian. You will make at least one powerful friend in this cycle.

It's possible that you will learn more about people politics and power games through friends — or others in the group — than any other source. Be aware that any network, club, team or association you are involved with around 2009 is inevitably going to go through massive changes. Reshuffles, departures, power struggles and even the odd loss here and there are all classic Pluto Eleventh House outcomes.

Unless you want to waste a lot of time and energy, don't get into string-pulling, manipulation or intrigue in the group in these years. It could all get surprisingly deep, dark and complicated, in a way you had not anticipated.

JUPITER — CYCLES OF LUCK AND OPPORTUNITY

WORKING WITH YOUR JUPITER RETURNS

When Jupiter returns to the same spot it was in in your horoscope at birth, you'll get lucky, and it will change your life. It happens around every twelve years. What took place for you between eleven and thirteen? That was your first taste of what Jupiter can do. Expect more opportunities around age twenty-four, thirty-six, forty-eight, sixty and so on.

The area of life Jupiter triggers depends on the house (the slice of the horoscope wheel) it was in at the minute of birth. If you are curious, go to www.astro.com and look for this symbol on your horoscope wheel ♃. Which segment of the wheel is it in? That's your good karma!

House One — Image

House Two — Cash

House Three — Ideas

House Four — Home

House Five — Kids

House Six — Work

House Seven — Partnership

House Eight — Finance

House Nine — Travel

House Ten — Success

House Eleven — Friends

House Twelve — Secrets

House One begins at the 9:00 p.m. position on the wheel. Count anti-clockwise to find the other houses — House Seven should be almost opposite it.

JUPITER AND YOUR SUN SIGN (SOLAR) CHART

Jupiter always works well with your Sun sign (solar) chart, which is the one that media astrologers use to predict the future. Where's the luck in your life going to come from? Here's a full Jupiter cycle for you to analyse.

2007	Jupiter in Sagittarius
2008	Jupiter in Capricorn
2009	Jupiter in Aquarius
2010	Jupiter in Pisces
2011	Jupiter in Aries
2012	Jupiter in Taurus
2013	Jupiter in Gemini
2014	Jupiter in Cancer
2015	Jupiter in Leo
2016	Jupiter in Virgo
2017	Jupiter in Libra
2018	Jupiter in Scorpio
2019	Jupiter in Sagittarius

Jupiter in Cycle One — Jupiter is in your sign

In 2007 this is you, Sagittarius. In 2016 it's you, Virgo. You'll have opportunities to make more of your image. Lucky connections and situations will help boost your appearance.

Jupiter in Cycle Two — Jupiter is in the sign after yours

In 2009 this is you, Capricorn. In 2014 it's you, Gemini. You'll have opportunities to make more of your cashflow. Lucky connections and situations will help boost your bank account.

Jupiter in Cycle Three — Jupiter is two signs after yours

In 2013 this is you, Aries. In 2019 it's you, Libra. You'll have opportunities to take more short trips. Lucky connections and situations will help your ideas and your way with words.

Jupiter in Cycle Four — Jupiter is three signs after yours

In 2009 this is you, Scorpio. In 2017 it's you, Cancer. You'll have opportunities to make more of your home. Lucky connections and situations will help real estate, rentals or renovations.

Jupiter in Cycle Five — Jupiter is four signs after yours

In 2008 this is you, Virgo. In 2019 it's you, Leo. You'll have opportunities to make more of your children, or other people's children. Your luck is in with sexual growth and learning.

Jupiter in Cycle Six — Jupiter is five signs after yours

In 2012 this is you, Sagittarius. And in 2013 it's you, Capricorn. You'll have opportunities to make more of an old or new job. Luck will help you find better health and wellbeing.

Jupiter in Cycle Seven — Jupiter is six signs after yours

In 2010 this is you, Virgo. And in 2012 it's you, Scorpio. You'll have opportunities to make more of a marriage or relationship — or get out of one. A business partnership will pay off.

Jupiter in Cycle Eight — Jupiter is seven signs after yours

In 2007 this is you, Taurus. In 2009 it's you, Cancer. You'll have opportunities to make more of other people's cash, possessions, houses or flats. Family or a partner's money may help.

Jupiter in Cycle Nine — Jupiter is eight signs after yours

In 2018 it's you, Pisces. In 2019 it's you, Aries. You'll have opportunities to make more of travel, relocation or people from miles away. Publishing or education could be lucky too.

Jupiter in Cycle Ten — Jupiter is nine signs after yours

In 2013 it's you, Virgo. In 2018 it's you, Aquarius. You'll have opportunities to make more of your old job, or a big new position. Luck will help you to greater success or status now.

Jupiter in Cycle Eleven — Jupiter is ten signs after yours

In 2018 it's you, Capricorn. In 2019 it's you, Aquarius. You'll have opportunities to make more of the group now, or your friends. New friends could be incredibly lucky for you.

Jupiter in Cycle Twelve — Jupiter is eleven signs after yours

In 2007 it's you, Capricorn. In 2009 it's you, Pisces. You'll have opportunities to make more of what is secret, confidential or private. What you get up to alone helps growth and luck.

YOUR JUPITER RETURN — AROUND AGE 24, 36, 48, 60, 72

This is a big opportunity to exploit a big opportunity. It may be a makeover, a pay rise, your first car, a mortgage, a baby, a new job, a marriage, an inheritance, a trip, an award, a new social life or a spiritual awakening. It depends on your own chart, really. When Jupiter travels around the sky to come back to the very same place it was in at the moment of your birth, stuff happens. Doors swing open. All you have to do is push yourself through.

How to spot it

A general feeling that life is flowing your way, that thinking big is a good idea, and that being positive can take you places.

And don't forget

Jupiter keeps on coming back. The expansion, optimism, luck and 'open doors' feeling will be with you approximately every twelve years, on a regular basis. It shouldn't be too hard to pinpoint the months that you really feel Jupiter operating, though.

THE URANUS OPPOSITION — YOUR FORTIES

Happy with Jupiter? How about your Uranus Opposition, around age thirty-eight to forty-two?

When people describe a mid-life crisis, it's usually about this: Uranus, the planet of liberation, doing all sorts of bizarre things to your chart as it travels through the zodiac. It typically happens as you go into your forties.

Uranus may feel like an itch you have to scratch. You may feel wired, practically buzzing as you lie in bed at night, unable to stand the compromises you have made or unwilling to go on in the same old ways. At this point, women classically do something that leaves those around them reeling. In the '70s, a lot of them 'got' women's liberation. Basically, Uranus is a massive lie detector. If some part of your life entails you faking it — for whatever reason — then Uranus will shake everything up.

Your mantra at this time will be 'freedom, freedom, freedom'. As a general rule, the more free and honest your life has been to date, the less dramatic this period will feel. But if you've managed to lock yourself in a box, or if you're off on a life path which isn't really authentic or 'alive', then expect electrifying changes. You'll be minding your own business, trundling along the street one day, and — BAM! Suddenly you're stopped in your tracks. Uranus really is the giant foot of the zodiac.

To find out the exact time that Uranus will oppose Uranus, call or e-mail your friendly astrologer. It's a massive milestone in your life, and in your horoscope, and you may need some personal assistance with it!

YOUR RISING SIGN AND YOUR PERSONAL LIFE PATH

Your Rising sign (also known as your Ascendant) tells you about the fate that has been fixed for you, from the moment of birth. If you have Cancer Rising, destiny says that you will keep on experiencing family issues, and particularly key situations involving your mother. Your own parenting potential is also going to be a big part of your journey on the planet if you have Cancer on the Ascendant.

If you have Aries Rising, destiny might throw you into a chain of situations where it always seems that you have to compete, to fight, to win. There will be battles and competitions in your personal life or professional life.

Look up your Rising sign below. For total accuracy, though, go to www.astro.com and type in your time, date and place of birth. The sign on the 9pm position on the wheel that comes back is your Rising Sign. Otherwise, what follows is a good rough guide.

FIND YOUR RISING SIGN HERE

Aries born around dawn — Aries Rising

Aries born after dawn — Taurus Rising

Aries born mid-morning — Gemini Rising

Aries born around noon — Cancer Rising

Aries born early afternoon — Leo Rising

Aries born mid-afternoon — Virgo Rising

Aries born around sunset — Libra Rising

Aries born after dinner — Scorpio Rising

Aries born mid-evening — Sagittarius Rising

Aries born around midnight — Capricorn Rising

Aries born in the small hours — Aquarius Rising

Aries born before dawn — Pisces Rising

Taurus born around dawn — Taurus Rising

Taurus born after dawn — Gemini Rising

Taurus born mid-morning — Cancer Rising

Taurus born around noon — Leo Rising

Taurus born early afternoon — Virgo Rising

Taurus born mid-afternoon — Libra Rising

Taurus born around sunset — Scorpio Rising

Taurus born after dinner — Sagittarius Rising

Taurus born mid-evening — Capricorn Rising

Taurus born around midnight — Aquarius Rising

Taurus born in the small hours — Pisces Rising

Taurus born before dawn — Aries Rising

Gemini born around dawn — Gemini Rising

Gemini born after dawn — Cancer Rising

Gemini born mid-morning — Leo Rising

Gemini born around noon — Virgo Rising

Gemini born early afternoon — Libra Rising

Gemini born mid-afternoon — Scorpio Rising

Gemini born around sunset– Sagittarius Rising

Gemini born after dinner — Capricorn Rising

Gemini born mid-evening — Aquarius Rising

Gemini born around midnight — Pisces Rising

Gemini born in the small hours — Aries Rising

Gemini born before dawn — Taurus Rising

Cancer born around dawn — Cancer Rising

Cancer born after dawn — Leo Rising

Cancer born mid-morning — Virgo Rising

Cancer born around noon — Libra Rising

Cancer born early afternoon — Scorpio Rising

Cancer born mid-afternoon — Sagittarius Rising

Cancer born around sunset — Capricorn Rising

Cancer born after dinner — Aquarius Rising

Cancer born mid-evening — Pisces Rising

Cancer born around midnight — Aries Rising

Cancer born in the small hours — Taurus Rising

Cancer born before dawn — Gemini Rising

Leo born around dawn — Leo Rising

Leo born after dawn — Virgo Rising

Leo born mid-morning — Libra Rising

Leo born around noon — Scorpio Rising

Leo born early afternoon — Sagittarius Rising

Leo born mid-afternoon — Capricorn Rising

Leo born around sunset — Aquarius Rising

Leo born after dinner — Pisces Rising

Leo born mid-evening — Aries Rising

Leo born around midnight — Taurus Rising

Leo born in the small hours — Gemini Rising

Leo born before dawn — Cancer Rising

Virgo born around dawn — Virgo Rising

Virgo born after dawn — Libra Rising

Virgo born mid-morning — Scorpio Rising

Virgo born around noon — Sagittarius Rising

Virgo born early afternoon — Capricorn Rising

Virgo born mid-afternoon — Aquarius Rising

Virgo born around sunset — Pisces Rising

Virgo born after dinner — Aries Rising
Virgo born mid-evening — Taurus Rising
Virgo born around midnight — Gemini Rising
Virgo born in the small hours — Cancer Rising
Virgo born before dawn — Leo Rising
Libra born around dawn — Libra Rising
Libra born after dawn — Scorpio Rising
Libra born mid-morning — Sagittarius Rising
Libra born around noon — Capricorn Rising
Libra born early afternoon — Aquarius Rising
Libra born mid-afternoon — Pisces Rising
Libra born around sunset — Aries Rising
Libra born after dinner — Taurus Rising
Libra born mid-evening — Gemini Rising
Libra born around midnight — Cancer Rising
Libra born in the small hours — Leo Rising
Libra born before dawn — Virgo Rising
Scorpio born around dawn — Scorpio Rising
Scorpio born after dawn — Sagittarius Rising
Scorpio born mid-morning — Capricorn Rising
Scorpio born around noon — Aquarius Rising
Scorpio born early afternoon — Pisces Rising
Scorpio born mid-afternoon — Aries Rising
Scorpio born around sunset — Taurus Rising
Scorpio born after dinner — Gemini Rising
Scorpio born mid-evening — Cancer Rising
Scorpio born around midnight — Leo Rising
Scorpio born in the small hours — Virgo Rising
Scorpio born before dawn — Libra Rising
Sagittarius born around dawn — Sagittarius Rising
Sagittarius born after dawn — Capricorn Rising
Sagittarius born mid-morning — Aquarius Rising
Sagittarius born around noon — Pisces Rising
Sagittarius born early afternoon — Aries Rising

Sagittarius born mid-afternoon — Taurus Rising
Sagittarius born around sunset — Gemini Rising
Sagittarius born after dinner — Cancer Rising
Sagittarius born mid-evening — Leo Rising
Sagittarius born around midnight — Virgo Rising
Sagittarius born in the small hours — Libra Rising
Sagittarius born before dawn — Scorpio Rising
Capricorn born around dawn — Capricorn Rising
Capricorn born after dawn — Aquarius Rising
Capricorn born mid-morning — Pisces Rising
Capricorn born around noon — Aries Rising
Capricorn born early afternoon — Taurus Rising
Capricorn born mid-afternoon — Gemini Rising
Capricorn born around sunset — Cancer Rising
Capricorn born after dinner — Leo Rising
Capricorn born mid-evening — Virgo Rising
Capricorn born around midnight — Libra Rising
Capricorn born in the small hours — Scorpio Rising
Capricorn born before dawn — Sagittarius Rising
Aquarius born around dawn — Aquarius Rising
Aquarius born after dawn — Pisces Rising
Aquarius born mid-morning — Aries Rising
Aquarius born around noon — Taurus Rising
Aquarius born early afternoon — Gemini Rising
Aquarius born mid-afternoon — Cancer Rising
Aquarius born around sunset — Leo Rising
Aquarius born after dinner — Virgo Rising
Aquarius born mid-evening — Libra Rising
Aquarius born around midnight — Scorpio Rising
Aquarius born in the small hours — Sagittarius Rising
Aquarius born before dawn — Capricorn Rising
Pisces born around dawn — Pisces Rising
Pisces born after dawn — Aries Rising
Pisces born mid-morning — Taurus Rising

Pisces born around noon — Gemini Rising
Pisces born early afternoon — Cancer Rising
Pisces born mid-afternoon — Leo Rising
Pisces born around sunset — Virgo Rising
Pisces born after dinner — Libra Rising
Pisces born mid-evening — Scorpio Rising
Pisces born around midnight — Sagittarius Rising
Pisces born in the small hours — Capricorn Rising
Pisces born before dawn — Aquarius Rising

YOU KNOW YOU'VE GOT ARIES RISING IF . . .

You see the world as a competitive place, and you believe you have to be faster or tougher than other people to hold your own. You like clothes, accessories or cars that let people know how energetic and 'out there' you are. If people want to get to know the real you, you're well aware that they must first get past the act you sometimes put on — that of the bold, fearless, go-getter action woman. Your first approach to people is usually fast and gutsy.

YOUR DESTINY: Contests, battles and victories.

YOU KNOW YOU'VE GOT TAURUS RISING IF . . .

You see the world as a place where money rules pretty much everything. To feel at home in this world, you either have to have a strong set of values that goes beyond money and materialism, or you have to have a very good accountant and investment portfolio! You like clothes, accessories or cars that let people know you value the good things in life. If people want to get to know the real you, they have to get past your down-to-earth, practical act.

YOUR DESTINY: Wealth, or wealth that goes beyond money.

YOU KNOW YOU'VE GOT GEMINI RISING IF . . .

You see the world as a place to make connections in, a place to make contact, swap gossip, exchange information and news, and then be on your way. To feel at home in this world you have to have good communication skills — written or verbal. You like clothes, accessories or cars that let people know that you're just a little more intelligent or well-informed than the average person. School or the education process was a big deal for you.

YOUR DESTINY: A lifetime involvement with the written or spoken word.

YOU KNOW YOU'VE GOT CANCER RISING IF . . .

You see the world as a place where everything leads back to the family and childhood — you can't help this psychological view of the world. To feel at home out there, you feel you have to have some kind of place to call your own — a particular region, homeland or a treasured house or flat. You like clothes, accessories or cars that protect you. If people want to get to know the real you, they have to get past that caring, sensitive persona first.

YOUR DESTINY: Everything will always come back to the family.

YOU KNOW YOU'VE GOT LEO RISING IF . . .

You see the world as a place where you have to be confident about what you do and who you are — or nothing works. To feel as if you belong out there, you automatically look for a career or calling (which may have nothing to do with your job) where you can take a respected, leading role. Finding an outlet for creative self-expression is also vital, in your opinion. To get to know the real you, people have to get past the impressive exterior first.

YOUR DESTINY: A place in the spotlight.

YOU KNOW YOU'VE GOT VIRGO RISING IF . . .

You see the world as a place where a job worth doing is worth doing well. Your approach to life is basically about fulfilling the high expectations you set yourself, and if that occasionally makes you look like a workaholic to other people, you'll put up with it. You like to present an exterior which is as good as you can get it, so the details of your body, hair, face and wardrobe count for a lot. To feel at home in the world, you pursue perfection.

YOUR DESTINY: Health and wellbeing will rule your biggest choices.

YOU KNOW YOU'VE GOT LIBRA RISING IF . . .

You see the world as a place where people stand or fall by their charm, their outer image, and their ability to glide smoothly and easily through life. To feel as if you belong in this world, you develop a popular persona — lots of smiles and good manners. To get past this to the real you, people must look beyond the glossy surface, and you probably know that by now. Looking presentable, or even well-designed and put together, is part of the deal.

YOUR DESTINY: One major partnership (or several).

YOU KNOW YOU'VE GOT SCORPIO RISING IF . . .

You see the world as a place where a certain amount of secrecy, discretion and confidentiality is the key to staying in control. You're so aware of the sexual vibes that flow between people that you either deliberately dress to play it all down, or you go the other way and crank it up. To get past the image to the real you, people must first deal with your intensity, which is quite noticeable on a first meeting. You may even use it on purpose.

YOUR DESTINY: An amazingly powerful job or marriage.

YOU KNOW YOU'VE GOT SAGITTARIUS RISING IF . . .

You see the world as a place to explore, take adventures in and find meaning in. To feel at home in this world, you believe it's important to travel, either in and around your own area or venturing overseas. To get past the outer you to the real person underneath, people have to look beyond the sense of humour and the positive persona you project. You like clothes, accessories or cars which say you're a world citizen, or you've explored life a bit.

YOUR DESTINY: Lots of travel, or emigration.

YOU KNOW YOU'VE GOT CAPRICORN RISING IF . . .

You feel that the world is quite a structured place, and you're fairly shrewd about the way the whole thing works. You certainly understand the part that hierarchy plays, no matter if you're talking about the world of work or the world of status and social standing. To get to know the real you, people have to get past the ambitious, feet-on-the-ground persona you send out. You prefer a wardrobe which allows people to take you seriously.

YOUR DESTINY: A long, slow crawl to the top.

YOU KNOW YOU'VE GOT AQUARIUS RISING IF . . .

You see the world as an interesting, challenging place, but the main challenge is being true to yourself when all around would like you to conform or compromise — in other words, to fit in. To make things work for you in this world, you've come to accept that you have to do your own thing, in your own way. To get to know what you're really like underneath, people have to get past the odd bit of weirdness or eccentricity. You're your own person.

YOUR DESTINY: A life which is unique, free and unconventional.

YOU KNOW YOU'VE GOT PISCES RISING IF . . .

You see the world as a mysterious, fascinating place where there is more to practically everything than meets the eye. If an Impressionist painting doesn't convince you of that, then a psychic reading or a scuba-diving session will. To get to know what you're really like, people must first see past the sensitivity, the emotion and the occasional vagueness or elusiveness. You prefer a look which says you're imaginative rather than boringly practical.

YOUR DESTINY: A life which is spiritual or creative.

HOW YOUR RISING SIGN INFLUENCES YOUR PERSONALITY

Your Rising Sign isn't the real you. That's your Sun, Moon, Mercury, Venus and Mars signs. But it moulds you and shapes you, so that strangers might sometimes mistake you for your Rising Sign instead of the other factors.

Here's the lowdown on your personality, and the sign which was rising at the minute of your birth.

ARIES RISING

If you were born when the sign of Aries was rising on the horizon, you came into the world at a time when this kind of journey was being mapped out for you — fast, full of challenges and a real competition to be number one. Your Sun, Moon, Mercury, Venus and Mars signs will describe the resources you have to deal with this kind of life journey!

Learning to Win

Because life will often put you in situations which feel like a contest or a battle, you will discover that there is a part of you that won't accept coming second. Competitive sport is one department of life that seems to have an interesting effect on Aries Rising types, as it is here that you play out some of the tensions, and pleasures, of this sign. Feeling that life is a race, or a contest, is something that will become more familiar to you as time goes by. You will also have something to learn about winning and losing.

Part of you may intensely dislike lagging behind, or being left at the start. So one of the challenges with this Rising sign is to reward yourself for the victories, but also to understand that being a poor loser, or a 'difficult' finisher, is not going to help you in the next race you face. Arguing with the opposition, or arguing with the umpire (whoever is playing that role), will not do you any favours either. The first taste of success, or the greatest victory, is something that will stay in your memory for a long time. There will be quite a few of these events in your lifetime, but it may be the memory of the last one along that gives you the inspiration to keep going for the next time.

Your Energy Levels

Very few Aries Rising women like waiting around. This is partly because, after a certain age, the fates will have accustomed you to getting out there and getting what you need. You learn to push, push, push your way through life. This may occasionally earn you a reputation for being aggressive or self-interested. But to drag your feet, or lie in bed, would be unthinkable. Destiny says you always have to get out there, and keep moving. Psychologically, too, a strong sense of enthusiasm is one of your characteristics.

Good Timing

With this Rising sign, it is inevitable that you will always leave someone, somewhere, behind. But even though this has the flattering effect of making you a leader, or an Amazon type, you need to watch out for the patches when you leap ahead so quickly that you end up clumsily falling over and having to start again. For more information and a stronger Arian 'feel', you may want to scan the chapters on Aries as a lot of this will apply to you.

TAURUS RISING

You will often be put in financial high and low situations where you must work out a different sense of values each time. Eventually, the Material Girl days will be balanced by a concern for the things that money cannot purchase. Your deep enjoyment of that elusive thing, Quality of Life, may swing between having the right kind of CDs in your collection, having all that is sensual, creative and artistic around you, and . . . just having a good life! You will be put in many professional or personal situations where the dilemma is being rich in material things, but poor in other areas. In this way, you learn to find your limits. You will go through your madly hedonistic periods, and you will also spend a great deal more than you have to. Equally, you will have to become used to the idea that someone is always going to see you as a provider — the woman who brings the money home for others. There will be moments when this feels rather like meeting a quota.

Your Value System

Because you like natural things — and Taurus is, after all, an Earth sign — you will ultimately have to decide how much it costs to be able to stop and smell the roses occasionally. Some women with Taurus Rising have also become involved with the conservation movement for this reason, but there are an equal number who just enjoy being where the trees are. Still, one cannot enjoy the natural world if there is money to be made, or shopping to be done, and at some stage in your life you are going to have to choose. Equally, perhaps, there will come a point when you realise that some aspects of your lifestyle are just not compatible with the earth's welfare — or the ocean's.

Selling Out

The singular, instructive experience in your life will be the prospect of Selling Out. Some of you will, and some of you won't, but it will remain a crucial stage in your journey. Often, you face this decision on a professional level. Going where the money is, you find yourself compromising other values. You price yourself into one market, but price yourself out of another market, which does not rest on money for its values, but on the things which are beyond price. If this does not occur on a professional level, it may do so in your private life. Your partner's financial status, and the question of your mutual lifestyle, or income, will be a big one. The Taurus Rising journey is full of these kinds of decisions. One client of mine from years ago was in the odd position of enjoying a huge annual salary in a corporate position she loathed and wanting to give everything up to work for an overseas charity. Your journey is about being an accountant or stockbroker, on a symbolic level. You will be doing a lot of adding up or subtracting, but what you are dealing with is not shares in an oil company but shares in your own life. Only you can decide which shares are worth what!

GEMINI RISING

If you were born when the sign of Gemini was on the ascendant, you will spend your life in the world of words, before anything else. Your enjoyment of good books and good conversation will be a big part of the journey. You'll be on the move a lot too, and will become one of life's jugglers. Your Sun, Moon, Mercury, Venus and Mars signs will describe the resources you have to deal with this kind of life journey.

Witty and Verbal

The pen is mightier than the sword. Wit is a weapon. Because life will often be tough, you develop a sharp, amusing response to it. It's more than a way of seeing the world; it's also a particular talent for expressing your view of it. The typical Gemini Rising woman is witty, an entertaining correspondent or phone companion and full of quotable quotes. This sign can be sarcastic and acidic too. If anybody underestimates your intelligence, they are likely to find themselves on the receiving end of another quotable quote from you. Gossipy diaries, letters and journals — or blogging — may be a part of your journey.

The Life of the Mind

Some Geminian women develop minds like filing cabinets, and this may occur because of the profession you find yourself in, or because of a particular sense of vocation or calling. Because people will often be seeking the facts from you, you will go to some lengths to make sure you are well-informed. Because you discover, when young, how good it feels to know the answer, you will get into the habit of always needing to know. Information and loose news always seems to follow you around. It can operate on any level too, as gossip or hard news.

Sibling Figures or Twins

You will pick up a big sibling or 'twin' issue with this Rising sign. Gemini is the sign of the twins, and if you had this sign rising at the moment you were born, destiny says a brother or sister will be a Very Big Deal. Some of you find a cousin takes on that role too. Or you acquire a 'brother' or 'sister' figure in your life who seems to perform the twin function. In the original myths surrounding Gemini, there is rivalry between the twins, but also a special bond. For some of you with this Rising sign, the big issue may have been the brother or sister you didn't get. But in the end, you find a twin figure anyway — a substitute sibling, who presents you with all the issues of competition, attachment and complexity that go with the territory.

Have Suitcase, Will Travel

Your journey is going to be full of short hops, regular zipping around the local scene, and plenty of changes of pace. Gemini is associated with the connection of individuals, ideas and places. This is the country–city Rising sign, but also the Sydney–Melbourne and the London–Paris and the New York–Los Angeles. It really is a case of 'have suitcase, will travel' with Gemini Rising, but planes, trains and automobiles are as strongly connected to your journey as anything else. A mobile phone wouldn't go astray either.

CANCER RISING

How did you learn to be so protective? Probably by having a series of lame ducks, needy people and lost sheep wandering across your path. The Cancer Rising journey is a little like this. It is, however, also about becoming a great cook and moving an awful lot of furniture around.

Creating a Home

At various times in your life, you will be living in spaces which just yelp for a decorator, a renovator or an interior designer. That person is going to be you. The Cancer Rising journey is about turning houses and flats into homes. Some of you may become involved with property, housing, environment or accommodation issues along the way. Others will be content to take the Cancerian journey by hanging around hardware stores and guiding removal trucks into the driveway.

A Sense of Place

Your Cancer Rising journey also involves finding a sense of place on a national level — culturally or geographically — and working out what it means to be patriotic, or identified with your country of choice. The word *homeland* strongly applies to the Cancer Rising life path. You may occasionally feel as if you are playing hostess to all of life's travellers, wanderers and tourists. Life will hand you several chances to define your own sense of home and country to yourself, and welcoming others — comparing notes on a variety of homelands — is one way of achieving this. The Cancer Rising journey always seems to include several dramatic homecomings too. By travelling away, you better understand what it is to be *home*.

The Cancer Rising journey also involves a lot of feeding. The Moon, your ruler, is associated with food, and this may have a special meaning on many different levels for you. On a more basic note, your life will involve more stirring, serving and washing up than most. The feeding that you do will also be emotional. Because you will be intimately involved with the kinds of lame ducks and lost sheep mentioned at the beginning, you will develop a shoulder to lean on, a supportive listening style, the strong arms of a nurse, and the good timing of a natural cook.

The Maternal Role

Playing Mother, or being Mother, is natural on a Cancer Rising journey. The 'feeding' theme may be quite literal too. Not every woman with Cancer Rising finds herself on the path to motherhood, but you are there to nourish people — and even the occasional animal — as part of the journey. Because nobody else cares, you will have to. Because people are hungry, you will have to provide. Because waifs and strays need adopting, destiny asks you to do it. Somehow, the

Cancer Rising journey always seems to ask for a combination of psychologist, cook, cleaner and nurse from you. If you do have a child, it will probably be the biggest journey of your life. If you do not, you will gather other kinds of dependents and 'offspring' around you.

Family and Clan

Dynasties are important in the Cancer Rising journey. For one reason or another, family members will exercise a great deal of influence over what you do with your life and the choices you make. Your relationship with your mother, and all other 'mother' figures within the clan, will be particularly vital, and could have a lot to say about the various turning points you reach in childhood, adolescence and adulthood.

LEO RISING

Destiny says that Leo Rising women have a journey that puts them on display a lot of the time. Your Sun, Moon, Mercury, Venus and Mars signs will explain how comfortable you feel about that!

Winning Respect

Life can be pretty low, and people can be pretty undignified, and this will often strike you as you live your life. Dealing with the distasteful people or situations in life in a gracious way will be part of your journey. You can expect to encounter several challenges, either in your career or in your personal life, where you must exhibit grace under pressure. The situation may be disguised in different ways each time, but the issue is the same: human nature can be low — keep your standards high. Your Leo Rising journey is designed to teach you that you can win respect, recognition and appreciation by holding your head high. Also, perhaps, keeping a stiff upper lip. Spinal complaints are associated with a Leo Rising journey, and I think it may be because women born to this life path strain so much to keep this posture and maintain their grace.

Self-Expression

Because others will ask to be entertained or diverted, you will find you have to oblige. The Leo Rising journey is very much about self-expression, and it arises partly because you have no choice but to accept that there is a crowd, or an audience, out there — and partly because of this phenomenon: the blank canvas. This may be a blank canvas quite literally, and you may dabble in painting or make it your life's pursuit. The 'blank' can also be found on a sheet of paper, a film negative, an empty stage, or in a deserted sports arena.

Drama and Diversion

Several times in your life, you will get this message very strongly: people are looking for drama, style and diversion. Awkward experiences where you *know* you have turned in a less than fabulous performance will occur repeatedly until you do the proper Leonine thing and decide that you can dramatise the ordinary and elevate the mundane. This is partly what you are here for. The way in which you do this will be described by your Sun, Moon, Mercury, Venus or Mars signs. These planets may point to particular talents or abilities, and it is up to destiny to provide the setting for them — which it often will. This 'chance' side of the Leo Rising journey may feel rather like a series of signposts. It 'just happens' that fate will repeatedly hand you opportunities and chances to express yourself.

VIRGO RISING

If you were born with Virgo Rising, then your journey will be about working hard, using your brain, communicating and being healthy. Virgo rules House Six of the horoscope, which is where bodies are perfected, healed and repaired, and work gets done. Your Sun, Moon, Mercury, Venus and Mars signs will describe the resources you have to deal with this kind of life journey.

Attention to Detail

As a great deal of your journey will be spent locked in your own head, you may decide to get things right from day one and become a natural researcher or analyst. Because you will often need to get things absolutely right in your working life, you will find that life asks you to apply your mind as often as possible. In this way, you develop an orderly thinking style. Lists will probably be a big part of your life too. The kind of career you end up choosing — or having chosen for you — will demand an early start or a late finish. An enormous amount of detailed work will be involved, and you may also find that your quest for perfection keeps you there much longer, perhaps, than others are prepared to tolerate.

Brothers and Sisters

Because Mercury is the ruler of Virgo, this god (and symbol) has a huge say over your journey. The myth explains that Mercury stole from his brother, Apollo, but then charmed his way back into his affections again. If you have a brother or sister in your life, there may be some tough issues here, as well as an unusually special bond. If you have Virgo Rising and destiny passed on a brother or sister for you, you may develop a complex, platonic relationship with a man over the course of your life (literally, like a brother) or a 'sisterly' bond with another woman.

Body-Consciousness

Things seem to work in two directions here: either you have an uncanny ability to understand skin, bone, iron count and muscle resistance from the start, or you end up dragging your body into such unhealthy territory that you have to virtually become your own doctor or dietitian. Some of you even end up in the caring or health professions as a result of it. While an astrologer can accurately say that body-consciousness will be a big part of your life, it will happen for different reasons — destiny says you will be put in touch with your body by whatever means possible. This may happen because you enter a career, or an interest area, where bodies are the centre of all known existence. It may also happen when you survive time out in hospital, or at home: the repair and restoration process has something to say about how you will regard your body in future.

Looking for Perfection

In your teens and twenties, there will be quite a few episodes where you feel you have personally fallen down, or others have missed the mark. These stick in your consciousness more strongly than others might expect, and may be a turning point in the way you manage your life and times after that. Your Virgo-influenced journey is really about looking for the ultimate, for the best, for the most precise and orderly result.

LIBRA RISING

If you were born when the sign of Libra was on the ascendant, having a husband, soulmate or business partner (or maybe all three) will be a big part of your journey. Your taste, and sense of aesthetics, will also be important. Your Sun, Moon, Mercury, Venus and Mars signs will describe the ways in which you will make the most of this kind of life journey, but here's what's in store.

Balancing Partnerships

I don't know if you've ever heard the music written for the ballet *Romeo and Juliet*, but it may as well be your theme song. With this Rising sign, you're always looking for the harmony between people. In your own life, you can expect a cradle-to-grave quest for your missing half or opposite number. Because you will often be put in situations where balance, peace or harmony is threatened, you will learn some remarkable diplomacy skills. Because it's the threat of discord that affects you most strongly, you learn to take the soft handle with people — especially that person you consider to be your mate.

Libra Rising is something of a destiny pointer, as it will throw you certain people who naturally end up on the other end of the seesaw with you. Many women with this Rising sign spend their life in units, doubles and couples. For more information on this tendency to double up, you may want to scan the section on Libra. If you also have the Sun, Moon, Mercury, Venus or Mars in this sign, then one particular marriage, relationship or balancing act will be the big defining statement of your life.

Relating Skills

Because you go out into the world wanting people to accompany you, and travel with you, it's crucial that you have some handbook of relating skills — a mental list of what passes for gentleness and charm in this world of car alarms and single-digit gestures. Libra Rising women I have known are natural PR experts. With this sign rising, you know how to establish social harmony, and how to smooth things over between people.

Dealing with Injustices

The Libra Rising journey involves righting wrongs. Destiny says you'll see some blatantly unfair things in your life, and perhaps the occasional serious miscarriage of justice. Because of this, you develop a passion for balancing the scales, and the only time you will break your famous rule of 'smoothing, smiling and nodding' is when you realise you have to declare war to get peace. It rankles when you believe that you or others have been unfairly accused. Or if one group, or species, is suffering at the hands of another's prejudice and bias.

Sound and Vision

Your feeling for colours, textures, sounds and forms will be an integral part of what you do with your life. There are art collectors with this rising sign, but also musicians, and women who are passionate about music. You may find your career sidetracks you into all that is easy on the eye or ear, or it may be your life outside work which provides the backdrop. Beauty counts!

SCORPIO RISING

Fate says that part of your journey is going to be quite intense. Scorpio is closely tied to the story of the phoenix, which rose from its own ashes. Surviving crises, and becoming a new woman as a result of them, is part of your life story too.

Sexuality

Scorpionic sexuality tends to be taboo, for one reason or another. Because what is taboo in our society is pretty much decided by the church and the Establishment, it would not be surprising if you encountered lessons and learning experiences related to these areas: prostitution, adultery, group sex, erotica and pornography, rape fantasy and sadomasochism — or any of the aspects of life which polite society would prefer to censor. You may be drawn to homosexuality in some way. There may even be shades of sexual danger or violence in your life: incest, paedophilia, sexual assault. Obviously, some aspects of human sexuality and desire will be more palatable for you than others. Your Scorpio Rising journey will tend to involve you quite intensely in your own physical wants and needs. You may also find that you become an experienced expert on the drives and desires of other people, which often seem to fall into a file labelled 'Off Limits' as far as the rest of the world is concerned.

Rising from the Ashes

The Scorpio Rising journey is inevitably associated with death, and some women who have this life path may have to deal with the reality of the death of someone close, or they may themselves survive a brush with death or a life-threatening illness. The deeper meaning of the Scorpio Rising journey, though, is actually death and resurrection. Death is just another word for an ending, followed by a new beginning — you may find this happens to you a lot, in your career or in your personal life.

The kind of crises you encounter are transformative by nature. Scorpio Rising women will commonly describe life-changing events as times of real pain and darkness, but something quite extraordinary happens after the long trawl through the depths: they become new versions of their old selves. The Scorpio Rising journey is about *survival*, above all other things.

A Woman of Passion

Your life journey is associated with incredible passions and desires — not always physical, often professional or vocational. Astrologers associate Scorpio with passion because Pluto, your ruler, was always a slave to desire. Apart from the obvious working-out of the sign — the incredible romantic obsessions and longings — you also have the capacity for *total involvement* in your goals. Because you cannot deliver half-measures, you have to give everything. 'Better than sex' is how one Scorpio Rising woman described her obsession with her business to me. Your journey will throw you into situations, time and time again, where you know your success or failure depends on complete dedication.

The fates will send you a memo that says: 'This goal requires everything you have. If you cannot take it with you to breakfast, lunch, dinner and bed — don't bother.' Not surprisingly, Scorpio Rising women end up doing amazing things with their lives because of this quality. You will need to fine-tune your life, though. You are vulnerable to fanaticism. You can also punish yourself for not trying hard enough. Somewhere in between manic obsession and scratching the surface, you will find just the right amount of intensity. That is what destiny will ask you to give to your life.

SAGITTARIUS RISING

There will be plenty of journeys within your life journey, as Sagittarius Rising points to travel. Your Sun, Moon, Mercury, Venus and Mars signs will describe the ways in which you will make the most of these experiences.

Awfully Big Adventures

You go out into the world wanting to take more of it in — it's as simple as that. So you wander as far as you can, save up for overseas treks, or find a career which takes in all of the world, not just the end of the street. Destiny may intervene and send you off on cross-cultural adventures anyway. Some of you end up near the Taj Mahal others disappear in the depths of Darwin. A Sagittarius Rising sign is a passport to other passports, though, and well worth taking advantage of.

A Sense of Humour

Your natural sense of comedy and the absurdity of life could lead you to a career where light entertainment makes you money — or, more likely, into a life which is full of people who come to rely on your hilarious perspective on the world.

Along with Gemini, Sagittarius is the sign which occurs most frequently in the charts of famous funny men and women. It's often the Rising sign too, so if you do feel like becoming a comedienne, the door is open.

A lot of your inherent ability to amuse — and your need to be amused — comes from Jupiter, the planet which rules your Rising sign. Jupiter is all about exaggeration, and a lot of who (and what) you find funny comes from your natural tendency to make trivial things very big — or big, important things very small. Both can keep you entertained.

Lifelong Education

You are destined to live a life where you are constantly learning about the world, even if you left school at the age of sixteen. Lots of Sagittarius Rising people go on to become academics or lecturers (another way to learn forever), but there are also lots of you who just take perpetual seminars, classes and courses.

If school was a happy experience for you, then you may well get into the education system and stay there. If not, you will get your education in other ways. You are unlikely to choose anything which is too mundane or ordinary on the list of subjects, though.

Some of your education will be done on the road, in other countries, or by surrounding yourself with people who have a totally different background to your own. Foreign influences will be around you for a substantial part of your life, and at every step you will want to take in more, if you are typical of your Rising sign.

CAPRICORN RISING

The long, slow crawl to the top is your destiny, and fate will have a way of taking you there. The other planet signs in your chart — the Sun, Moon, Mercury, Venus and Mars signs — will describe the resources you use in order to deal with your destiny. It will be an ambitious life, full of impressive achievement — but always taken the hard way!

Your Success

Capricorn Rising usually sends you on a journey to the top of the professional or career ladder. If you don't have a job, you'll marry up (see what I have to say about status, later in this section). Most Capricorn Rising women can't wait to get stuck into their own business or a compelling career, however. You choose industries or professions where it's easier for women to smash through the glass ceiling. Nevertheless, it all takes time.

One of the rules with this Rising sign is that success will never come quickly or easily. At the same time, when it comes, it won't be a flash in the pan either! This can be frustrating, as you are extremely ambitious and want to be the best, or have the best. Nevertheless, as Saturn rules your Rising sign, you will spend a lot of time waiting for the calendar to turn over before you can be sure that you are on the next rung of the ladder.

Making friends with time is one way to be more comfortable with your destiny. If you grow to appreciate what time can do (anything from sculpt marble to turn silly girls into wise old women) then your Capricorn Rising life path will seem easier. We live in a world where everyone wants everything now, which is why you often feel like a fish out of water. It doesn't come to you that easily — every achievement you have on your CV has been slowly, patiently and carefully built up! Nevertheless, time will also tell who has staying power and real rock-solid achievement under their wing — and who was just another five-minute wonder.

Your Status

You will move up a social class in your lifetime, or possibly several. It's quite normal for Capricorn Rising women to start off as working class, or lower middle-class, and then end up (for financial or marital reasons) miles above their old classmates or schoolfriends. Even those of you who begin life on a fairly high social platform will continue to move on up (to quote Curtis Mayfield) through the decades to come.

Living in the Real World

You will have to live in the real world a lot more than other women. There is a grittiness about Capricorn Rising women which speaks volumes about all they have to go through; you think it's hilarious when sweet young things carry on as if life is one long free lunch. Through various twists of fate in your life, you will learn the hard way about how things really are. This in turn helps you develop a kind of knowing — a mature wisdom — that can be worth its weight in gold to less experienced people. You make a wonderful natural agony aunt or advisor to people who are more naïve than you, as you typically see and experience so much in your life. You can seem like everyone's smartest aunty at the age of nineteen — often because your childhood and teen years taught you to grow up fast.

You are skilled at the practical management of life, the way it really is — not the way the television advertisements pretend it should be. Your greatest temptation is pessimism, though. Don't succumb! There's a difference between your natural caution and a pointless negativity about the future. If you're not careful, that negativity will stand between you and success. In the meantime, keep on being real. The world needs more Capricorn Rising women to tell them how life *really* is!

AQUARIUS RISING

You're here to change the world, and you may already be on the way. You do this by taking a different path to other women, and remaining independent of what your family, friends or partners are up to. You can change our planet in small, local ways — or big, far-ranging, political ways. However, you will always use your other planet signs to help you achieve it.

A Better World

You want a better world, and as a child or teenager may have felt this very strongly. In some cases, it comes in later life — in your forties, for example, when Uranus opposes Uranus in your chart, and radical changes come thick and fast. Most Aquarius Rising women are definitely on the path of change by their thirties, however.

How do you get those changes? It really depends on how big your world is, how much time you have, and how much cash you have to spend. Some of you are destined to become major business, political or non-government organisation players. Others will focus on their children's schools, their own workplace or their social lives.

Acts of rebellion will be common in your destiny. Sometimes this means you quite literally live a shocking life — you may be the only lesbian in your village, or a militant right-winger in a town full of gentle hippies.

Your philosophy and ideas are uniquely your own. From time to time you will feel the call of a group (see later in this section) and adapt your theories to suit the leaders. Mostly, though, your own version of how life should be is independently created, which is why your conversations are unique. You just don't seem to see the world in the same way as other people. And how you think life should be is often a hybrid of your own concepts, along with some standard political, spiritual or academic theories.

Group Chemistry

You'll join quite a few groups, classes, associations, clubs and teams over the course of your life, looking for the same elusive group 'mind' that you've found in other places. Alternatively, you'll find one and stick to it — anything from a rock band, to a political party, to a netball team. It's in your life path to travel with a tribe, and even in childhood and adolescence, the typical Aquarius Rising woman has her 'gang'.

You may achieve more through a group than you ever could alone. If you are single, you may also use a group of friends as a family substitute, or a relationship gap-filler. You won't do this in a calculated way — it just seems to happen. Your destiny in life is frequently independent of husbands or partners, because Aquarius is a free-spirited sign, and when it is on the horizon at the moment of your birth, fate often decrees that you'll fly solo. You can do this even when you're married, of course — lots of Aquarius Rising women seem to have vaguely single lives, even with rings on their fingers.

Being Your Own Woman

Uranus is the planet which rules your Rising sign, Aquarius. Uranus came along at the time of the French Revolution and it has a lot to do with women's liberation as well. It also rules electricity. Destiny says you will be your own woman in this lifetime, which often means rebellion, revolution and electric shocks for those around you!

PISCES RISING

You will be asked to use your imagination on your life journey, either through a job, or a specific interest or hobby. So you may end up working with computer images — or having a normal job, but living for the cinema on the weekends. Along with imagination, compassion is part of your life's path. So, once again, you may find a job in the caring professions, or find a non-caring job, but devote your spare time to people or animals who need you. In all cases, your other planet signs will help you to live out your Pisces Rising destiny.

Alternative Realities

When we all get bogged down by mortgages, the television news, or the boring, daily grind, it's your job to show us your life and inspire us. Your life path is destined to lift you into an alternative reality, a lot of the time. That means a bit of magic and a lot of miracles — it may even be why you picked up this book, as astrology may be your path into that.

Other examples of your alternative realities probably include your interests and passions, which could take you into any area from poetry to painting. Or maybe you're interested in escaping from life in other ways, by looking for something far more spiritual and uplifting. You might find that through Buddhism, or by volunteering for the RSPCA.

The possibilities on your life path are endless because each Pisces Rising woman needs to find her own niche. You may even have an alternative reality just by marrying a prince — or constructing your own theme park. Maybe you'll end up with a home which is near the sea, with a spa — or you'll get heavily into role-playing games and spend your weekends dressed up as Queen Guinevere. Travelling like a gypsy can help you find another world out there too — or just closing your eyes and escaping into your own private world after dark, with lit candles and a running bath.

Have drugs or alcohol found you yet, or vice versa? It's a common outcome with this Rising sign. Only you can decide if they make the real world an easier place to live, or if they complicate things.

Compassion and Empathy

Fate will take you into jobs, into relationships, into friendships — or into a family — where you need to explore your compassion and empathy. Animals may cross your path (strays or mistreated pets, for example) which trigger the same destiny. For this reason, Pisces Rising women often end up with people around them who are dependent in some way. Sacrifice is probably a word that means a lot to you. It's part of the Pisces Rising destiny, as Neptune, the planet which rules Pisces, always asks you to give up, or give in — sometimes in the most dramatic way. Self-sacrifice may very well be part of your journey in this life. You might do it for a husband, for a parent, for a colleague, or for some other close connection.

The Sixth Sense

Pisces rules psychic ability, so there are a lot of Pisces Rising women wandering around with a pack of tarot cards in their handbag — or such a deep trust of their hunches that their colleagues sometimes wonder what planet they are on. You may have had this ability since you were a small child. If not, it may take some years to show itself properly.

Where does it come from? Neptune, the ruler of Pisces, is also associated with the ocean, and with water in general. For Pisces Rising women, there is often a feeling of bobbing around in a vast ocean full of other people's thoughts and feelings, with none of the usual rules that prevent us from seeing into each other's souls, minds and hearts.

BIRTHDAY TABLES

Sun, Mercury, Venus and Mars Signs

PLANET SIGN TABLES 1950 TO 2000

Start here to find out your Sun, Mercury, Venus and Mars signs. If you were born before 1950, or you need to look up a baby born after 2000, please visit www.jessicaadams.com for extra planet sign tables.

Each date shows the day that a planet changed signs — it's that simple.

FAMOUS EXAMPLES

Angelina Jolie — 4 June 1975
> Sun in Gemini, Mercury in Gemini, Venus in Cancer, Mars in Aries

Madonna — 16 August 1958
> Sun in Leo, Mercury in Virgo, Venus in Leo, Mars in Taurus

Oprah Winfrey — 29 January 1954
> Sun in Aquarius, Mercury in Aquarius, Venus in Aquarius, Mars in Scorpio

Condoleezza Rice — 14 November 1954
Sun in Scorpio, Mercury in Scorpio, Venus in Scorpio,
Mars in Aquarius

You can find your Moon sign in the special section after this. Again, if the date you want is not listed in the tables, please go to www.jessicaadams.com.

What follows are planet signs, averaged for all time zones. If you were born on the last or first day that a planet was changing signs, there is a small chance that what you see listed here will be out by one sign. To double-check, remember you can always calculate your full birth horoscope free at www.astro.com.

If you see the R symbol it means a planet is retrograding (stuck) in the previous sign. If you see the D symbol it means a planet is direct (moving through) the previous sign.

EXAMPLE

A person born on 9 January 1950 has Mercury in Aquarius.

A person born on 30 January 1950 has Mercury in Capricorn.

If you see a D or R symbol with no sign listed at all, just go back to the previous sign — that's yours too! If you were born in January, this may involve going back to the previous sign, as listed in December of the previous year.

EXAMPLE

A person born on 13 January 1951 has Mercury in Capricorn, because Mercury is D (direct) in Capricorn from the end of 1950, the year before.

All the planet sign tables follow on, from year to year. So if you were born in the first days of any year, there is a chance you will need to look at December of the previous year to find out which sign Mercury, Venus or Mars is in.

EXAMPLE

A person born on 1 January 1999 has Venus in Capricorn — following on from where it was in December 1998.

THE SUN

The Sun's position through the signs is averaged from year to year, which is why Sun Signs turn up in magazines and newspapers with slightly varying start and end dates. Were you born on the cusp? It doesn't mean you are two signs at once — but it does mean you need to check your true Sun Sign at www.astro.com. In the meantime, here are the twelve classic Sun Sign date brackets, averaged for your day of birth.

ARIES 21 March to 20 April

TAURUS 21 April to 21 May

GEMINI 22 May to 21 June

CANCER 22 June to 22 July

LEO 23 July to 23 August

VIRGO 24 August to 22 September

LIBRA 23 September to 22 October

SCORPIO 23 October to 21 November

SAGITTARIUS 22 November to 21 December

CAPRICORN 22 December to 20 January

AQUARIUS 21 January to 19 February

PISCES 20 February to 20 March

1950

	SUN			MERCURY			VENUS			MARS	
dy	mth	sign	dy	mth	sign	dy	mth	sign	dy	mth	sign
1	JAN	Cap	1	JAN	Aqu	1	JAN	Aqu	1	JAN	Lib
20	JAN	Aqu	15	JAN	Cap	6	APR	Pis	28	MAR	Vir
19	FEB	Pis	14	FEB	Aqu	5	MAY	Ari	3	MAY	D
21	MAR	Ari	7	MAR	Pis	1	JUN	Tau	11	JUN	Lib
20	APR	Tau	24	MAR	Ari	27	JUN	Gem	10	AUG	Sco
21	MAY	Gem	8	APR	Tau	22	JUL	Can	25	SEP	Sag
21	JUN	Can	3	MAY	R	16	AUG	Leo	6	NOV	Cap
23	JUL	Leo	27	MAY	D	10	SEP	Vir	15	DEC	Aqu
23	AUG	Vir	14	JUN	Gem	4	OCT	Lib			
23	SEP	Lib	2	JUL	Can	28	OCT	Sco			
23	OCT	Sco	16	JUL	Leo	21	NOV	Sag			
22	NOV	Sag	2	AUG	Vir	14	DEC	Cap			
22	DEC	Cap	27	AUG	Lib						
			4	SEP	R						
			10	SEP	Vir						
			26	SEP	D						
			9	OCT	Lib						
			27	OCT	Sco						
			15	NOV	Sag						
			5	DEC	Cap						
			23	DEC	R						

1951

	SUN			MERCURY			VENUS			MARS	
dy	mth	sign	dy	mth	sign	dy	mth	sign	dy	mth	sign
1	JAN	Cap	12	JAN	D	7	JAN	Aqu	22	JAN	Pis
20	JAN	Aqu	9	FEB	Aqu	31	JAN	Pis	1	MAR	Ari
19	FEB	Pis	28	FEB	Pis	24	FEB	Ari	10	APR	Tau
21	MAR	Ari	16	MAR	Ari	21	MAR	Tau	21	MAY	Gem
20	APR	Tau	2	APR	Tau	15	APR	Gem	3	JUL	Can
21	MAY	Gem	14	APR	R	11	MAY	Can	18	AUG	Leo
22	JUN	Can	1	MAY	Ari	7	JUN	Leo	5	OCT	Vir
23	JUL	Leo	8	MAY	D	8	JUL	Vir	24	NOV	Lib
23	AUG	Vir	15	MAY	Tau	13	AUG	R			
23	SEP	Lib	9	JUN	Gem	25	SEP	D			
24	OCT	Sco	24	JUN	Can	9	NOV	Lib			
23	NOV	Sag	8	JUL	Leo	8	DEC	Sco			
22	DEC	Cap	27	JUL	Vir						
			17	AUG	R						
			9	SEP	D						
			2	OCT	Lib						
			19	OCT	Sco						
			8	NOV	Sag						
			1	DEC	Cap						
			7	DEC	R						
			12	DEC	Sag						
			27	DEC	D						

1952

	SUN			MERCURY			VENUS			MARS	
dy	mth	sign	dy	mth	sign	dy	mth	sign	dy	mth	sign
1	JAN	Cap	13	JAN	Cap	2	JAN	Sag	20	JAN	Sco
21	JAN	Aqu	3	FEB	Aqu	27	JAN	Cap	25	MAR	R
19	FEB	Pis	20	FEB	Pis	21	FEB	Aqu	10	JUN	D
20	MAR	Ari	7	MAR	Ari	16	MAR	Pis	27	AUG	Sag
20	APR	Tau	26	MAR	R	9	APR	Ari	12	OCT	Cap
21	MAY	Gem	19	APR	D	4	MAY	Tau	21	NOV	Aqu
21	JUN	Can	14	MAY	Tau	28	MAY	Gem	30	DEC	Pis
22	JUL	Leo	31	MAY	Gem	22	JUN	Can			
23	AUG	Vir	14	JUN	Can	16	JUL	Leo			
23	SEP	Lib	30	JUN	Leo	9	AUG	Vir			
23	OCT	Sco	29	JUL	R	3	SEP	Lib			
22	NOV	Sag	22	AUG	D	27	SEP	Sco			
21	DEC	Cap	7	SEP	Vir	22	OCT	Sag			
			23	SEP	Lib	15	NOV	Cap			
			11	OCT	Sco	10	DEC	Aqu			
			1	NOV	Sag						
			20	NOV	R						
			10	DEC	D						

1953

	SUN			MERCURY			VENUS			MARS	
dy	mth	sign	dy	mth	sign	dy	mth	sign	dy	mth	sign
1	JAN	Cap	6	JAN	Cap	5	JAN	Pis	8	FEB	Ari
20	JAN	Aqu	25	JAN	Aqu	2	FEB	Ari	20	MAR	Tau
18	FEB	Pis	11	FEB	Pis	14	MAR	Tau	1	MAY	Gem
20	MAR	Ari	2	MAR	Ari	23	MAR	R	14	JUN	Can
20	APR	Tau	9	MAR	R	31	MAR	Ari	29	JUL	Leo
21	MAY	Gem	15	MAR	Pis	4	MAY	D	14	SEP	Vir
21	JUN	Can	1	APR	D	5	JUN	Tau	1	NOV	Lib
23	JUL	Leo	17	APR	Ari	7	JUL	Gem	20	DEC	Sco
23	AUG	Vir	8	MAY	Tau	4	AUG	Can			
23	SEP	Lib	23	MAY	Gem	30	AUG	Leo			
23	OCT	Sco	6	JUN	Can	24	SEP	Vir			
22	NOV	Sag	26	JUN	Leo	18	OCT	Lib			
22	DEC	Cap	11	JUL	R	11	NOV	Sco			
			28	JUL	Can	5	DEC	Sag			
			4	AUG	D	29	DEC	Cap			
			11	AUG	Leo						
			30	AUG	Vir						
			15	SEP	Lib						
			4	OCT	Sco						
			31	OCT	Sag						
			3	NOV	R						
			6	NOV	Sco						
			23	NOV	D						
			10	DEC	Sag						
			30	DEC	Cap						

1954

	SUN			MERCURY			VENUS			MARS	
dy	mth	sign	dy	mth	sign	dy	mth	sign	dy	mth	sign
1	JAN	Cap	18	JAN	Aqu	22	JAN	Aqu	9	FEB	Sag
20	JAN	Aqu	4	FEB	Pis	15	FEB	Pis	12	APR	Cap
19	FEB	Pis	20	FEB	R	11	MAR	Ari	23	MAY	R
21	MAR	Ari	14	MAR	D	4	APR	Tau	3	JUL	Sag
20	APR	Tau	13	APR	Ari	28	APR	Gem	29	JUL	D
21	MAY	Gem	30	APR	Tau	23	MAY	Can	24	AUG	Cap
21	JUN	Can	14	MAY	Gem	17	JUN	Leo	21	OCT	Aqu
23	JUL	Leo	30	MAY	Can	13	JUL	Vir	4	DEC	Pis
23	AUG	Vir	23	JUN	R	9	AUG	Lib			
23	SEP	Lib	17	JUL	D	6	SEP	Sco			
23	OCT	Sco	7	AUG	Leo	23	OCT	Sag			
22	NOV	Sag	22	AUG	Vir	25	OCT	R			
22	DEC	Cap	8	SEP	Lib	27	OCT	Sco			
			29	SEP	Sco	5	DEC	D			
			18	OCT	R						
			4	NOV	Lib						
			7	NOV	D						
			11	NOV	Sco						
			4	DEC	Sag						
			23	DEC	Cap						

1955

	SUN			MERCURY			VENUS			MARS	
dy	mth	sign	dy	mth	sign	dy	mth	sign	dy	mth	sign
1	JAN	Cap	10	JAN	Aqu	6	JAN	Sag	15	JAN	Ari
20	JAN	Aqu	3	FEB	R	6	FEB	Cap	26	FEB	Tau
19	FEB	Pis	25	FEB	D	4	MAR	Aqu	10	APR	Gem
21	MAR	Ari	17	MAR	Pis	30	MAR	Pis	26	MAY	Can
20	APR	Tau	6	APR	Ari	24	APR	Ari	11	JUL	Leo
21	MAY	Gem	22	APR	Tau	19	MAY	Tau	27	AUG	Vir
22	JUN	Can	6	MAY	Gem	13	JUN	Gem	13	OCT	Lib
23	JUL	Leo	3	JUN	R	8	JUL	Can	29	NOV	Sco
23	AUG	Vir	27	JUN	D	1	AUG	Leo			
23	SEP	Lib	13	JUL	Can	25	AUG	Vir			
24	OCT	Sco	30	JUL	Leo	18	SEP	Lib			
23	NOV	Sag	14	AUG	Vir	13	OCT	Sco			
22	DEC	Cap	1	SEP	Lib	6	NOV	Sag			
			1	OCT	R	30	NOV	Cap			
			22	OCT	D	24	DEC	Aqu			
			8	NOV	Sco						
			27	NOV	Sag						
			16	DEC	Cap						

1956

	SUN			MERCURY			VENUS			MARS	
dy	mth	sign	dy	mth	sign	dy	mth	sign	dy	mth	sign
1	JAN	Cap	4	JAN	Aqu	17	JAN	Pis	14	JAN	Sag
21	JAN	Aqu	18	JAN	R	11	FEB	Ari	28	FEB	Cap
19	FEB	Pis	2	FEB	Cap	7	MAR	Tau	14	APR	Aqu
20	MAR	Ari	8	FEB	D	4	APR	Gem	3	JUN	Pis
20	APR	Tau	15	FEB	Aqu	8	MAY	Can	10	AUG	R
21	MAY	Gem	11	MAR	Pis	31	MAY	R	10	OCT	D
21	JUN	Can	28	MAR	Ari	23	JUN	Gem	6	DEC	Ari
22	JUL	Leo	12	APR	Tau	13	JUL	D			
23	AUG	Vir	29	APR	Gem	4	AUG	Can			
23	SEP	Lib	14	MAY	R	8	SEP	Leo			
23	OCT	Sco	7	JUN	D	6	OCT	Vir			
22	NOV	Sag	6	JUL	Can	31	OCT	Lib			
21	DEC	Cap	21	JUL	Leo	25	NOV	Sco			
			5	AUG	Vir	19	DEC	Sag			
			26	AUG	Lib						
			13	SEP	R						
			29	SEP	Vir						
			5	OCT	D						
			11	OCT	Lib						
			31	OCT	Sco						
			18	NOV	Sag						
			8	DEC	Cap						

1957

	SUN			MERCURY			VENUS			MARS	
dy	mth	sign	dy	mth	sign	dy	mth	sign	dy	mth	sign
1	JAN	Cap	1	JAN	R	12	JAN	Cap	28	JAN	Tau
20	JAN	Aqu	21	JAN	D	5	FEB	Aqu	17	MAR	Gem
18	FEB	Pis	12	FEB	Aqu	1	MAR	Pis	4	MAY	Can
20	MAR	Ari	4	MAR	Pis	25	MAR	Ari	21	JUN	Leo
20	APR	Tau	20	MAR	Ari	19	APR	Tau	8	AUG	Vir
21	MAY	Gem	4	APR	Tau	13	MAY	Gem	24	SEP	Lib
21	JUN	Can	25	APR	R	6	JUN	Can	8	NOV	Sco
23	JUL	Leo	19	MAY	D	1	JUL	Leo	23	DEC	Sag
23	AUG	Vir	12	JUN	Gem	26	JUL	Vir			
23	SEP	Lib	28	JUN	Can	20	AUG	Lib			
23	OCT	Sco	12	JUL	Leo	14	SEP	Sco			
22	NOV	Sag	30	JUL	Vir	10	OCT	Sag			
22	DEC	Cap	27	AUG	R	5	NOV	Cap			
			19	SEP	D	6	DEC	Aqu			
			6	OCT	Lib						
			23	OCT	Sco						
			11	NOV	Sag						
			2	DEC	Cap						
			16	DEC	R						
			28	DEC	Sag						

1958

SUN			MERCURY			VENUS			MARS		
dy	mth	sign	dy	mth	sign	dy	mth	sign	dy	mth	sign
1	JAN	Cap	5	JAN	D	8	JAN	R	3	FEB	Cap
20	JAN	Aqu	14	JAN	Cap	18	FEB	D	17	MAR	Aqu
19	FEB	Pis	6	FEB	Aqu	6	APR	Pis	27	APR	Pis
21	MAR	Ari	24	FEB	Pis	5	MAY	Ari	7	JUN	Ari
20	APR	Tau	12	MAR	Ari	1	JUN	Tau	21	JUL	Tau
21	MAY	Gem	2	APR	Tau	26	JUN	Gem	21	SEP	Gem
21	JUN	Can	6	APR	R	22	JUL	Can	10	OCT	R
23	JUL	Leo	10	APR	Ari	16	AUG	Leo	28	OCT	Tau
23	AUG	Vir	30	APR	D	9	SEP	Vir	20	DEC	D
23	SEP	Lib	17	MAY	Tau	3	OCT	Lib			
23	OCT	Sco	5	JUN	Gem	27	OCT	Sco			
22	NOV	Sag	20	JUN	Can	20	NOV	Sag			
22	DEC	Cap	4	JUL	Leo	14	DEC	Cap			
			26	JUL	Vir						
			9	AUG	R						
			23	AUG	Leo						
			2	SEP	D						
			11	SEP	Vir						
			28	SEP	Lib						
			16	OCT	Sco						
			5	NOV	Sag						
			30	NOV	R						
			20	DEC	D						

1959

SUN			MERCURY			VENUS			MARS		
dy	mth	sign	dy	mth	sign	dy	mth	sign	dy	mth	sign
1	JAN	Cap	10	JAN	Cap	7	JAN	Aqu	10	FEB	Gem
20	JAN	Aqu	30	JAN	Aqu	31	JAN	Pis	10	APR	Can
19	FEB	Pis	17	FEB	Pis	24	FEB	Ari	1	JUN	Leo
21	MAR	Ari	5	MAR	Ari	20	MAR	Tau	20	JUL	Vir
20	APR	Tau	19	MAR	R	14	APR	Gem	5	SEP	Lib
21	MAY	Gem	12	APR	D	10	MAY	Can	21	OCT	Sco
22	JUN	Can	12	MAY	Tau	6	JUN	Leo	3	DEC	Sag
23	JUL	Leo	28	MAY	Gem	8	JUL	Vir			
23	AUG	Vir	11	JUN	Can	10	AUG	R			
23	SEP	Lib	28	JUN	Leo	20	SEP	Leo			
24	OCT	Sco	22	JUL	R	22	SEP	D			
23	NOV	Sag	15	AUG	D	25	SEP	Vir			
22	DEC	Cap	5	SEP	Vir	9	NOV	Lib			
			21	SEP	Lib	7	DEC	Sco			
			9	OCT	Sco						
			31	OCT	Sag						
			14	NOV	R						
			25	NOV	Sco						
			3	DEC	D						
			13	DEC	Sag						

1960

	SUN			MERCURY			VENUS			MARS	
dy	mth	sign	dy	mth	sign	dy	mth	sign	dy	mth	sign
1	JAN	Cap	4	JAN	Cap	2	JAN	Sag	14	JAN	Cap
21	JAN	Aqu	23	JAN	Aqu	27	JAN	Cap	23	FEB	Aqu
19	FEB	Pis	9	FEB	Pis	20	FEB	Aqu	2	APR	Pis
20	MAR	Ari	1	MAR	R	16	MAR	Pis	11	MAY	Ari
20	APR	Tau	24	MAR	D	9	APR	Ari	20	JUN	Tau
21	MAY	Gem	16	APR	Ari	3	MAY	Tau	2	AUG	Gem
21	JUN	Can	4	MAY	Tau	28	MAY	Gem	21	SEP	Can
22	JUL	Leo	19	MAY	Gem	21	JUN	Can	20	NOV	R
23	AUG	Vir	2	JUN	Can	16	JUL	Leo			
23	SEP	Lib	1	JUL	Leo	9	AUG	Vir			
23	OCT	Sco	3	JUL	R	2	SEP	Lib			
22	NOV	Sag	6	JUL	Can	27	SEP	Sco			
21	DEC	Cap	27	JUL	D	21	OCT	Sag			
			10	AUG	Leo	15	NOV	Cap			
			27	AUG	Vir	10	DEC	Aqu			
			12	SEP	Lib						
			1	OCT	Sco						
			27	OCT	R						
			16	NOV	D						
			7	DEC	Sag						
			27	DEC	Cap						

1961

	SUN			MERCURY			VENUS			MARS	
dy	mth	sign	dy	mth	sign	dy	mth	sign	dy	mth	sign
1	JAN	Cap	14	JAN	Aqu	5	JAN	Pis	1	JAN	Can
20	JAN	Aqu	1	FEB	Pis	2	FEB	Ari	5	FEB	Gem
18	FEB	Pis	24	FEB	Aqu	5	JUN	Tau	7	FEB	Can
20	MAR	Ari	18	MAR	Pis	7	JUL	Gem	6	MAY	Leo
20	APR	Tau	10	APR	Ari	3	AUG	Can	28	JUN	Vir
21	MAY	Gem	26	APR	Tau	29	AUG	Leo	17	AUG	Lib
21	JUN	Can	10	MAY	Gem	23	SEP	Vir	1	OCT	Sco
23	JUL	Leo	28	MAY	Can	18	OCT	Lib	13	NOV	Sag
23	AUG	Vir	4	AUG	Leo	11	NOV	Sco	24	DEC	Cap
23	SEP	Lib	18	AUG	Vir	5	DEC	Sag			
23	OCT	Sco	4	SEP	Lib	29	DEC	Cap			
22	NOV	Sag	27	SEP	Sco						
22	DEC	Cap	22	OCT	Lib						
			10	NOV	Sco						
			30	NOV	Sag						
			20	DEC	Cap						

1962

	SUN			MERCURY			VENUS			MARS	
dy	mth	sign	dy	mth	sign	dy	mth	sign	dy	mth	sign
1	JAN	Cap	7	JAN	Aqu	21	JAN	Aqu	1	FEB	Aqu
20	JAN	Aqu	15	MAR	Pis	14	FEB	Pis	12	MAR	Pis
19	FEB	Pis	3	APR	Ari	10	MAR	Ari	19	APR	Ari
21	MAR	Ari	18	APR	Tau	3	APR	Tau	28	MAY	Tau
20	APR	Tau	3	MAY	Gem	28	APR	Gem	9	JUL	Gem
21	MAY	Gem	11	JUL	Can	23	MAY	Can	22	AUG	Can
21	JUN	Can	26	JUL	Leo	17	JUN	Leo	11	OCT	Leo
23	JUL	Leo	10	AUG	Vir	12	JUL	Vir			
23	AUG	Vir	29	AUG	Lib	8	AUG	Lib			
23	SEP	Lib	5	NOV	Sco	7	SEP	Sco			
23	OCT	Sco	23	NOV	Sag						
22	NOV	Sag	12	DEC	Cap						
22	DEC	Cap									

1963

	SUN			MERCURY			VENUS			MARS	
dy	mth	sign	dy	mth	sign	dy	mth	sign	dy	mth	sign
1	JAN	Cap	2	JAN	Aqu	6	JAN	Sag	1	JAN	Leo
20	JAN	Aqu	20	JAN	Cap	5	FEB	Cap	3	JUN	Vir
19	FEB	Pis	15	FEB	Aqu	4	MAR	Aqu	27	JUL	Lib
21	MAR	Ari	9	MAR	Pis	30	MAR	Pis	12	SEP	Sco
20	APR	Tau	26	MAR	Ari	24	APR	Ari	25	OCT	Sag
21	MAY	Gem	9	APR	Tau	19	MAY	Tau	5	DEC	Cap
22	JUN	Can	3	MAY	Gem	12	JUN	Gem			
23	JUL	Leo	10	MAY	Tau	7	JUL	Can			
23	AUG	Vir	14	JUN	Gem	31	JUL	Leo			
23	SEP	Lib	4	JUL	Can	25	AUG	Vir			
24	OCT	Sco	18	JUL	Leo	18	SEP	Lib			
23	NOV	Sag	3	AUG	Vir	12	OCT	Sco			
22	DEC	Cap	26	AUG	Lib	5	NOV	Sag			
			16	SEP	Vir	29	NOV	Cap			
			10	OCT	Lib	23	DEC	Aqu			
			28	OCT	Sco						
			16	NOV	Sag						
			6	DEC	Cap						

1964

	SUN			MERCURY			VENUS			MARS	
dy	mth	sign	dy	mth	sign	dy	mth	sign	dy	mth	sign
1	JAN	Cap	10	FEB	Aqu	17	JAN	Pis	13	JAN	Aqu
21	JAN	Aqu	29	FEB	Pis	10	FEB	Ari	20	FEB	Pis
19	FEB	Pis	16	MAR	Ari	7	MAR	Tau	29	MAR	Ari
20	MAR	Ari	2	APR	Tau	4	APR	Gem	7	MAY	Tau
20	APR	Tau	9	JUN	Gem	9	MAY	Can	17	JUN	Gem
21	MAY	Gem	24	JUN	Can	17	JUN	Gem	30	JUL	Can
21	JUN	Can	9	JUL	Leo	5	AUG	Can	15	SEP	Leo
22	JUL	Leo	27	JUL	Vir	8	SEP	Leo	6	NOV	Vir
23	AUG	Vir	3	OCT	Lib	5	OCT	Vir			
23	SEP	Lib	20	OCT	Sco	31	OCT	Lib			
23	OCT	Sco	8	NOV	Sag	25	NOV	Sco			
22	NOV	Sag	30	NOV	Cap	19	DEC	Sag			
21	DEC	Cap	16	DEC	Sag						

1965

	SUN			MERCURY			VENUS			MARS	
dy	mth	sign	dy	mth	sign	dy	mth	sign	dy	mth	sign
1	JAN	Cap	13	JAN	Cap	12	JAN	Cap	1	JAN	Vir
20	JAN	Aqu	3	FEB	Aqu	5	FEB	Aqu	29	JUN	Lib
18	FEB	Pis	21	FEB	Pis	1	MAR	Pis	20	AUG	Sco
20	MAR	Ari	9	MAR	Ari	25	MAR	Ari	4	OCT	Sag
20	APR	Tau	15	MAY	Tau	18	APR	Tau	14	NOV	Cap
21	MAY	Gem	2	JUN	Gem	12	MAY	Gem	23	DEC	Aqu
21	JUN	Can	16	JUN	Can	6	JUN	Can			
23	JUL	Leo	1	JUL	Leo	30	JUN	Leo			
23	AUG	Vir	31	JUL	Vir	25	JUL	Vir			
23	SEP	Lib	3	AUG	Leo	19	AUG	Lib			
23	OCT	Sco	8	SEP	Vir	13	SEP	Sco			
22	NOV	Sag	25	SEP	Lib	9	OCT	Sag			
22	DEC	Cap	12	OCT	Sco	5	NOV	Cap			
			2	NOV	Sag	7	DEC	Aqu			

1966

SUN			MERCURY			VENUS			MARS		
dy	mth	sign	dy	mth	sign	dy	mth	sign	dy	mth	sign
1	JAN	Cap	7	JAN	Cap	6	FEB	Cap	30	JAN	Pis
20	JAN	Aqu	27	JAN	Aqu	25	FEB	Aqu	9	MAR	Ari
19	FEB	Pis	13	FEB	Pis	6	APR	Pis	17	APR	Tau
21	MAR	Ari	3	MAR	Ari	5	MAY	Ari	28	MAY	Gem
20	APR	Tau	22	MAR	Pis	31	MAY	Tau	11	JUL	Can
21	MAY	Gem	17	APR	Ari	26	JUN	Gem	25	AUG	Leo
21	JUN	Can	9	MAY	Tau	21	JUL	Can	12	OCT	Vir
23	JUL	Leo	24	MAY	Gem	15	AUG	Leo	4	DEC	Lib
23	AUG	Vir	7	JUN	Can	8	SEP	Vir			
23	SEP	Lib	26	JUN	Leo	3	OCT	Lib			
23	OCT	Sco	1	SEP	Vir	27	OCT	Sco			
22	NOV	Sag	17	SEP	Lib	20	NOV	Sag			
22	DEC	Cap	5	OCT	Sco	13	DEC	Cap			
			30	OCT	Sag						
			13	NOV	Sco						
			11	DEC	Sag						

1967

SUN			MERCURY			VENUS			MARS		
dy	mth	sign	dy	mth	sign	dy	mth	sign	dy	mth	sign
1	JAN	Cap	1	JAN	Cap	6	JAN	Aqu	12	FEB	Sco
20	JAN	Aqu	19	JAN	Aqu	30	JAN	Pis	31	MAR	Lib
19	FEB	Pis	6	FEB	Pis	23	FEB	Ari	19	JUL	Sco
21	MAR	Ari	14	APR	Ari	20	MAR	Tau	10	SEP	Sag
20	APR	Tau	1	MAY	Tau	10	MAY	Can	23	OCT	Cap
21	MAY	Gem	16	MAY	Gem	14	APR	Gem	1	DEC	Aqu
22	JUN	Can	31	MAY	Can	6	JUN	Leo			
23	JUL	Leo	8	AUG	Leo	8	JUL	Vir			
23	AUG	Vir	24	AUG	Vir	9	SEP	Leo			
23	SEP	Lib	9	SEP	Lib	1	OCT	Vir			
24	OCT	Sco	30	SEP	Sco	9	NOV	Lib			
23	NOV	Sag	5	DEC	Sag	7	DEC	Sco			
22	DEC	Cap	24	DEC	Cap						

1968

	SUN			MERCURY			VENUS			MARS	
dy	mth	sign	dy	mth	sign	dy	mth	sign	dy	mth	sign
1	JAN	Cap	12	JAN	Aqu	1	JAN	Sag	9	JAN	Pis
20	JAN	Aqu	1	FEB	Pis	26	JAN	Cap	17	FEB	Ari
19	FEB	Pis	11	FEB	Aqu	20	FEB	Aqu	27	MAR	Tau
20	MAR	Ari	17	MAR	Pis	15	MAR	Pis	8	MAY	Gem
20	APR	Tau	7	APR	Ari	8	APR	Ari	21	JUN	Can
21	MAY	Gem	22	APR	Tau	3	MAY	Tau	5	AUG	Leo
21	JUN	Can	6	MAY	Gem	27	MAY	Gem	21	SEP	Vir
22	JUL	Leo	29	MAY	Can	21	JUN	Can	9	NOV	Lib
23	AUG	Vir	13	JUN	Gem	15	JUL	Leo	29	DEC	Sco
22	SEP	Lib	13	JUL	Can	8	AUG	Vir			
23	OCT	Sco	31	JUL	Leo	2	SEP	Lib			
22	NOV	Sag	15	AUG	Vir	26	SEP	Sco			
21	DEC	Cap	1	SEP	Lib	21	OCT	Sag			
			28	SEP	Sco	14	NOV	Cap			
			7	OCT	Lib	9	DEC	Aqu			
			8	NOV	Sco						
			27	NOV	Sag						
			16	DEC	Cap						

1969

	SUN			MERCURY			VENUS			MARS	
dy	mth	sign	dy	mth	sign	dy	mth	sign	dy	mth	sign
1	JAN	Cap	1	JAN	Cap	4	JAN	Pis	25	FEB	Sag
20	JAN	Aqu	5	JAN	Aqu	2	FEB	Ari	21	SEP	Cap
18	FEB	Pis	13	MAR	Pis	6	JUN	Tau	4	NOV	Aqu
20	MAR	Ari	31	MAR	Ari	6	JUL	Gem	15	DEC	Pis
20	APR	Tau	15	APR	Tau	3	AUG	Can			
21	MAY	Gem	1	MAY	Gem	29	AUG	Leo			
21	JUN	Can	9	JUL	Can	23	SEP	Vir			
23	JUL	Leo	23	JUL	Leo	17	OCT	Lib			
23	AUG	Vir	8	AUG	Vir	10	NOV	Sco			
23	SEP	Lib	28	AUG	Lib	4	DEC	Sag			
23	OCT	Sco	8	OCT	Vir	28	DEC	Cap			
22	NOV	Sag	10	OCT	Lib						
22	DEC	Cap	2	NOV	Sco						
			21	NOV	Sag						
			10	DEC	Cap						

1970

	SUN			MERCURY			VENUS			MARS	
dy	mth	sign	dy	mth	sign	dy	mth	sign	dy	mth	sign
1	JAN	Cap	1	JAN	Cap	21	JAN	Aqu	24	JAN	Ari
20	JAN	Aqu	14	FEB	Aqu	14	FEB	Pis	7	MAR	Tau
19	FEB	Pis	6	MAR	Pis	10	MAR	Ari	18	APR	Gem
21	MAR	Ari	23	MAR	Ari	3	APR	Tau	2	JUN	Can
20	APR	Tau	7	APR	Tau	27	APR	Gem	18	JUL	Leo
21	MAY	Gem	14	JUN	Gem	22	MAY	Can	3	SEP	Vir
21	JUN	Can	1	JUL	Can	16	JUN	Leo	20	OCT	Lib
23	JUL	Leo	15	JUL	Leo	12	JUL	Vir	6	DEC	Sco
23	AUG	Vir	1	AUG	Vir	8	AUG	Lib			
23	SEP	Lib	8	OCT	Lib	7	SEP	Sco			
23	OCT	Sco	26	OCT	Sco						
22	NOV	Sag	14	NOV	Sag						
22	DEC	Cap	4	DEC	Cap						

1971

	SUN			MERCURY			VENUS			MARS	
dy	mth	sign	dy	mth	sign	dy	mth	sign	dy	mth	sign
1	JAN	Cap	2	JAN	Sag	7	JAN	Sag	23	JAN	Sag
20	JAN	Aqu	14	JAN	Cap	5	FEB	Cap	12	MAR	Cap
19	FEB	Pis	7	FEB	Aqu	4	MAR	Aqu	3	MAY	Aqu
21	MAR	Ari	26	FEB	Pis	29	MAR	Pis	6	NOV	Pis
20	APR	Tau	14	MAR	Ari	23	APR	Ari	26	DEC	Ari
21	MAY	Gem	1	APR	Tau	18	MAY	Tau			
22	JUN	Can	18	APR	Ari	12	JUN	Gem			
23	JUL	Leo	17	MAY	Tau	6	JUL	Can			
23	AUG	Vir	7	JUN	Gem	31	JUL	Leo			
23	SEP	Lib	21	JUN	Can	17	SEP	Lib			
24	OCT	Sco	6	JUL	Leo	11	OCT	Sco			
22	NOV	Sag	26	JUL	Vir	5	NOV	Sag			
22	DEC	Cap	29	AUG	Leo	29	NOV	Cap			
			11	SEP	Vir	23	DEC	Aqu			
			30	SEP	Lib						
			17	OCT	Sco						
			6	NOV	Sag						

1972

	SUN			MERCURY			VENUS			MARS	
dy	mth	sign	dy	mth	sign	dy	mth	sign	dy	mth	sign
1	JAN	Cap	11	JAN	Cap	16	JAN	Pis	10	FEB	Tau
20	JAN	Aqu	31	JAN	Aqu	10	FEB	Ari	27	MAR	Gem
19	FEB	Pis	18	FEB	Pis	7	MAR	Tau	12	MAY	Can
20	MAR	Ari	5	MAR	Ari	3	APR	Gem	28	JUN	Leo
19	APR	Tau	12	MAY	Tau	10	MAY	Can	15	AUG	Vir
20	MAY	Gem	29	MAY	Gem	11	JUN	Gem	30	SEP	Lib
21	JUN	Can	12	JUN	Can	6	AUG	Can	15	NOV	Sco
22	JUL	Leo	28	JUN	Leo	7	SEP	Leo	30	DEC	Sag
23	AUG	Vir	5	SEP	Vir	5	OCT	Vir			
22	SEP	Lib	21	SEP	Lib	30	OCT	Lib			
23	OCT	Sco	9	OCT	Sco	24	NOV	Sco			
22	NOV	Sag	30	OCT	Sag	18	DEC	Sag			
21	DEC	Cap	29	NOV	Sco						
			12	DEC	Sag						

1973

	SUN			MERCURY			VENUS			MARS	
dy	mth	sign	dy	mth	sign	dy	mth	sign	dy	mth	sign
1	JAN	Cap	4	JAN	Cap	11	JAN	Cap	12	FEB	Cap
20	JAN	Aqu	23	JAN	Aqu	4	FEB	Aqu	26	MAR	Aqu
18	FEB	Pis	9	FEB	Pis	28	FEB	Pis	8	MAY	Pis
20	MAR	Ari	16	APR	Ari	24	MAR	Ari	20	JUN	Ari
20	APR	Tau	6	MAY	Tau	18	APR	Tau	12	AUG	Tau
21	MAY	Gem	20	MAY	Gem	12	MAY	Gem	29	OCT	Ari
21	JUN	Can	4	JUN	Can	5	JUN	Can	24	DEC	Tau
22	JUL	Leo	27	JUN	Leo	30	JUN	Leo			
23	AUG	Vir	16	JUL	Can	25	JUL	Vir			
23	SEP	Lib	11	AUG	Leo	19	AUG	Lib			
23	OCT	Sco	28	AUG	Vir	13	SEP	Sco			
22	NOV	Sag	13	SEP	Lib	9	OCT	Sag			
22	DEC	Cap	2	OCT	Sco	5	NOV	Cap			
			8	DEC	Sag	7	DEC	Aqu			
			28	DEC	Cap						

1974

	SUN			MERCURY			VENUS			MARS	
dy	mth	sign	dy	mth	sign	dy	mth	sign	dy	mth	sign
1	JAN	Cap	16	JAN	Aqu	29	JAN	Cap	27	FEB	Gem
20	JAN	Aqu	2	FEB	Pis	28	FEB	Aqu	20	APR	Can
19	FEB	Pis	2	MAR	Aqu	6	APR	Pis	9	JUN	Leo
21	MAR	Ari	17	MAR	Pis	4	MAY	Ari	27	JUL	Vir
20	APR	Tau	11	APR	Ari	31	MAY	Tau	12	SEP	Lib
21	MAY	Gem	28	APR	Tau	25	JUN	Gem	28	OCT	Sco
21	JUN	Can	12	MAY	Gem	21	JUL	Can	10	DEC	Sag
23	JUL	Leo	29	MAY	Can	14	AUG	Leo			
23	AUG	Vir	5	AUG	Leo	8	SEP	Vir			
23	SEP	Lib	20	AUG	Vir	2	OCT	Lib			
23	OCT	Sco	6	SEP	Lib	26	OCT	Sco			
22	NOV	Sag	28	SEP	Sco	19	NOV	Sag			
22	DEC	Cap	26	OCT	Lib	13	DEC	Cap			
			11	NOV	Sco						
			2	DEC	Sag						
			21	DEC	Cap						

1975

	SUN			MERCURY			VENUS			MARS	
dy	mth	sign	dy	mth	sign	dy	mth	sign	dy	mth	sign
1	JAN	Cap	8	JAN	Aqu	6	JAN	Aqu	21	JAN	Cap
20	JAN	Aqu	16	MAR	Pis	30	JAN	Pis	3	MAR	Aqu
19	FEB	Pis	4	APR	Ari	23	FEB	Ari	11	APR	Pis
21	MAR	Ari	19	APR	Tau	19	MAR	Tau	21	MAY	Ari
20	APR	Tau	4	MAY	Gem	13	APR	Gem	1	JUL	Tau
21	MAY	Gem	12	JUL	Can	9	MAY	Can	14	AUG	Gem
22	JUN	Can	28	JUL	Leo	6	JUN	Leo	17	OCT	Can
23	JUL	Leo	12	AUG	Vir	9	JUL	Vir	25	NOV	Gem
23	AUG	Vir	30	AUG	Lib	2	SEP	Leo			
23	SEP	Lib	6	NOV	Sco	4	OCT	Vir			
24	OCT	Sco	25	NOV	Sag	9	NOV	Lib			
22	NOV	Sag	14	DEC	Cap	7	DEC	Sco			
22	DEC	Cap									

1976

SUN			MERCURY			VENUS			MARS		
dy	mth	sign	dy	mth	sign	dy	mth	sign	dy	mth	sign
1	JAN	Cap	1	JAN	Cap	1	JAN	Sag	1	JAN	Gem
20	JAN	Aqu	3	JAN	Aqu	26	JAN	Cap	18	MAR	Can
19	FEB	Pis	26	JAN	Cap	19	FEB	Aqu	16	MAY	Leo
20	MAR	Ari	16	FEB	Aqu	15	MAR	Pis	6	JUL	Vir
19	APR	Tau	10	MAR	Pis	8	APR	Ari	24	AUG	Lib
20	MAY	Gem	27	MAR	Ari	2	MAY	Tau	8	OCT	Sco
21	JUN	Can	11	APR	Tau	27	MAY	Gem	20	NOV	Sag
22	JUL	Leo	30	APR	Gem	20	JUN	Can			
23	AUG	Vir	20	MAY	Tau	14	JUL	Leo			
22	SEP	Lib	14	JUN	Gem	8	AUG	Vir			
23	OCT	Sco	5	JUL	Can	1	SEP	Lib			
22	NOV	Sag	19	JUL	Leo	26	SEP	Sco			
21	DEC	Cap	4	AUG	Vir	20	OCT	Sag			
			26	AUG	Lib	14	NOV	Cap			
			22	SEP	Vir	9	DEC	Aqu			
			11	OCT	Lib						
			30	OCT	Sco						
			17	NOV	Sag						
			7	DEC	Cap						

1977

SUN			MERCURY			VENUS			MARS		
dy	mth	sign	dy	mth	sign	dy	mth	sign	dy	mth	sign
1	JAN	Cap	10	FEB	Aqu	4	JAN	Pis	1	JAN	Cap
20	JAN	Aqu	2	MAR	Pis	2	FEB	Ari	9	FEB	Aqu
18	FEB	Pis	18	MAR	Ari	6	JUN	Tau	20	MAR	Pis
20	MAR	Ari	3	APR	Tau	6	JUL	Gem	27	APR	Ari
20	APR	Tau	10	JUN	Gem	2	AUG	Can	6	JUN	Tau
21	MAY	Gem	26	JUN	Can	28	AUG	Leo	17	JUL	Gem
21	JUN	Can	10	JUL	Leo	22	SEP	Vir	1	SEP	Can
22	JUL	Leo	28	JUL	Vir	17	OCT	Lib	26	OCT	Leo
23	AUG	Vir	4	OCT	Lib	10	NOV	Sco			
23	SEP	Lib	21	OCT	Sco	4	DEC	Sag			
23	OCT	Sco	9	NOV	Sag	27	DEC	Cap			
22	NOV	Sag	1	DEC	Cap						
21	DEC	Cap	21	DEC	Sag						

1978

	SUN			MERCURY			VENUS			MARS	
dy	mth	sign	dy	mth	sign	dy	mth	sign	dy	mth	sign
1	JAN	Cap	13	JAN	Cap	20	JAN	Aqu	26	JAN	Can
20	JAN	Aqu	4	FEB	Aqu	13	FEB	Pis	10	APR	Leo
19	FEB	Pis	22	FEB	Pis	9	MAR	Ari	14	JUN	Vir
20	MAR	Ari	10	MAR	Ari	2	APR	Tau	4	AUG	Lib
20	APR	Tau	16	MAY	Tau	27	APR	Gem	19	SEP	Sco
21	MAY	Gem	3	JUN	Gem	22	MAY	Can	2	NOV	Sag
21	JUN	Can	17	JUN	Can	16	JUN	Leo	12	DEC	Cap
23	JUL	Leo	2	JUL	Leo	12	JUL	Vir			
23	AUG	Vir	27	JUL	Vir	8	AUG	Lib			
23	SEP	Lib	13	AUG	Leo	7	SEP	Sco			
23	OCT	Sco	9	SEP	Vir						
22	NOV	Sag	26	SEP	Lib						
22	DEC	Cap	14	OCT	Sco						
			3	NOV	Sag						

1979

	SUN			MERCURY			VENUS			MARS	
dy	mth	sign	dy	mth	sign	dy	mth	sign	dy	mth	sign
1	JAN	Cap	8	JAN	Cap	7	JAN	Sag	20	JAN	Aqu
20	JAN	Aqu	28	JAN	Aqu	5	FEB	Cap	27	FEB	Pis
19	FEB	Pis	14	FEB	Pis	3	MAR	Aqu	7	APR	Ari
21	MAR	Ari	3	MAR	Ari	29	MAR	Pis	16	MAY	Tau
20	APR	Tau	28	MAR	Pis	23	APR	Ari	26	JUN	Gem
21	MAY	Gem	17	APR	Ari	18	MAY	Tau	8	AUG	Can
21	JUN	Can	10	MAY	Tau	11	JUN	Gem	24	SEP	Leo
23	JUL	Leo	26	MAY	Gem	6	JUL	Can	19	NOV	Vir
23	AUG	Vir	9	JUN	Can	30	JUL	Leo			
23	SEP	Lib	27	JUN	Leo	24	AUG	Vir			
24	OCT	Sco	2	SEP	Vir	17	SEP	Lib			
22	NOV	Sag	18	SEP	Lib	11	OCT	Sco			
22	DEC	Cap	7	OCT	Sco	4	NOV	Sag			
			30	OCT	Sag	28	NOV	Cap			
			18	NOV	Sco	22	DEC	Aqu			
			12	DEC	Sag						

1980

dy	SUN mth	sign	dy	MERCURY mth	sign	dy	VENUS mth	sign	dy	MARS mth	sign
1	JAN	Cap	2	JAN	Cap	16	JAN	Pis	1	JAN	Vir
20	JAN	Aqu	21	JAN	Aqu	9	FEB	Ari	11	MAR	Leo
19	FEB	Pis	7	FEB	Pis	6	MAR	Tau	4	MAY	Vir
20	MAR	Ari	14	APR	Ari	3	APR	Gem	10	JUL	Lib
19	APR	Tau	2	MAY	Tau	12	MAY	Can	29	AUG	Sco
20	MAY	Gem	16	MAY	Gem	5	JUN	Gem	12	OCT	Sag
21	JUN	Can	31	MAY	Can	6	AUG	Can	22	NOV	Cap
22	JUL	Leo	9	AUG	Leo	7	SEP	Leo	30	DEC	Aqu
22	AUG	Vir	24	AUG	Vir	4	OCT	Vir			
22	SEP	Lib	10	SEP	Lib	30	OCT	Lib			
23	OCT	Sco	30	SEP	Sco	24	NOV	Sco			
22	NOV	Sag	5	DEC	Sag	18	DEC	Sag			
21	DEC	Cap	25	DEC	Cap						

1981

dy	SUN mth	sign	dy	MERCURY mth	sign	dy	VENUS mth	sign	dy	MARS mth	sign
1	JAN	Cap	12	JAN	Aqu	11	JAN	Cap	6	FEB	Pis
20	JAN	Aqu	31	JAN	Pis	4	FEB	Aqu	17	MAR	Ari
18	FEB	Pis	16	FEB	Aqu	28	FEB	Pis	25	APR	Tau
20	MAR	Ari	18	MAR	Pis	24	MAR	Ari	5	JUN	Gem
20	APR	Tau	8	APR	Ari	17	APR	Tau	18	JUL	Can
21	MAY	Gem	24	APR	Tau	11	MAY	Gem	2	SEP	Leo
21	JUN	Can	8	MAY	Gem	5	JUN	Can	21	OCT	Vir
22	JUL	Leo	28	MAY	Can	29	JUN	Leo	16	DEC	Lib
23	AUG	Vir	22	JUN	Gem	24	JUL	Vir			
23	SEP	Lib	12	JUL	Can	18	AUG	Lib			
23	OCT	Sco	1	AUG	Leo	12	SEP	Sco			
22	NOV	Sag	16	AUG	Vir	8	OCT	Sag			
21	DEC	Cap	2	SEP	Lib	5	NOV	Cap			
			27	SEP	Sco	8	DEC	Aqu			
			14	OCT	Lib						
			9	NOV	Sco						
			28	NOV	Sag						
			17	DEC	Cap						

1982

SUN			MERCURY			VENUS			MARS		
dy	mth	sign	dy	mth	sign	dy	mth	sign	dy	mth	sign
1	JAN	Cap	5	JAN	Aqu	23	JAN	Cap	1	JAN	Lib
20	JAN	Aqu	13	MAR	Pis	2	MAR	Aqu	3	AUG	Sco
18	FEB	Pis	31	MAR	Ari	6	APR	Pis	20	SEP	Sag
20	MAR	Ari	15	APR	Tau	4	MAY	Ari	31	OCT	Cap
20	APR	Tau	1	MAY	Gem	30	MAY	Tau	10	DEC	Aqu
21	MAY	Gem	9	JUL	Can	20	JUN	Gem			
21	JUN	Can	24	JUL	Leo	20	JUL	Can			
23	JUL	Leo	8	AUG	Vir	14	AUG	Leo			
23	AUG	Vir	28	AUG	Lib	7	SEP	Vir			
23	SEP	Lib	3	NOV	Sco	2	OCT	Lib			
23	OCT	Sco	21	NOV	Sag	26	OCT	Sco			
22	NOV	Sag	10	DEC	Cap	18	NOV	Sag			
22	DEC	Cap				12	DEC	Cap			

1983

SUN			MERCURY			VENUS			MARS		
dy	mth	sign	dy	mth	sign	dy	mth	sign	dy	mth	sign
1	JAN	Cap	1	JAN	Aqu	5	JAN	Aqu	17	JAN	Pis
20	JAN	Aqu	12	JAN	Cap	29	JAN	Pis	25	FEB	Ari
19	FEB	Pis	14	FEB	Aqu	22	FEB	Ari	5	APR	Tau
21	MAR	Ari	7	MAR	Pis	19	MAR	Tau	16	MAY	Gem
20	APR	Tau	23	MAR	Ari	13	APR	Gem	29	JUN	Can
21	MAY	Gem	7	APR	Tau	9	MAY	Can	13	AUG	Leo
21	JUN	Can	14	JUN	Gem	6	JUN	Leo	30	SEP	Vir
23	JUL	Leo	1	JUL	Can	10	JUL	Vir	18	NOV	Lib
23	AUG	Vir	15	JUL	Leo	27	AUG	Leo			
23	SEP	Lib	1	AUG	Vir	5	OCT	Vir			
23	OCT	Sco	29	AUG	Lib	9	NOV	Lib			
22	NOV	Sag	6	SEP	Vir	6	DEC	Sco			
22	DEC	Cap	8	OCT	Lib						
			26	OCT	Sco						
			14	NOV	Sag						
			4	DEC	Cap						

1984

	SUN			MERCURY			VENUS			MARS	
dy	mth	sign	dy	mth	sign	dy	mth	sign	dy	mth	sign
1	JAN	Cap	9	FEB	Aqu	1	JAN	Sag	11	JAN	Sco
20	JAN	Aqu	27	FEB	Pis	25	JAN	Cap	17	AUG	Sag
19	FEB	Pis	14	MAR	Ari	19	FEB	Aqu	5	OCT	Cap
20	MAR	Ari	31	MAR	Tau	14	MAR	Pis	15	NOV	Aqu
19	APR	Tau	25	APR	Ari	7	APR	Ari	25	DEC	Pis
20	MAY	Gem	15	MAY	Tau	2	MAY	Tau			
21	JUN	Can	7	JUN	Gem	26	MAY	Gem			
22	JUL	Leo	22	JUN	Can	20	JUN	Can			
22	AUG	Vir	6	JUL	Leo	14	JUL	Leo			
22	SEP	Lib	26	JUL	Vir	7	AUG	Vir			
23	OCT	Sco	30	SEP	Lib	1	SEP	Lib			
22	NOV	Sag	18	OCT	Sco	25	SEP	Sco			
21	DEC	Cap	6	NOV	Sag	20	OCT	Sag			
			1	DEC	Cap	13	NOV	Cap			
			7	DEC	Sag	9	DEC	Aqu			

1985

	SUN			MERCURY			VENUS			MARS	
dy	mth	sign	dy	mth	sign	dy	mth	sign	dy	mth	sign
1	JAN	Cap	11	JAN	Cap	4	JAN	Pis	2	FEB	Ari
20	JAN	Aqu	1	FEB	Aqu	2	FEB	Ari	15	MAR	Tau
18	FEB	Pis	18	FEB	Pis	6	JUN	Tau	26	APR	Gem
20	MAR	Ari	7	MAR	Ari	6	JUL	Gem	9	JUN	Can
20	APR	Tau	14	MAY	Tau	2	AUG	Can	25	JUL	Leo
21	MAY	Gem	30	MAY	Gem	28	AUG	Leo	10	SEP	Vir
21	JUN	Can	13	JUN	Can	22	SEP	Vir	27	OCT	Lib
22	JUL	Leo	29	JUN	Leo	16	OCT	Lib	14	DEC	Sco
23	AUG	Vir	6	SEP	Vir	9	NOV	Sco			
23	SEP	Lib	22	SEP	Lib	3	DEC	Sag			
23	OCT	Sco	10	OCT	Sco	27	DEC	Cap			
22	NOV	Sag	31	OCT	Sag						
21	DEC	Cap	4	DEC	Sco						
			12	DEC	Sag						

1986

	SUN			MERCURY			VENUS			MARS	
dy	mth	sign	dy	mth	sign	dy	mth	sign	dy	mth	sign
1	JAN	Cap	5	JAN	Cap	20	JAN	Aqu	2	FEB	Sag
20	JAN	Aqu	25	JAN	Aqu	13	FEB	Pis	28	MAR	Cap
18	FEB	Pis	11	FEB	Pis	9	MAR	Ari	8	JUN	R
20	MAR	Ari	3	MAR	Ari	2	APR	Tau	12	AUG	D
20	APR	Tau	7	MAR	R	26	APR	Gem	9	OCT	Aqu
21	MAY	Gem	11	MAR	Pis	21	MAY	Can	26	NOV	Pis
21	JUN	Can	30	MAR	D	15	JUN	Leo			
23	JUL	Leo	17	APR	Ari	11	JUL	Vir			
23	AUG	Vir	7	MAY	Tau	7	AUG	Lib			
23	SEP	Lib	22	MAY	Gem	7	SEP	Sco			
23	OCT	Sco	5	JUN	Can	15	OCT	R			
22	NOV	Sag	26	JUN	Leo	26	NOV	D			
22	DEC	Cap	9	JUL	R						
			23	JUL	Can						
			3	AUG	D						
			11	AUG	Leo						
			30	AUG	Vir						
			15	SEP	Lib						
			4	OCT	Sco						
			2	NOV	R						
			22	NOV	D						
			10	DEC	Sag						
			29	DEC	Cap						

1987

	SUN			MERCURY			VENUS			MARS	
dy	mth	sign	dy	mth	sign	dy	mth	sign	dy	mth	sign
1	JAN	Cap	17	JAN	Aqu	7	JAN	Sag	8	JAN	Ari
20	JAN	Aqu	4	FEB	Pis	5	FEB	Cap	20	FEB	Tau
19	FEB	Pis	18	FEB	R	3	MAR	Aqu	5	APR	Gem
21	MAR	Ari	12	MAR	Aqu	28	MAR	Pis	21	MAY	Can
20	APR	Tau	12	MAR	D	22	APR	Ari	6	JUL	Leo
21	MAY	Gem	13	MAR	Pis	17	MAY	Tau	22	AUG	Vir
21	JUN	Can	12	APR	Ari	11	JUN	Gem	8	OCT	Lib
23	JUL	Leo	29	APR	Tau	5	JUL	Can	24	NOV	Sco
23	AUG	Vir	13	MAY	Gem	30	JUL	Leo			
23	SEP	Lib	30	MAY	Can	23	AUG	Vir			
23	OCT	Sco	21	JUN	R	16	SEP	Lib			
22	NOV	Sag	15	JUL	D	10	OCT	Sco			
22	DEC	Cap	6	AUG	Leo	3	NOV	Sag			
			21	AUG	Vir	28	NOV	Cap			
			7	SEP	Lib	22	DEC	Aqu			
			28	SEP	Sco						
			16	OCT	R						
			1	NOV	Lib						
			6	NOV	D						
			11	NOV	Sco						
			3	DEC	Sag						
			22	DEC	Cap						

1988

	SUN			MERCURY			VENUS			MARS	
dy	**mth**	**sign**	**dy**	**mth**	**sign**	**dy**	**mth**	**sign**	**dy**	**mth**	**sign**
1	JAN	Cap	10	JAN	Aqu	15	JAN	Pis	8	JAN	Sag
20	JAN	Aqu	2	FEB	R	9	FEB	Ari	22	FEB	Cap
19	FEB	Pis	23	FEB	D	6	MAR	Tau	6	APR	Aqu
20	MAR	Ari	16	MAR	Pis	3	APR	Gem	22	MAY	Pis
19	APR	Tau	4	APR	Ari	17	MAY	Can	13	JUL	Ari
20	MAY	Gem	20	APR	Tau	22	MAY	R	26	AUG	R
21	JUN	Can	4	MAY	Gem	27	MAY	Gem	23	OCT	Pis
22	JUL	Leo	31	MAY	R	4	JUL	D	28	OCT	D
22	AUG	Vir	24	JUN	D	6	AUG	Can	1	NOV	Ari
22	SEP	Lib	12	JUL	Can	7	SEP	Leo			
23	OCT	Sco	28	JUL	Leo	4	OCT	Vir			
22	NOV	Sag	12	AUG	Vir	29	OCT	Lib			
21	DEC	Cap	30	AUG	Lib	23	NOV	Sco			
			28	SEP	R	17	DEC	Sag			
			20	OCT	D						
			6	NOV	Sco						
			25	NOV	Sag						
			14	DEC	Cap						

1989

	SUN			MERCURY			VENUS			MARS	
dy	**mth**	**sign**	**dy**	**mth**	**sign**	**dy**	**mth**	**sign**	**dy**	**mth**	**sign**
1	JAN	Cap	2	JAN	Aqu	10	JAN	Cap	19	JAN	Tau
20	JAN	Aqu	16	JAN	R	3	FEB	Aqu	11	MAR	Gem
18	FEB	Pis	29	JAN	Cap	27	FEB	Pis	29	APR	Can
20	MAR	Ari	5	FEB	D	23	MAR	Ari	16	JUN	Leo
20	APR	Tau	14	FEB	Aqu	16	APR	Tau	3	AUG	Vir
21	MAY	Gem	10	MAR	Pis	11	MAY	Gem	19	SEP	Lib
21	JUN	Can	28	MAR	Ari	4	JUN	Can	4	NOV	Sco
22	JUL	Leo	11	APR	Tau	29	JUN	Leo	18	DEC	Sag
23	AUG	Vir	29	APR	Gem	24	JUL	Vir			
23	SEP	Lib	12	MAY	R	18	AUG	Lib			
23	OCT	Sco	28	MAY	Tau	12	SEP	Sco			
22	NOV	Sag	5	JUN	D	8	OCT	Sag			
21	DEC	Cap	12	JUN	Gem	5	NOV	Cap			
			6	JUL	Can	10	DEC	Aqu			
			20	JUL	Leo	29	DEC	R			
			5	AUG	Vir						
			26	AUG	Lib						
			11	SEP	R						
			26	SEP	Vir						
			3	OCT	D						
			11	OCT	Lib						
			30	OCT	Sco						
			18	NOV	Sag						
			7	DEC	Cap						
			30	DEC	R						

1990

SUN			MERCURY			VENUS			MARS		
dy	mth	sign	dy	mth	sign	dy	mth	sign	dy	mth	sign
1	JAN	Cap	1	JAN	Cap	16	JAN	Cap	29	JAN	Cap
20	JAN	Aqu	12	FEB	Aqu	8	FEB	D	11	MAR	Aqu
18	FEB	Pis	3	MAR	Pis	3	MAR	Aqu	20	APR	Pis
20	MAR	Ari	20	MAR	Ari	6	APR	Pis	31	MAY	Ari
20	APR	Tau	4	APR	Tau	4	MAY	Ari	12	JUL	Tau
21	MAY	Gem	23	APR	R	30	MAY	Tau	31	AUG	Gem
21	JUN	Can	17	MAY	D	25	JUN	Gem	20	OCT	R
23	JUL	Leo	12	JUN	Gem	20	JUL	Can	14	DEC	Tau
23	AUG	Vir	27	JUN	Can	13	AUG	Leo			
23	SEP	Lib	11	JUL	Leo	7	SEP	Vir			
23	OCT	Sco	29	JUL	Vir	1	OCT	Lib			
22	NOV	Sag	25	AUG	R	25	OCT	Sco			
22	DEC	Cap	17	SEP	D	18	NOV	Sag			
			5	OCT	Lib	12	DEC	Cap			
			23	OCT	Sco						
			11	NOV	Sag						
			2	DEC	Cap						
			14	DEC	R						
			25	DEC	Sag						

1991

SUN			MERCURY			VENUS			MARS		
dy	mth	sign	dy	mth	sign	dy	mth	sign	dy	mth	sign
1	JAN	Cap	1	JAN	Sag	5	JAN	Aqu	1	JAN	Tau
20	JAN	Aqu	14	JAN	Cap	29	JAN	Pis	21	JAN	Gem
19	FEB	Pis	5	FEB	Aqu	22	FEB	Ari	3	APR	Can
21	MAR	Ari	24	FEB	Pis	18	MAR	Tau	26	MAY	Leo
20	APR	Tau	11	MAR	Ari	13	APR	Gem	15	JUL	Vir
21	MAY	Gem	4	APR	R	9	MAY	Can	1	SEP	Lib
21	JUN	Can	28	APR	D	6	JUN	Leo	16	OCT	Sco
23	JUL	Leo	16	MAY	Tau	11	JUL	Vir	29	NOV	Sag
23	AUG	Vir	5	JUN	Gem	1	AUG	R			
23	SEP	Lib	19	JUN	Can	21	AUG	Leo			
23	OCT	Sco	4	JUL	Leo	13	SEP	D			
22	NOV	Sag	26	JUL	Vir	6	OCT	Vir			
22	DEC	Cap	7	AUG	R	9	NOV	Lib			
			19	AUG	Leo	6	DEC	Sco			
			31	AUG	D	31	DEC	Sag			
			10	SEP	Vir						
			28	SEP	Lib						
			15	OCT	Sco						
			4	NOV	Sag						
			28	NOV	R						
			18	DEC	D						

1992

SUN			MERCURY			VENUS			MARS		
dy	mth	sign	dy	mth	sign	dy	mth	sign	dy	mth	sign
1	JAN	Cap	10	JAN	Cap	25	JAN	Cap	9	JAN	Cap
20	JAN	Aqu	29	JAN	Aqu	18	FEB	Aqu	18	FEB	Aqu
19	FEB	Pis	16	FEB	Pis	13	MAR	Pis	28	MAR	Pis
20	MAR	Ari	3	MAR	Ari	7	APR	Ari	5	MAY	Ari
19	APR	Tau	17	MAR	R	1	MAY	Tau	14	JUN	Tau
20	MAY	Gem	4	APR	Pis	26	MAY	Gem	26	JUL	Gem
21	JUN	Can	9	APR	D	19	JUN	Can	12	SEP	Can
22	JUL	Leo	14	APR	Ari	13	JUL	Leo	28	NOV	R
22	AUG	Vir	11	MAY	Tau	7	AUG	Vir			
22	SEP	Lib	26	MAY	Gem	31	AUG	Lib			
23	OCT	Sco	9	JUN	Can	25	SEP	Sco			
22	NOV	Sag	27	JUN	Leo	19	OCT	Sag			
21	DEC	Cap	20	JUL	R	13	NOV	Cap			
			13	AUG	D	8	DEC	Aqu			
			3	SEP	Vir						
			19	SEP	Lib						
			7	OCT	Sco						
			29	OCT	Sag						
			11	NOV	R						
			21	NOV	Sco						
			1	DEC	D						
			12	DEC	Sag						

1993

SUN			MERCURY			VENUS			MARS		
dy	mth	sign	dy	mth	sign	dy	mth	sign	dy	mth	sign
1	JAN	Cap	2	JAN	Cap	3	JAN	Pis	1	JAN	Can
20	JAN	Aqu	21	JAN	Aqu	2	FEB	Ari	27	APR	Leo
18	FEB	Pis	7	FEB	Pis	11	MAR	R	23	JUN	Vir
20	MAR	Ari	27	FEB	R	22	APR	D	12	AUG	Lib
20	APR	Tau	22	MAR	D	6	JUN	Tau	27	SEP	Sco
21	MAY	Gem	15	APR	Ari	6	JUL	Gem	9	NOV	Sag
21	JUN	Can	3	MAY	Tau	1	AUG	Can	20	DEC	Cap
22	JUL	Leo	18	MAY	Gem	27	AUG	Leo			
23	AUG	Vir	2	JUN	Can	21	SEP	Vir			
23	SEP	Lib	1	JUL	R	16	OCT	Lib			
23	OCT	Sco	25	JUL	D	9	NOV	Sco			
22	NOV	Sag	10	AUG	Leo	2	DEC	Sag			
21	DEC	Cap	26	AUG	Vir	26	DEC	Cap			
			11	SEP	Lib						
			1	OCT	Sco						
			25	OCT	R						
			15	NOV	D						
			7	DEC	Sag						
			26	DEC	Cap						

1994

	SUN			MERCURY			VENUS			MARS	
dy	mth	sign	dy	mth	sign	dy	mth	sign	dy	mth	sign
1	JAN	Cap	14	JAN	Aqu	19	JAN	Aqu	28	JAN	Aqu
20	JAN	Aqu	1	FEB	Pis	12	FEB	Pis	7	MAR	Pis
18	FEB	Pis	11	FEB	R	8	MAR	Ari	14	APR	Ari
20	MAR	Ari	21	FEB	Aqu	1	APR	Tau	23	MAY	Tau
20	APR	Tau	5	MAR	D	26	APR	Gem	3	JUL	Gem
21	MAY	Gem	18	MAR	Pis	21	MAY	Can	16	AUG	Can
21	JUN	Can	9	APR	Ari	15	JUN	Leo	4	OCT	Leo
23	JUL	Leo	25	APR	Tau	11	JUL	Vir	12	DEC	Vir
23	AUG	Vir	9	MAY	Gem	7	AUG	Lib			
23	SEP	Lib	28	MAY	Can	7	SEP	Sco			
23	OCT	Sco	12	JUN	R	13	OCT	R			
22	NOV	Sag	2	JUL	Gem	23	NOV	D			
22	DEC	Cap	6	JUL	D						
			10	JUL	Can						
			3	AUG	Leo						
			18	AUG	Vir						
			4	SEP	Lib						
			27	SEP	Sco						
			9	OCT	R						
			19	OCT	Lib						
			30	OCT	D						
			10	NOV	Sco						
			30	NOV	Sag						
			19	DEC	Cap						

1995

	SUN			MERCURY			VENUS			MARS	
dy	mth	sign	dy	mth	sign	dy	mth	sign	dy	mth	sign
1	JAN	Cap	6	JAN	Aqu	7	JAN	Sag	1	JAN	Vir
20	JAN	Aqu	26	JAN	R	4	FEB	Cap	22	JAN	Leo
19	FEB	Pis	16	FEB	D	2	MAR	Aqu	25	MAY	Vir
21	MAR	Ari	14	MAR	Pis	28	MAR	Pis	21	JUL	Lib
20	APR	Tau	2	APR	Ari	22	APR	Ari	7	SEP	Sco
21	MAY	Gem	17	APR	Tau	16	MAY	Tau	20	OCT	Sag
21	JUN	Can	2	MAY	Gem	10	JUN	Gem	30	NOV	Cap
23	JUL	Leo	24	MAY	R	5	JUL	Can			
23	AUG	Vir	17	JUN	D	29	JUL	Leo			
23	SEP	Lib	10	JUL	Can	23	AUG	Vir			
23	OCT	Sco	25	JUL	Leo	16	SEP	Lib			
22	NOV	Sag	10	AUG	Vir	10	OCT	Sco			
22	DEC	Cap	29	AUG	Lib	3	NOV	Sag			
			22	SEP	R	27	NOV	Cap			
			14	OCT	D	21	DEC	Aqu			
			4	NOV	Sco						
			22	NOV	Sag						
			12	DEC	Cap						

1996

SUN			MERCURY			VENUS			MARS		
dy	mth	sign	dy	mth	sign	dy	mth	sign	dy	mth	sign
1	JAN	Cap	1	JAN	Aqu	15	JAN	Pis	8	JAN	Aqu
20	JAN	Aqu	9	JAN	R	9	FEB	Ari	15	FEB	Pis
19	FEB	Pis	17	JAN	Cap	6	MAR	Tau	24	MAR	Ari
20	MAR	Ari	30	JAN	D	3	APR	Gem	2	MAY	Tau
19	APR	Tau	15	FEB	Aqu	20	MAY	R	12	JUN	Gem
20	MAY	Gem	7	MAR	Pis	2	JUL	D	25	JUL	Can
21	JUN	Can	24	MAR	Ari	7	AUG	Can	9	SEP	Leo
22	JUL	Leo	8	APR	Tau	7	SEP	Leo	30	OCT	Vir
22	AUG	Vir	3	MAY	R	4	OCT	Vir			
22	SEP	Lib	27	MAY	D	29	OCT	Lib			
23	OCT	Sco	13	JUN	Gem	23	NOV	Sco			
22	NOV	Sag	2	JUL	Can	17	DEC	Sag			
21	DEC	Cap	16	JUL	Leo						
			1	AUG	Vir						
			26	AUG	Lib						
			4	SEP	R						
			12	SEP	Vir						
			26	SEP	D						
			9	OCT	Lib						
			27	OCT	Sco						
			14	NOV	Sag						
			4	DEC	Cap						
			23	DEC	R						

1997

SUN			MERCURY			VENUS			MARS		
dy	mth	sign	dy	mth	sign	dy	mth	sign	dy	mth	sign
1	JAN	Cap	1	JAN	Cap	10	JAN	Cap	3	JAN	Lib
20	JAN	Aqu	9	FEB	Aqu	3	FEB	Aqu	6	FEB	R
18	FEB	Pis	28	FEB	Pis	27	FEB	Pis	8	MAR	Vir
20	MAR	Ari	16	MAR	Ari	23	MAR	Ari	27	APR	D
20	APR	Tau	1	APR	Tau	16	APR	Tau	19	JUN	Lib
21	MAY	Gem	15	APR	R	10	MAY	Gem	14	AUG	Sco
21	JUN	Can	5	MAY	Ari	4	JUN	Can	28	SEP	Sag
22	JUL	Leo	8	MAY	D	28	JUN	Leo	9	NOV	Cap
23	AUG	Vir	12	MAY	Tau	23	JUL	Vir	18	DEC	Aqu
22	SEP	Lib	8	JUN	Gem	17	AUG	Lib			
23	OCT	Sco	23	JUN	Can	12	SEP	Sco			
22	NOV	Sag	8	JUL	Leo	8	OCT	Sag			
21	DEC	Cap	27	JUL	Vir	5	NOV	Cap			
			17	AUG	R	12	DEC	Aqu			
			10	SEP	D	26	DEC	R			
			2	OCT	Lib						
			19	OCT	Sco						
			7	NOV	Sag						
			30	NOV	Cap						
			7	DEC	R						
			13	DEC	Sag						
			27	DEC	D						

1998

	SUN			MERCURY			VENUS			MARS	
dy	mth	sign	dy	mth	sign	dy	mth	sign	dy	mth	sign
1	JAN	Cap	12	JAN	Cap	9	JAN	Cap	25	JAN	Pis
20	JAN	Aqu	2	FEB	Aqu	5	FEB	D	4	MAR	Ari
18	FEB	Pis	20	FEB	Pis	4	MAR	Aqu	13	APR	Tau
20	MAR	Ari	8	MAR	Ari	6	APR	Pis	24	MAY	Gem
20	APR	Tau	27	MAR	R	3	MAY	Ari	6	JUL	Can
21	MAY	Gem	20	APR	D	29	MAY	Tau	20	AUG	Leo
21	JUN	Can	15	MAY	Tau	24	JUN	Gem	7	OCT	Vir
23	JUL	Leo	1	JUN	Gem	19	JUL	Can	27	NOV	Lib
23	AUG	Vir	15	JUN	Can	13	AUG	Leo			
23	SEP	Lib	30	JUN	Leo	6	SEP	Vir			
23	OCT	Sco	31	JUL	R	30	SEP	Lib			
22	NOV	Sag	23	AUG	D	24	OCT	Sco			
22	DEC	Cap	8	SEP	Vir	17	NOV	Sag			
			24	SEP	Lib	11	DEC	Cap			
			12	OCT	Sco						
			1	NOV	Sag						
			21	NOV	R						
			11	DEC	D						

1999

	SUN			MERCURY			VENUS			MARS	
dy	mth	sign	dy	mth	sign	dy	mth	sign	dy	mth	sign
1	JAN	Cap	7	JAN	Cap	4	JAN	Aqu	26	JAN	Sco
20	JAN	Aqu	26	JAN	Aqu	28	JAN	Pis	18	MAR	R
19	FEB	Pis	12	FEB	Pis	21	FEB	Ari	5	MAY	Lib
21	MAR	Ari	2	MAR	Ari	18	MAR	Tau	4	JUN	D
20	APR	Tau	10	MAR	R	12	APR	Gem	5	JUL	Sco
21	MAY	Gem	18	MAR	Pis	8	MAY	Can	2	SEP	Sag
21	JUN	Can	2	APR	D	5	JUN	Leo	17	OCT	Cap
23	JUL	Leo	17	APR	Ari	12	JUL	Vir	26	NOV	Aqu
23	AUG	Vir	8	MAY	Tau	30	JUL	R			
23	SEP	Lib	23	MAY	Gem	15	AUG	Leo			
23	OCT	Sco	7	JUN	Can	11	SEP	D			
22	NOV	Sag	26	JUN	Leo	7	OCT	Vir			
22	DEC	Cap	12	JUL	R	9	NOV	Lib			
			31	JUL	Can	5	DEC	Sco			
			6	AUG	D	31	DEC	Sag			
			11	AUG	Leo						
			31	AUG	Vir						
			16	SEP	Lib						
			5	OCT	Sco						
			30	OCT	Sag						
			5	NOV	R						
			9	NOV	Sco						
			25	NOV	D						
			11	DEC	Sag						
			31	DEC	Cap						

2000

	SUN			MERCURY			VENUS			MARS	
dy	**mth**	**sign**	**dy**	**mth**	**sign**	**dy**	**mth**	**sign**	**dy**	**mth**	**sign**
1	JAN	Cap	18	JAN	Aqu	24	JAN	Cap	4	JAN	Pis
20	JAN	Aqu	5	FEB	Pis	18	FEB	Aqu	12	FEB	Ari
19	FEB	Pis	21	FEB	R	13	MAR	Pis	23	MAR	Tau
20	MAR	Ari	14	MAR	D	6	APR	Ari	3	MAY	Gem
19	APR	Tau	13	APR	Ari	1	MAY	Tau	16	JUN	Can
20	MAY	Gem	30	APR	Tau	25	MAY	Gem	1	AUG	Leo
21	JUN	Can	14	MAY	Gem	18	JUN	Can	17	SEP	Vir
22	JUL	Leo	30	MAY	Can	13	JUL	Leo	4	NOV	Lib
22	AUG	Vir	23	JUN	R	6	AUG	Vir	23	DEC	Sco
22	SEP	Lib	17	JUL	D	31	AUG	Lib			
23	OCT	Sco	7	AUG	Leo	24	SEP	Sco			
22	NOV	Sag	22	AUG	Vir	19	OCT	Sag			
21	DEC	Cap	7	SEP	Lib	13	NOV	Cap			
			28	SEP	Sco	8	DEC	Aqu			
			18	OCT	R						
			7	NOV	Lib						
			8	NOV	D						
			8	NOV	Sco						
			3	DEC	Sag						
			23	DEC	Cap						

Moon Signs

To find your Moon Sign, look up the sign relevant to your month and year of birth. Then, moving clockwise around the wheel, count forward the number of signs indicated on table two. Begin with the next sign along as the '1' position when you count forward.

Example

25 July 1964

Look-up sign is Pisces

Number of signs to count forward — 11

Counting clockwise around the wheel, this results in the Moon in Aquarius. This is the Moon sign for most people born on 25 July 1964. To allow for slight changes within time zones, though, always check at www.astro.com.

YEAR AND MONTH OF BIRTH

	JAN	FEB	MAR	APR	MAY	JUN	JUL	AUG	SEP	OCT	NOV	DEC
1930	Cap	Pis	Pis	Tau	Gem	Leo	Vir	Sco	Sag	Cap	Pis	Ari
1931	Tau	Can	Can	Vir	Lib	Sag	Cap	Pis	Ari	Tau	Can	Leo
1932	Lib	Sag	Sag	Aqu	Pis	Tau	Gem	Can	Vir	Lib	Sag	Cap
1933	Pis	Ari	Tau	Gem	Can	Vir	Lib	Sag	Cap	Pis	Ari	Tau
1934	Can	Leo	Vir	Lib	Sag	Cap	Pis	Ari	Gem	Can	Leo	Vir
1935	Sco	Cap	Cap	Pis	Ari	Gem	Can	Leo	Lib	Sco	Cap	Aqu

	JAN	FEB	MAR	APR	MAY	JUN	JUL	AUG	SEP	OCT	NOV	DEC
1936	Ari	Tau	Gem	Leo	Vir	Lib	Sco	Cap	Pis	Ari	Gem	Can
1937	Leo	Lib	Lib	Sag	Cap	Aqu	Ari	Tau	Can	Leo	Lib	Sco
1938	Cap	Aqu	Aqu	Ari	Tau	Can	Leo	Lib	Sco	Cap	Aqu	Pis
1939	Tau	Gem	Can	Leo	Lib	Sco	Cap	Aqu	Ari	Tau	Gem	Leo
1940	Vir	Sco	Sag	Cap	Aqu	Ari	Tau	Can	Leo	Lib	Sco	Cap
1941	Aqu	Ari	Ari	Tau	Gem	Leo	Vir	Sco	Cap	Aqu	Ari	Tau
1942	Gem	Leo	Leo	Lib	Sco	Cap	Aqu	Ari	Tau	Gem	Leo	Vir
1943	Lib	Sag	Sag	Aqu	Pis	Tau	Gem	Leo	Vir	Lib	Sag	Cap
1944	Pis	Tau	Tau	Can	Leo	Lib	Sco	Sag	Aqu	Pis	Tau	Gem
1945	Leo	Vir	Lib	Sco	Sag	Aqu	Pis	Tau	Can	Leo	Vir	Lib
1946	Sag	Cap	Aqu	Pis	Tau	Gem	Leo	Vir	Sco	Sag	Cap	Aqu
1947	Ari	Gem	Gem	Leo	Vir	Sco	Sag	Cap	Pis	Ari	Gem	Can
1948	Vir	Lib	Sco	Cap	Aqu	Pis	Ari	Gem	Leo	Vir	Sco	Sag
1949	Cap	Pis	Pis	Tau	Gem	Leo	Vir	Sco	Sag	Cap	Pis	Ari
1950	Gem	Can	Can	Vir	Lib	Sag	Cap	Pis	Ari	Gem	Can	Leo
1951	Lib	Sag	Sag	Aqu	Pis	Ari	Gem	Can	Vir	Lib	Sco	Cap
1952	Pis	Ari	Tau	Gem	Can	Vir	Lib	Sag	Cap	Pis	Ari	Gem
1953	Can	Vir	Vir	Lib	Sag	Cap	Pis	Ari	Gem	Can	Vir	Lib
1954	Sco	Cap	Cap	Pis	Ari	Gem	Can	Vir	Lib	Sco	Cap	Aqu
1955	Ari	Tau	Gem	Can	Vir	Lib	Sco	Cap	Aqu	Pis	Tau	Gem
1956	Leo	Lib	Sco	Sag	Cap	Pis	Ari	Tau	Can	Leo	Lib	Sco
1957	Cap	Aqu	Pis	Ari	Tau	Can	Leo	Lib	Sag	Cap	Aqu	Pis
1958	Tau	Gem	Can	Leo	Lib	Sag	Cap	Aqu	Ari	Tau	Gem	Leo
1959	Vir	Sco	Sco	Cap	Aqu	Ari	Tau	Gem	Leo	Vir	Sco	Sag
1960	Aqu	Ari	Ari	Gem	Can	Leo	Vir	Sco	Cap	Aqu	Ari	Tau
1961	Can	Leo	Leo	Lib	Sco	Cap	Aqu	Ari	Gem	Can	Leo	Vir
1962	Sco	Sag	Sag	Aqu	Pis	Tau	Gem	Leo	Vir	Sco	Sag	Cap
1963	Pis	Tau	Tau	Can	Leo	Lib	Sco	Sag	Aqu	Pis	Tau	Gem
1964	Leo	Vir	Lib	Sco	Sag	Aqu	Pis	Tau	Can	Leo	Lib	Sco
1965	Sag	Aqu	Aqu	Ari	Tau	Gem	Leo	Lib	Sco	Sag	Aqu	Pis
1966	Ari	Gem	Gem	Leo	Vir	Sco	Sag	Aqu	Pis	Ari	Gem	Can
1967	Vir	Sco	Sco	Cap	Aqu	Pis	Ari	Gem	Can	Vir	Lib	Sag
1968	Cap	Pis	Ari	Tau	Gem	Leo	Vir	Sco	Sag	Aqu	Pis	Ari
1969	Gem	Can	Leo	Vir	Lib	Sag	Cap	Pis	Tau	Gem	Can	Leo
1970	Lib	Sco	Sag	Aqu	Pis	Tau	Gem	Can	Vir	Lib	Sag	Cap
1971	Aqu	Ari	Tau	Gem	Can	Vir	Lib	Sco	Cap	Aqu	Ari	Tau
1972	Can	Vir	Vir	Sco	Sag	Cap	Pis	Ari	Gem	Can	Vir	Lib
1973	Sag	Cap	Cap	Pis	Ari	Gem	Can	Vir	Lib	Sag	Cap	Aqu
1974	Ari	Tau	Gem	Can	Vir	Lib	Sag	Cap	Pis	Ari	Tau	Gem
1975	Leo	Lib	Lib	Sag	Cap	Pis	Ari	Tau	Can	Leo	Lib	Sco
1976	Cap	Aqu	Pis	Ari	Tau	Can	Leo	Lib	Sag	Cap	Pis	Ari
1977	Tau	Can	Can	Vir	Lib	Sag	Cap	Pis	Ari	Tau	Can	Leo
1978	Vir	Sco	Sco	Cap	Aqu	Ari	Tau	Can	Leo	Vir	Sco	Sag

410

	JAN	FEB	MAR	APR	MAY	JUN	JUL	AUG	SEP	OCT	NOV	DEC
1979	Aqu	Ari	Ari	Pis	Can	Leo	Vir	Sco	Sag	Aqu	Pis	Tau
1980	Gem	Leo	Vir	Lib	Sco	Cap	Aqu	Ari	Gem	Can	Leo	Vir
1981	Sco	Sag	Cap	Aqu	Pis	Tau	Can	Leo	Lib	Sco	Sag	Cap
1982	Pis	Tau	Tau	Can	Leo	Lib	Sco	Sag	Aqu	Pis	Tau	Gem
1983	Leo	Vir	Lib	Sco	Sag	Aqu	Pis	Ari	Gem	Can	Vir	Lib
1984	Sag	Aqu	Aqu	Ari	Tau	Gem	Leo	Lib	Sco	Sag	Aqu	Pis
1985	Tau	Gem	Gem	Leo	Vir	Sco	Sag	Aqu	Pis	Tau	Gem	Can

DAY OF BIRTH

Day of birth	Count forward
1	0
2	1
3	1
4	1
5	2
6	2
7	3
8	3
9	4
10	4
11	5
12	5
13	5
14	6
15	6
16	7
17	7
18	8
19	8
20	9
21	9
22	10
23	10
24	10
25	11
26	11
27	12
28	12
29	1
30	1
31	2

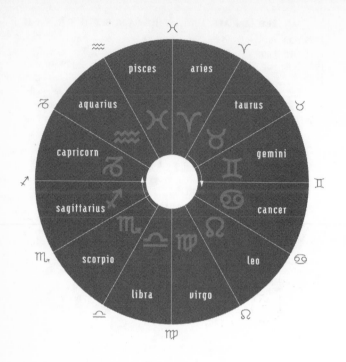

RESOURCES

ASTROLOGY ON THE INTERNET

There are so many astrology sites on the web that it's hard to know where to begin. People tell me they want to visit sites written in plain English, with specific, accurate predictions. They don't want a hard sell, though. Nor do they want lots of flashing advertisements — or registration forms — or requests for their personal e-mail addresses. And, it seems, the more extra features, the better!

Here are some sites, chosen by me — or recommended to me by other people — which fit the bill. Free, accurate and astrologically sound, they often offer personal readings too. They're generally regarded as five-star in the astrological world — why not check them out?

MADALYN ASLAN
Author of *What's Your Sign*, *Madalyn Aslan's Jupiter Signs* and resident *CosmoGirl* Astrologer.

www.madalynaslan.com

DEBORAH HOULDING

Author of *The Houses — Temples of the Sky* and hostess of a hugely popular website.

www.skyscript.co.uk

MICHAEL LUTIN

Astrologer for *Vanity Fair* and vastly experienced international lecturer and author.

www.michaellutin.com

KATHERINE MERLIN

Astrologer for *Town and Country* magazine in America, with an impressive client list.

http://magazines.ivillage.com/townandcountry

SUSAN MILLER

Author of *Planets and Possibilities* and luxuriously long monthly forecasts.

www.astrologyzone.com

MYSTIC MEDUSA

Author of *Mystic Medusa's Astroguide* and *Mystic Medusa's Soulmating*.

www.mysticmedusa.com

MARJORIE ORR

Author of *The Astrological History of the World* and *Daily Mail* columnist in the UK.

www.marjorieorr.com

LEIGH OSWALD

Astrologer for *Harper's Bazaar* — with an impressive academic background too.

www.astroanalysis.co.uk

ADAM SMITH

Author and astrologer for *Sunday Life* in *The Sunday Age* and *The Sun-Herald*.

www.astroboogie.com

NEIL SPENCER

Author of *True as the Stars Above*, and regular horoscope columnist at *The Observer.*

http://lifeandhealth.guardian.co.uk/experts/neilspencer

JAN SPILLER

Author of *New Moon Astrology*, *Spiritual Astrology* and *Astrology for the Soul*.

www.janspiller.com

PENNY THORNTON

Author of numerous books, Princess Diana's astrologer, and *Who Weekly* columnist.

www.astrolutely.com

JULIAN VENABLES

BBC radio astrologer, teacher, columnist and editorial consultant for this book.

www.julestheastrologer.co.uk

Finally, don't forget you can find lots of free psychic and astrological features at my site, www.jessicaadams.com — including weekly and monthly predictions, and a blog. Email me there to let me know about your favourite horoscope website too.

BIBLIOGRAPHY

The Astrolabe World Ephemeris: 2001–2050 at Noon, Whitford Press, Atglen, Pennsylvania, USA 1998

Keven W. Barrett, *Ancient Astrological Vedic Wisdom: Understanding the Moon's Nodes Rahu and Ketu*, Astrolabe Australia, Wentworth Falls, New South Wales, Australia, 1996

Caroline W. Casey, *Making the Gods Work For You: The Astrological Language of the Psyche*, Piatkus, London, UK, 1998

Hart Defouw and Robert Svoboda, *Light On Life*, Penguin, New Delhi, India, 1996

Robert Hand, *Horoscope Symbols*, Whitford Press, Atglen, Pennsylvania, USA, 1981

Lynda Hill, *360 Degrees of Wisdom: Charting Your Destiny with the Sabian Oracle*, Plume, Penguin USA, New York, USA, 2004

Kwan Lau, *Secrets of Chinese Astrology: A Handbook for Self-Discovery*, Tengu Books, Trumbull, Connecticut, USA, 1994

Lois M. Rodden, *Profiles of Women, Astro-Data 1*, Data News Press, Yucaipa, California, USA, 1979